THE PENGUIN BOOK OF INDIAN
JOURNEYS

THE PENGUIN BOOK OF
INDIAN JOURNEYS

EDITED WITH AN INTRODUCTION
BY DOM MORAES

VIKING

VIKING

Penguin Books India (P) Ltd., 11 Community Centre, Panchsheel Park, New Delhi
110017, India
Penguin Books Ltd., 27 Wrights Lane, London W8 5TZ, UK
Penguin Putnam Inc., 375 Hudson Street, New York, New York 10014, USA
Penguin Books Australia Ltd., Ringwood, Victoria, Australia
Penguin Books Canada Ltd., 10 Alcorn Avenue, Suite 300, Toronto, Ontario MAV
3B2, Canada
Penguin Books (NZ) Ltd., Cnr Rosedale & Airborne Roads, Albany, Auckland, New
Zealand

First published in Viking by Penguin Books India 2001
This anthology copyright © Penguin Books India 2001
The copyright for individual pieces vests with the authors or their estates.

Page viii is an extension of the copyright page.

Typeset in Sabon by Mantra Virtual Services, New Delhi
Printed at Rekha Printers Pvt. Ltd., New Delhi 110 020

CONTENTS

ACKNOWLEDGEMENTS

Grateful acknowledgement is made to the following for permission to reprint copyright material:

The Random House Group Limited for the extracts from *What Am I Doing Here* by Bruce Chatwin and *Travels with My Elephant* by Mark Shand, both published by Jonathan Cape;

Curtis Brown on behalf of William Dalrymple for the extract from *The Age of Kali* by William Dalrymple, published by Flamingo;

A.P. Watt Ltd on behalf of Jan Morris for the extract from *Among the Cities* by Jan Morris, published by Penguin Books;

Sheil Land Associates Ltd on behalf of Charlie Pye-Smith for the extract from *Rebels and Outcasts: A Journey Through Christian India* by Charlie Pye-Smith, published by Penguin Books;

Profile Books for the extract from *Three-Quarters of a Footprint: Travels in South India* by Joe Roberts, published by Profile Books;

Penguin Books Ltd for the extracts from the following books, all published by Penguin Books: *Imaginary Homelands* by Salman Rushdie, *An Area of Darkness* by V.S. Naipaul, *No Full Stops in India* by Mark Tully, *The Great Railway Bazaar* by Paul Theroux, *Chasing the Monsoon* by Alexander Frater and *Indian Summer* by James Cameron.

INTRODUCTION

I once lunched in Mumbai with two Japanese businessmen. Like many other businessmen, not necessarily Japanese, they seemed cloned from a prototype, from what they thought, wore, and were, to what they ate: T-bone steaks and *tiramisu*. I've forgotten how I met them; but one unusual observation they made (jointly, so to speak) has stayed in my mind for years.

At some point they said they found it difficult to understand the minds of Indian businessmen, because Indians weren't Asians. I may have seemed surprised, for they explained the remark. Physically, they said, Indians were different from other Asians. In the north of the subcontinent, some true Asians lived, such as the people of Nepal, Sikkim, and Bhutan, and the Assamese. But the other Indians didn't look like Asians, or think like them.

Semitic peoples who followed Islam lived west of India, and the 'true Asians', mostly Buddhists, lived east of it. The Hindus, according to the Japanese, were unique to the subcontinent, a separate race. They had persecuted the Buddhists; only a few were left. The Muslims and Christians who lived in India were mostly converts from Hinduism. Therefore most of the Indian population was Hindu, or of Hindu descent, but not Asian.

The idea that India is somehow different from other countries has fascinated travellers, from prehistory to the present. It has always been several countries in one, with distinct regional cultures and a definite divide between the Dravidian south and the Aryan north. Travellers have continually been startled, annoyed, and attracted by its colossal, inexplicable diversities. But they are understandable, for India is bigger than Europe.

India describes itself as a secular state. At the moment it isn't. It has been Hindu, as my Japanese friends said, since the religion first evolved, and Indians and the people of the Indian subcontinent, some of whom are widely scattered, are the only ones in the world who practise it. (There are also, of course, a few eccentric foreign converts, followers of Hindu-based cults, and the Balinese, descended from Indian colonists.)

Some writers have said Hinduism made its followers docile and submissive. Certainly the Hindus remained passive under successive conquests and occupations for nearly a millennium. Some are now returning to their original roots, though in very disquieting ways, for they are fed a violent, recidivistic version of Hinduism. Some of the essays in this book discuss its genesis.

Many people over the centuries undertook journeys to India. It came under longer, stronger cultural influences from Europe than any other Asian country. More was written about it than any other; more was known about it. Foreign writers (from a number of nations) produced more literature about India than Indians did. Its differences and oddities, so often described, became slightly devalued by time. So did the literature about it.

The generation of Indians that followed midnight's children has shown more curiosity about its country than its forebears did. These younger writers are able to bypass exotica. They are able to describe what life in India feels like, day by day, because they live it. The journeys they make are to some extent intellectual, to examine issues that affect India. But they examine these issues by talking to the people affected by them.

All good travel literature describes the discoveries made by the writer: of things or of places, of other people, or of himself. Most good travel writing on India today, whether by foreigners or Indians, discovers and reveals—sometimes with surprise—the people of the country. Earlier, most foreign writers had limited access to rural people, or to the urban middle class and poor. The Indians they knew were almost entirely privileged Indians.

India is curious in that it has always had an invisible majority. Travel literature of the past showed it only as a faceless mass, present but unidentifiable. Perhaps foreign writers are more adventurous now, or perhaps they could never reach beyond the privileged classes before. But they write more about the underprivileged these days. For them it is the discovery of another India that always existed, but nobody visited or knew.

The Indian travel writers are better equipped to enter this India. They know it more closely (though not always) than foreigners do. Some of the essays in this book portray small people, neglected and helpless in their lives, or belligerent and brutal, and report what they say. They reveal that there is not only a second, unexplored India, but another, larger nation of Indians whose views, unreported by the media, are largely unknown.

In some ways India has become even more mysterious as it becomes better known. It has developed even more problems than it already had. They are partly identified in this book, and have mostly to do with the emergence of a form of Hinduism that is militant, minatory, and regressive, and that never existed before. Travel writers today have a new theme to explore, and their journeys will have to be into the Indian mind and psyche.

As a young man I lived in England and America, and when I wrote about India, did so as an observer from outside, almost from another planet. I exulted in atmospheric descriptions of unfamiliar places and extraordinary events. Later on I found much richer material in the lives of ordinary Indians who lived, suffered, and endured. Neither they nor their ancestors had ever, over thousands of years, been asked for their opinions.

Some of the essays in this book have a personal relevance to me. I first read the piece by James Cameron when he showed it to me in London, while recovering from the ordeal it describes. I accompanied Bruce Chatwin, who was staying with me in Delhi at the time, on the blackly comic trip to Pantnagar that he writes of here. These old friends of mine are dead, but they will remain alive through their work, and like the other authors in this book, be Virgils to all those who may traverse the subcontinent in the years to come, with words and adventures in their minds.

DOM MORAES

JAN MORRIS

HILL STATION: DARJEELING, 1970

*I have mixed feelings about the Indian hill stations,
some of which (Ootacamund for instance) are
altogether too neo-British for my taste. The marvellous
setting of Darjeeling, though, the most spectacular of
them all, easily puts history in its proper place.*

Darjeeling, the most celebrated of the Indian hill stations, is all
smallness. It is small physically, of course—hard even to find
upon the map of India, so tucked away is it like a trinket on the
northern frontiers. But it is still smaller figuratively. It is the
most deliberately diminutive town I know, as though it is always
trying to make itself less substantial still. One crosses vast
scorched plains to reach it from Calcutta, over colossally
winding rivers, through a landscape that has no end: but at the
foot of the hills Darjeeling sends a toy train to meet you—a gay
little blue-painted trundle of a train, which takes you
indefatigably puffing and chugging up through the forests and
the tea-gardens to the town.

Little people greet you at the top. Little ponies canter about
little streets. Hundreds and thousands of merry little children

JAN MORRIS is the author of the *Pax Britannica* trilogy; the autobiographical
Conundrum and *Pleasures of a Tangled Life*; works on Wales, Venice, Oxford,
Manhattan, Spain, Canada, Hong Kong and Sydney; six volumes of collected
travel essays; and the novel *Last Letters from Hav* (shortlisted for the Booker
Prize in 1985). 'Hill Station: Darjeeling, 1970' is from *Among the Cities*, a
collection of the best of her travel essays, written over thirty years, primarily
about the urban world.

tumble all about you. The town is perched upon a narrow ridge, about 7,000 feet up, with deep gorges falling away on either side, and when I arrived there for the first time I found it swirled all around by cloud. It felt curiously private and self-contained—like a childish fancy, I thought, a folly, a town magically reduced in scale and shut off from the world by vapour: but then, as to a crash of drums in a *coup de théâtre,* a gap momentarily appeared in the ever-shifting clouds, and there standing tremendously in the background, their snows flushed pink with sunlight, attended by range upon range of foothills and serenely surveying the expanse of the world, stood the divine mass of the Himalayan mountains.

I saw Darjeeling's point, and cut myself down to size.

Some visitors never see the snow peaks at all, for they are often invisible for days at a time. Anyway there is no need to go on about them. It is enough to say that to see Kanchenjunga and its peers from Darjeeling, in the cool of the morning, is one of the noblest experiences of travel. It is a kind of vision. It has moved generations of pilgrims to mysticism, and even more to overwriting.

Yet it is not the spectacle of the Himalayas that sets the style of Darjeeling. It is simply their presence. The town lives in the knowledge of them, and so acknowledges another scale of things. Its littleness is not inferiority complex, but self-awareness, and it gives the community a particular intensity and vivacity. Darjeeling is built in layers, neatly along its ridge like an exhibition town, from the posh hotels and the villas at the top to the jumbled bazaar quarter at the bottom: and all the way down this dense tiered mass of buildings life incessantly buzzes, hums and fizzes. Darjeeling's energies seem to burn the brighter for their smallness, and not a corner of the town is still, or empty, or dull.

It is a place of astonishing cheerfulness. Everybody seems to

be feeling simply splendid. Perhaps they all are, for the air is
magnificently brilliant, the heat is seldom too hot and the cold
not often icy. The nineteenth-century Welshman who first put
Darjeeling on the map saw it from the start as a sanatorium, and
the Rajas of Sikkim kindly handed it over to the British
Governor-General of India 'for the purpose of enabling the
servants of his government suffering from sickness to avail
themselves of its advantages'. Today Darjeeling's high spirits
never seem to flag. The children never stop playing, the youths
never end their horseplay, the tourists never tire of clattering
hilariously about the town on hired ponies. The cicadas sing all
day long in the gardens, and over and again from down the hill
come the hoots and puffs of the little trains (which prefer to
travel gregariously, and come merrily up from Siliguri two or
three at a time).

To the stranger it all seems intenser, more concentrated
than real life, and especially after dark, when the braziers are
aglow in the alleys of the bazaar, and the hotel lights
comfortably shine above. Then half Darjeeling turns out for a
stroll at Chaurasta, a triangular piazza half-way along the ridge,
and on my own first evening in Darjeeling I went and sat on a
bench there, and watched the town go by. Beyond the square the
ridge fell away abruptly into the night, and there were only the
dark foothills out there, and a suggestion of the snow-speaks,
and the stars that now and then appeared in unnatural brilliance
through the shifting clouds.

To and fro against this celestial backdrop the people of
Darjeeling loitered, strolled and gossiped like Spaniards on their
evening promenade, or more exotic Venetians at St Mark's.
There were tall flashing girls in saris and nose-clips. There were
brown gnome-like men in fur caps. There were slant-eyed
children of astonishing beauty, and boys with wild eager faces
like Gengis Khan. There were monks, and priests, and soldiers,
and grand Indian gentlemen in tweeds, and giggly Indian girls in
cotton party frocks. There were mountain porters hastening

back from work, carrying rucksacks and tent-poles. There were
ancient men with plaited pigtails. There were two hippies, and a
nun, and four French tourists, and me watching it all, as in
hallucination, from a corner bench beside the bandstand.

It was like a microcosm of the world, assembled up there
from the plains and mountains, ushered into that little square,
reduced to a neater and more manageable size, and given double
shots of adrenalin.

'What is your country?' a man peremptorily demanded, as we
met face to face and unavoidably on a narrow hill track, and
when I told him Wales, to the west of England, he asked further:
'Is it a high pass to get there?'

Unimaginably high are the passes, indescribably remote the
valleys, from which in the century since Captain Lloyd founded
Darjeeling the population of the town has found its way to the
ridge. This is a frontier settlement. Some of those snow peaks
are in India proper, some in Sikkim and Bhutan, some in the
Kingdom of Nepal, some in the People's Republic of Tibet. The
town stands on the edge of mysteries, and its people have
migrated from many parts of the eastern Himalayas, and from
the plains below. The old sanatorium of the memsahibs is far
more nowadays: not merely a celebrated resort, but an
important bazaar, a centre of local government and a kind of
ethnic demonstration.

No small town in the world can show so many kinds, and
types, and manners of people. The little Lepchas, the original
inhabitants of the region, are seldom more than five feet high,
but immensely strong and agile. The Sherpas from eastern
Nepal, the high-altitude porters of Everest and Kanchenjunga,
move with an inexorable striding impetus, as though they can't
stop. The Tibetans often look immensely sophisticated, trendy
almost, ready for any Chelsea discotheque with their flared
pants and impeccable complexions. The Gurkhas look soldiers

through and through, always marching, even off parade, with
head high and chest out. One sees few sleepy or dullard faces
among these Mongoloid peoples of the north: all seem
eminently capable—straight square-set people, who look as
though, deposited in a Brooklyn back-alley or one of the
remoter villages of the southern Urals, they would instantly find
their feet.

But they are only one element in the Darjeeling *mélange*.
There are many other kinds of Nepalese, for instance—
Gurungs, Magars, Tamangs, Newars. There are refugees from
Tibet proper, and Indian Army soldiers from the Punjab and
Rajasthan. Here comes a slim dark girl in blue pyjamas, who
might be Annamese, or perhaps Malay. Here are four Rajput
officers of the garrison, with their thin black Sandhurst
moustaches and their suede boots. The Hindu holy man beside
the lane is smeared mysteriously with yellow ochre. The Bengali
family being hoisted on to its ponies is all guileless anticipation,
proud young father holding the baby (who wears a pink peaked
cap with yellow velvet ribbons), mother in gold and red sari
assiduously combing the already immaculate hair of a small boy
apparently dressed for an exceptionally extravagant wedding.
The eyes that peer at you between bushy beard and bundled
turban are, of course, the eyes of a Sikh; the shy porcelain smile
from the lady at the next table is a smile from the palm trees and
sands of Madras.

In the autumn they have races at Darjeeling, and then one
may see this demographic jumble at its most cheerful. The
racecourse is endearingly claimed to be the smallest in the
world: at the end of a race the competitors run breakneck of the
course into the approach road, an unnerving experience for
newcomers. The meetings are not very formal. Young men play
football in the middle of the track. Between races the horses
graze casually on grassy spaces round about. A dribble of
racegoers stumbles down the mountain track from the town
above, carrying umbrellas and race cards, and a stream of jeeps

and rattly taxis blasts its way along the motor-road.

Still, the traditional procedures are honoured. The races are run by the Gymkhana Club of Darjeeling, and in the official stand the Stewards and Judges, mostly Army officers, sit in well-cut elegance with immensely superior ladies. Sometimes the senior steward takes a stroll about the enclosure, moving with the lordly benevolence common to racing bigwigs from Longchamps to Kentucky Downs. The race card is printed with every refinement of the recegoer's jargon and the rules are, of course, severe ('Trainers and Jockeys are hereby notified that Riotous Behaviour, Intemperance, or other Improper Conduct, although not occurring on the Race Course, will be taken cognizance of by the Stewards'). It would take an iconoclast indeed, to defy the decrees of the Darjeeling Gymkhana Club.

But all around that grandstand, swarming about the bookies at their little wooden stands, picnicking up the grassy slopes behind, haggling with the sellers of nuts or the purveyors of infallible tips, is the infinite variety of Darjeeling, impervious to regulation. Such a conglomeration of bone structures, life-styles, tastes, gestures! Such a cacophony of voices, deep, cracked, sing-song or bell-like! Such a marvellous fugue of history performed there, in the intersections of history, religion, or ambition that have brought this pot-pourri of the human kind to place its bets on the fourth race!

The bell rings; the flap drops; hurtling around the track in billows of dust come three or four black Tibetan ponies, ridden at desperate speed and with savage concentration by fierce little high-cheeked jockeys—brilliantly liveried in scarlets and yellows, visors low over their eyes—rocketing around that mini-track, as the crowd rises tip-toe with excitement, until they shoot out of sight, with cheers, laughter and catcalls, behind the grandstand and off the course. It is as though the scouts of Attila have passed through. The stranger may feel a certain sense of shock, but the stewards do not seem disconcerted. 'Jolly good show,' they say to each other. 'Hell of a good race, what?'

For the most dogmatic progressive will not deny to little Darjeeling a tug of nostalgia. It is harmless. It is only a fragrance of earlier times, a Victorian bouquet still lingering up here along the ridge. Darjeeling is largely built in that gabled semi-chalet style so dear to Victorian pleasure-seekers, and imposed upon its gallimaufry of peoples is a decorous, poke-bonnet, tea-and-biscuits style. Nobody in their senses would wish it otherwise. It is an essential part of Darjeeling's minuscule mystique, and used to suggest to me a musical-box town, where pretty little melodies would tinkle in the sunshine, while clockwork figures in top-hats and bustles jerkily proceeded along the Mall. The very names of the place carry this old evocation—the Esplanade, Happy Valley, Step Aside: and the main road to the plains is still known in Darjeeling as the Cart Road.

Some of the hotels are deliciously Victorian. The porridge at the Windamere [sic] Hotel is, I am told by unimpeachable authorities, unsurpassed in Scotland, while the tea at the Mount Everest is tea, my dear, just like we used to have it. Shopping in Darjeeling, too, is agreeably old-school. Patiently attentive are the assistants, instantly to hand is the chair for memsahib, and one almost expects to find, winging it across the Kashmiri shawls and the Tibetan prayer-wheels, one of those wire-pulley change receptacles one used to see in provincial English drapers' long ago.

Most of Darjeeling's pleasure (I except the illicit joys of the bazaar quarter) would perfectly satisfy our grandparents. There is the classic pleasure, for instance, which I abstemiously denied myself, of getting up at three in the morning to see the sunrise and the top of Everest from Tiger Hill. There are the pleasures of Excursions to Places of Interest, like Ghoom Rock or Kaventer's Dairy Farm. There are the pleasures of identifying wild flowers and trees, or sketching, or looking at animals in the outdoor zoo (where the Llama and the Siberian Tiger, returning one's inspection morosely from their enclosures, look as though they wish the Victorian era had never dawned). There are pony-rides, of course, and there is miniature golf, and when I was there *Ruddigore* was being performed by the pupils of St Paul's School.

There is the pleasure of walking. In most of Darjeeling no cars are allowed, and this is one of the walkingest towns on earth. One may walk decorously around the town itself, or through the Botanical Gardens. One may walk into the foothills for a picnic. Or one may, stocking up with tinned pineapple and sleeping bags, engage a team of Sherpas and stride off into the distant mountains. Every year more and more people go trekking from Darjeeling, and a very healthy pastime it must be. 'No place like Darjeeling,' one stalwart matron reproachfully observed as, staggering beneath the weight of her accoutrements, she passed me doing nothing in particular over a glass of lemonade—'nowhere like Darjeeling for blowing the cobwebs away!'

As I say, our grandparents would have loved it: and sometimes Darjeeling's scrapbook essence can be, to the sentimental visitor, distinctly moving. On Jalapahar Hill, at the eastern end of the ridge, there is a small military cantonment, complete with parade ground, garrison church and shops for the soldiery. I was once walking through this camp, enjoying its display of the military aesthetic—polished brass, regimental signs in white-washed pebbles, the clump of ammunition boots and the bristle of sergeantly moustaches—when an unexpected sound reached me from the parade ground behind. With a slow and melancholy introductory wail, the Gurkha pipe band broke into the sad, sad music of a Highland lament. I stopped dead in my dusty tracks, and the tears came to my eyes: for what generations of my own people, I thought, had stirred to that music in their exiles long ago, and how strange and sweet and lonely it sounded in these hills of the Indian frontier!

'Can I help you?' inquired a passer-by, seeing me standing there. 'You are not ill?' Not ill, I assured him as I moved on up the hill. Only susceptible!

Every morning before breakfast I used to walk up Observatory Hill. This wooded hump, rising directly above the Chaurasta, is holy to the Buddhists, who have a shrine upon its summit. All along the steep and winding path to the top mendicants invite the contributions of the pious—grave holy men who bow like archbishops, jolly old crones, coveys of chirpy inquisitive children. Two grinning stone lions guard the entrance to the holy compound, the trees are hung all over with white prayer flags, and mysteriously from the recesses of the shrine one may hear the incessant murmur of prayers and tinkling of bells. There are always people up there. Some are praying, some meditating, some reading sacred scripts, and one I met each day used to stand all alone among the bushes looking towards Tibet and writing in a large black notebook.

If the weather is clear there is a glorious view of Kanchenjunga and its peers, and while they were cooking my eggs in the hotel down below I used to sit on the grass alone and marvel at the immunity of Darjeeling. It has, it seemed to me, *escaped*. It knows its own dimension, and is satisfied. Though its name is famous everywhere, still it remains a small town of the Himalayan foothills, very close to the soil and the temple. There is material squalor enough, but seldom I think despair, still less degradation. The loads may be crippling, but still the porters find the energy to smile. The children and the chickens may be in and out of the kitchen, but the mothers never seem to get cross. The girls laugh as they laboriously chop firewood in the thickets, and the bundles of hay piled upon the backs of the labourers are speckled all over with flowers of pink and blue.

It is as though by an unconscious exertion of values

Darjeeling has selected what it wants from the world below, and rejected all the rest. And such is the inner variety of the place, so lavish are its colours, so remote is it even now from the pressures of the industrialized society, that within its own limits it can afford to be tolerant. There is nothing censorious about the place. One may look, behave, dress, believe more or less as one pleases. During my stay in Darjeeling I often saw a young American dressed in the habit of a Buddhist monk. He was studying at a nearby seminary, I was told, and wore the brown cloak, the sandals and the hair-bun as to the manner born. Nobody appeared the least surprised by this anomalous figure, and even his father, who was paying him a visit from the States, seemed entirely at home with the phenomenon. 'I'm going to drink, Jimmy,' I heard him saying to his son one day, puffing at his cigar and raising his glass, 'I'm going to drink to all these wonderful, wonderful people of Darjeeling!' (And 'Say,' he tactfully added as he put his glass down, rather hastily I thought, 'is this Indian wine? *Delicious!*')

For there is an innocent merit to the place. One feels better and kinder for a visit to Darjeeling. Those stupendous mountains in the clouds have set the scale right, and adjusted the balance. It's no good fussing, they seem to say. It can't last. And this sententious thought, which occurred to me every morning after ten minutes or so upon the hill, used to remind me that my eggs were waiting for me down the lane—and down I would hurry, past that merry line of beggars, tagged by swarms of children and encouraged by avuncular sages, to where the waiter in his red turban and his polished brass badge, looking anxiously from the dining-room door, was waiting to whisk the cover off my porridge.

V.S. NAIPAUL

ROMANCERS

We were paying guests. It was in Delhi, the city of symbols, first of the British Raj and now of the independent Indian republic: a jungle of black-and-white noticeboards mushrooming out of feverish administrative activity, the Indian Council for this and Academy for that, the Ministry for this and the Department for that, the buildings going up all the time, monstrous bird's nests of bamboo scaffolding: a city ever growing, as it has been for the last forty years, a city of civil servants and contractors. We were paying guests; and our host was Mrs Mahindra, the wife of a contractor.

She sent her car to meet us at the railway station. It was an attention we were grateful for. To step out of the third-class air-conditioned coach on to the smooth hot platform was to feel one's shirt instantly heated, to lose interest, to wonder with a dying flicker of intellectual curiosity why anyone in India bothered, why anyone had bothered with India. On that platform, oven-dry, competitive activity was yet maintained. The porters, blazing in red tunics and red turbans, hustled about

V.S. NAIPAUL's many novels include *The Mystic Masseur* (John Llewelyn Rhys Memorial Prize, 1957), *The Suffrage of Elvira, Miguel Street* (Somerset Maugham Award, 1959), *A House for Mr Biswas, Mr Stone and the Knights Companion* (Hawthornden Prize, 1963), *The Mimic Men* (W.H. Smith Award, 1968), *In a Free State* (Booker Prize, 1971) and *The enigma of Arrival*. In 1960 he began to travel, and has since produced several travel books, among them, *An Area of Darkness*—from which 'Romancers' is excerpted—*The Return of Eva Peron, Among the Believers: An Islamic Journey, A Turn in the South* and *India: A Million Mutinies Now*.

screeching for custom. The successful staggered beneath metal trunks sprayed with fine dust after the journey from Bombay: one trunk, two trunks, three trunks. The fans spun frenziedly above us. The beggars whined. The man from the Bhagirath Hotel waved his grubby folder. Remembering that for Antarctic explorers surrender was easy and that the enduring, the going on, was the act of bravery, I reached out for the folder and, standing in the midst of noise and activity in which I had lost interest and which now seemed to swing outwards from me in waves, I read with slow concentration, in which everything was distorted and dissolving:

> *Arrive a Delhi au terme d'un equisant voyage, c'est avec le plus grand plaisir que j'ai pris le meilleur des repos au Bahgitath Hotel, dant les installations permettent de se remettre de ses fetigues dans un cadre agreable. J'ai particulierment apprecie la gentillesse ei l'hospitolite de le direction et do personnel. Je ne peploie q'ue chose, c'est de n'avoir pu arroser les excellents repos des baissens alcoolirees aux quelles nous mettent le cour en joie.*
> *28-7-61*
>
> > *Fierre Bes Georges,*
> > *Gareme (Seine) France*

Baissens alcoolirees: yearning had glided into delirium. *Et Monsieur, qu'est-ce-qu-il peploie? Je ne peploie qu'ue chose. Arrosez les excellents repos.* On the shining concrete the figures were stretched out, Indian sleepers on an Indian railway station. The unemployed porters squatted. The beggar woman, whining, even she squatted. *Arrosez les excellents repos.* But there were no fountains. The streets were wide and grand, the roundabouts endless: a city built for giants, built for its vistas, for its symmetry: a city which remained its plan, unquickened and unhumanized, built for people who would be protected

from its openness, from the whiteness of its light, to whom the
trees were like the trees on an architect's drawing, decorations,
not intended to give shade: a city built like a monument. And
everything labelled, as on an architect's drawing; every moving
thing dwarfed, the man on his bicycle, with his black, black
shadow; an endless, ever-spreading city which encouraged no
repose, which sent people scuttling through its avenues and
malls, as these scooter-rickshaws scuttled noisily in and out of
the traffic, shrunk to less than human size in the presence of the
monumental city.

The house was in one of the New Delhi 'colonies' or
residential settlements, abrupt huddles of fantasy and riotous
modern lines after the exposed austerity of the centre. It was as
though an Indian village had been transformed into concrete
and glass, and magnified. The houses were not yet coherently
numbered; and the narrow nameless lanes were full of
bewildered Sikhs seeking houses by plot numbers, whose
sequence was chronological, indicating date of purchase. Dust;
concrete white and grey; no trees; each Sikh attached to a brisk,
black shadow.

We sat in front of an empty, unsmoked fireplace below an
electric fan and rested with glasses of Coca-Cola.

'Duffer, that Bihari boy,' Mrs Mahindra said, apologizing
for her chauffeur and making conversation.

She was plump, still young, with large staring eyes. She had
little English, and when words failed her she gave a giggle and
looked away. She said *Mm*, her eyes became vacant, and her
right hand went to her chin.

The house was new and on this ground floor smelled of
concrete and paint. The rooms were not yet fully decorated; the
furnishings were sparse. But there were fans everywhere; and
the bathroom fittings, from Germany, were rare and expensive.
'I am craze for foreign,' Mrs Mahindra said. 'Just craze for
foreign.'

She marvelled at our suitcases and at what they contained.

She fingered with reverence and delight.

'Craze, just craze for foreign.'

Widening her eyes, it might have been in fear, it might have been in admiration, she told us of her husband, the contractor. He had a hard life. He was always travelling about in forests and jungles and living in tents. She had to stay behind and do the housekeeping.

'Three thousand rupees a month allowance. These days cost-of-living that-is-no-joke.'

She was not really boasting. She came from a simple family and she accepted her new wealth as she would have accepted poverty. She was anxious to learn, anxious to do the correct thing, anxious for our foreign approval. Did we like the colour of her curtains? The colours of her walls? Look, that lamp bracket there was foreign, from Japan. There wasn't a thing which was not foreign except, as she confessed when we went up to her dining-room for lunch, for this brass dish-warmer.

She sat with us, not eating, staring at our plates, hand supporting her chin, widening her eyes dreamily and smiling whenever our glances met. She was new to the business, she said with a giggle. She had not had any paying guests before, and so we must forgive her if she treated us like her children.

Her sons arrived. They were in their teens, tall, and as cool towards us as their mother was demonstrative. They joined us at the table. Mrs Mahindra spooned out from the dishes into their plates, spooned out into our plates.

Suddenly she giggled and nodded towards her elder son.

'I want him to marry foreign.'

The boy didn't react.

We talked about the weather and the heat.

'The heat doesn't affect us,' the boy said. 'Our bedrooms are air-conditioned.'

Mrs Mahindra caught our eyes and gave a mischievous smile.

She insisted on taking us out with her that afternoon to do a little shopping. She wanted to buy curtains for one of the downstairs rooms. But, we said, the curtains she had shown us in that room were brand new and very elegant. No, no, she said; we were only being polite. She wanted to buy new curtains that afternoon and she wanted our foreign advice.

So we drove back into the centre. She pointed out the monuments: Humayun's Tomb, India Gate, Rashtrapati Bhavan.

'New Delhi, New Delhi,' she sighed. '*Capital* of India.'

We went from shop to shop, and I began to fade. Fading, I relapsed into mechanical speech. 'Look,' I said to the boy, pointing to a heap of slippers that were extravagantly of the orient, their tapering embroidered points curling back on themselves. 'Look, those are rather amusing.'

'They are too common for us.'

His mother was known to the shop assistants. She engaged them all in friendly conversation. They offered her chairs. She sat; she fingered; she talked. Bolt after bolt was unwrapped for her. Blandly she watched and blandly she walked away. Her movements were easy; no one appeared to be offended. She knew what she wanted, and at last she found it.

She asked us to study the fireplace that evening. It was of irregular shape and had been designed by her husband, who had also designed the irregular recesses, for electric lights, in the stone fence.

'Modern. Modern. *All* modern.'

In the morning the painters came to repaint the newly painted unused room to match the curtains that had been bought the previous afternoon.

She came into our room as we lay stripped below the ceiling fan after breakfast. She sat on the edge of the bed and talked. She examined this stocking, that shoe, that brassiere; she asked prices. She lured us out to watch the painters at work; she held the material against the paint and asked whether they went well together.

She had nothing to do except to spend three thousand rupees a month. She had one special friend. 'Mrs M. *Mehta. Secretary.* Women's *League.* Mrs M. Mehta. Air-conditioners and other electrical gadgets.' The name and the words were familiar from advertisements. Regularly Mrs Mahindra visited Mrs Mehta; regularly she consulted her astrologer; regularly she shopped and went to the temple. Her life was full and sweet.

A tall man of about fifty came to the house in the afternoon. He said he was answering an advertisement in the newspaper; he wished to lease the ground floor which we were occupying. He wore a double-breasted grey suit and spoke English with a strained army accent.

'Mm.' Mrs Mahindra looked away.

The man in the grey suit continued to speak in English. He represented a large firm, he said. A firm with foreign connections.

'Mm.' Her eyes became vacant; her palm went to her chin.

'No one will sleep here.' He was faltering a little; perhaps it had occurred to him that his firm was not as desirable as the 'diplomatic' foreigners so many advertisements solicited. 'We will give you a year's rent in advance and sign a lease for three years.'

'Mm.' She said, replying in Hindustani to his English, that she would have to talk to her husband. And then there were many other people who were interested.

'We intend to use the premises just as offices.' His dignity was beginning to yield to a certain exasperation. 'And all we would like is for a caretaker to sleep here at night. The house will remain as your home. We will give you twelve thousand rupees right away.'

She stared in her abstracted way, as though sniffing the new paint and thinking about the curtains.

'Duffer,' she said when he had gone. 'Talking English. *Barra sahib.* Duffer.'

The next morning she was glum.

'*Letter*. My husband's *father* is coming. Today. Tomorrow.' The prospect clearly depressed her. 'Talk, talk, thatisnojoke.'

When we came back to the house that afternoon we found her sitting, sad and dutiful, with a white-haired man in Indian dress. She already seemed to have shrunk a little; she looked chastened, even embarrassed. It was our foreignness she stressed when she introduced us. Then she looked away, became abstracted and took no further part in the conversation.

The white-haired man looked us over suspiciously. But he was, as Mrs Mahindra had hinted, a talker; and he regarded himself and especially his age, which was just over sixty, with wonder. It was not his adventures he spoke of so much as the habits he had formed in those sixty years. He rose at four every morning, he said; he went for a four- or five-mile walk; then he read some chapters of the Gita. He had followed this routine for forty years, and it was a routine he would recommend to any young man.

Mrs Mahindra sighed. I felt she had taken a lot already and I thought I would release her. I tried to get the old man to talk of his past to me. He had no adventures to relate; he just had a list of places he had lived in or worked in. I asked precise questions; I made him describe landscapes. But Mrs Mahindra, not understanding my purpose, not accepting—or perhaps by duty not able to accept—the release I offered, sat and suffered. In the end it was the old man whom I drove away. He went and sat by himself in the small front garden.

'Naughty, naughty,' Mrs Mahindra said, giving me a smile of pure exhaustion.

'Summer is here,' the old man said after dinner. 'I have been sleeping out in the open for a fortnight. I always find that I begin to sleep out in the open a few weeks before other people.'

'Will you be sleeping out in the open tonight?' I asked.

'Of course.'

He slept just outside the door. We could see him, and no

doubt he could see us. At four—so it was reasonable to
assume—we heard him rise and get ready for his walk: lavatory
chain, gargling, clattering, doors. We heard him return. And
when we got up we found him reading the Gita.

'I always read a few pages of the Gita after I come back from
my walk,' he said.

After that he idled about the house. He had nothing to do. It
was difficult to ignore him; he required to be spoken to. He
talked, but I began to feel that he also monitored.

We returned in the afternoon to a painful scene: the
interviewing of another applicant for the ground floor. The
applicant was uneasy; the old man, who was putting the
questions, was polite but reproving; and the object of his
reproof, I felt, was Mrs Mahindra, whose face was almost
hidden in the top end of her sari.

We lost some of Mrs Mahindra's attentions. In no time at
all she had dwindled into the Indian daughter-in-law. We heard
little now of her craze for foreign. We had become liabilities.
And when, attending to her father-in-law's conversation, she
caught our eyes, her smile was tired. It held no conspiracy, only
dutiful withdrawal. We had found her, on that first day, in a
brief moment of sparkle.

We had to go to the country that weekend, and it was with a
feeling almost of betrayal that we told her we were going to
leave her alone with her father-in-law for a few days. She
brightened at the news; she became active. We must just go, she
said, and not worry about a thing. We didn't have to pack
everything away; she would look after our room. She helped us
to get ready. She gave us a meal and stood in the irregularly
pointed stone gateway and waved while the Bihari chauffeur,
duffer as we remembered, drove us off. Plump, saddened,
wide-eyed Mrs Mahindra!

A weekend in the country! The words suggest cool clumps
of trees, green fields, streams. Our thoughts were all of water as
we left Delhi. But there was no water and little shade. The road

was a narrow metal strip between two lanes of pure dust. Dust
powdered the roadside trees and the fields. Once we drove for
miles over a flat brown wasteland. At the end of the journey lay
a town, and a communal killing. The Muslim murderer had fled;
the dead Hindu had to be mourned and cremated in swift
secrecy before daybreak; and afterwards troublemakers of both
sides had to be watched. This occupied our host for almost all
the weekend. We remained in the inspection house, grateful for
the high ceiling, below the spinning fan. On one wall there was a
framed typewritten digest of rules and regulations. Set into
another wall was a fireplace. The winters it promised seemed so
unlikely now; and it was as though one was forever doomed to
be in places at the wrong time, as though one was forever feeling
one's way through places where every label was false: the
confectionery machine on the railway platform that hadn't
worked for years, the advertisement for something that was no
longer made, the timetable which was out of date. Above the
mantelpiece there was a photograph of a tree standing on
eroded earth beside a meagre stream; and in that photograph, in
its message of exhaustion and persistence, there was something
which already we could recognize as of India.

We returned to Delhi by train below a darkening sky. We
waited for the storm to break. But what looked like raincloud
was only dust. The tea-boy cheated us (and on this run several
months later that same boy was to cheat us again); a passenger
complained of corruption; one story excited another. And the
wind blew and the dust penetrated everywhere, dust which, the
engineers tell us, can get in where water can't. We longed for the
town, for hot baths and air-conditioning and shuttered rooms.

The lower floor of the Mahindras' house was in darkness.
The door was locked. We had no key. We rang, and rang. After
some minutes a whispering, tiptoeing servant let us in as though
we were his private friends. Everything in our room was as we
had left it. The bed was unmade; the suitcases hadn't been
moved; letters and leaflets and full ashtrays were on the bedside

table; dust had settled on the static disarray. We were aware of muted activity upstairs, in the room with the Indian brass dish-warmer.

The sahib, the servant said, had returned from the jungle. And the sahib had quarrelled with the memsahib. 'He say, "You take *paying* guests? You take *money?*"'

We understood. We were Mrs Mahindra's first and last paying guests. We had been part of her idleness, perhaps like those men who had called to lease the ground floor. Perhaps Mrs M. Mehta, secretary of the Women's League, leased her ground floor; perhaps Mrs M. Mehta had a dazzling succession of foreign paying guests.

Dear Mrs Mahindra! She enjoyed her money and no doubt in her excitement had wished to make a little more. But her attentions had been touched with the genuine Indian warmth. We never saw her again; we never saw her sons again; we never saw her husband. Her father-in-law we only heard as, lurking in our room, we waited for him to settle down for the night. We heard him rise in the morning; we heard him leave for his walk. We gave him a few minutes. Then we crept out with our suitcases and roused one of the sleeping taxi-drivers in the taxi-rank not far off. Through a friend we later sent the money we owed.

The days in Delhi had been a blur of heat. The moments that stayed were those of retreat: darkened bedrooms, lunches, shuttered clubs, a dawn drive to the ruins of Tughlakabad, a vision of the Flame of the Forest. Sightseeing was not easy. Bare feet were required in too many places. The entrances to temples were wet and muddy and the courtyards of mosques were more scorching than tropical beaches in mid-afternoon. At every mosque and temple there were idlers waiting to pounce on those who did not take off their shoes. Their delight and their idleness infuriated me. So did one notice: 'If you think it is beneath your dignity to take off your shoes, slippers are provided.' At Rajghat, faced with an unnecessarily long walk over hot sand to the site of Gandhi's cremation, I refused to follow the Tourist Department's guide and sat, a fully shod heretic, in the shade. Blue-shirted schoolboys waited for the Americans among the tourists. The boys were well fed and well shod and carried their schoolbooks like emblems of their worthiness. They ran to the old ladies. The ladies, informed of India's poverty, stopped, opened their purses and smilingly distributed coins and notes, while from the road the professional beggars, denied entrance, watched enviously. The heat was unhinging me. I advanced towards the schoolboys, simple murder in my heart. They ran away, nimble in the heat. The Americans looked assessingly at me: the proud young Indian nationalist. Well, it would do. I walked back to the coach, converting exhaustion into anger and shame.

So it had been in Delhi. I was shouting now almost as soon as I entered government offices. At times the sight of rows of young men sitting at long tables, buried among sheaves of paper, young men checking slips of one sort or another, young men counting banknotes and tying them into bundles of a hundred, all India's human futility, was more than I could bear. 'Don't complain to me. Make your complaint through proper channel.' 'Through proper channel! Proper channel!' But it was hopeless; irony, mockery, was impossible in India. And: 'Don't complain to me. Complain to my officer.' 'Which is your bloody officer?' All this with a liberating sense that my violent mood was inviting violence. Yet so often it was met only with a cold, puncturing courtesy; and I was reduced to stillness, shame and exhaustion.

In Lutyens's city I required privacy and protection. Only then was I released from the delirium of seeing certain aspects of myself magnified out of recognition. I could sense the elegance of the city, in those colonnades hidden by signboards and straw blinds, in those vistas: the new tower at one end of the tree-lined avenue, the old dome at the other. I could sense the 'studious' atmosphere of which people had spoken in Bombay. I could sense its excitement as a new capital city, in the gatherings at the Gymkhana Club on a Sunday morning, the pro-consular talk about the abominations of the Congo from former United Nations officials, in the announcements in the newspapers of 'cultural' entertainments provided by the embassies of competing governments: a city to which importance had newly come, and all the new toys of the 'diplomatic'. But to me it was a city in which I could only escape from one darkened room to another, separate from the reality of out of doors, of dust and light and low-caste women in gorgeous saris—gorgeousness in saris being emblematic of lowness—working on building sites. A city doubly unreal, rising suddenly out of the plain: acres of seventeenth- and eighteenth-century ruins, then the ultra-contemporary exhibition buildings; a city whose emblematic grandeur spoke of a rich and settled hinterland and not of the poor, parched land through which we had been travelling for twenty-four hours.

Yet that evening, lying in my bunk in the aluminium coach of the Srinagar Express and waiting for the train to leave, I found that I had begun to take a perverse delight in the violence of it all: delight at the thought of the twenty-four-hour journey that had brought me to Delhi, the thirty-six-hour journey still farther north that awaited me, through all the flatness of the Punjab to the mightiest mountain range in the world; delight at the physical area of luxury I had managed to reserve for myself, the separation from the unpleasant which I was yet, through the easily operated rubber-beaded windows, able to see; the red-turbanned porters, the trolleys of books and magazines, the hawkers, the frenzied fans hanging low so that from my bunk the platform appeared to be ceilinged by spinning blades: once hated symbols of discomfort, now answering all my urgency and exaltation which, fraudulent though I knew it to be, I was already fearing to lose, for with a twenty degree drop in temperature all would subside to ordinariness.

The Punjab, intermittently glanced at during the night, was silent and featureless except for the moving oblongs of light from our train. A still hut, blacker against the flat black fields awaiting the day-long sun: what more had I expected? In the morning we were at Pathankot, the railhead—and how strange again and again to hear this solitary English word, to me so technical, industrial and dramatic, in a whole sentence of Hindustani—the railhead for Kashmir. It was cool at the station in the early morning; there was a hint of bush and, deceptive though it was, of mountains close at hand. And our passengers appeared in woollen shirts, sporty hats, jackets, cardigans, pullovers and even gloves, the woollen garments of the Indian summer holidays, not yet strictly needed, but an anticipation of the holiday that had almost begun.

At first it was only the army of whose presence we were aware on this flat scrub near the Pakistan border: signposted camps, all whitewash and straight lines, the rows of lorries and jeeps, the occasional manoeuvres of light tanks. These men in olive-green battledress and bush-hats might have belonged to another country. They walked differently; they were handsome. We stopped at Jammu for lunch. Thereafter we climbed, entering Kashmir by the road built by the Indian army in 1947 at the time of the Pakistan invasion. It grew cooler; there were hills and gorges and a broken view, hill beyond hill, receding planes of diminishing colour. We drove beside the Chenab river which, as we climbed, fell beneath us into a gorge, littered with logs.

'And where do you come from?'

It was the Indian question. I had been answering it five times a day. And now again I went through the explanations.

He was sitting across the aisle from me. He was respectably dressed in a suit. He was bald, with a sharp Gujerati nose, and he looked bitter.

'And what do you think of our great country?'

It was another Indian question; and the sarcasm had to be dismissed.

'Be frank. Tell me exactly what you think.'

'It's all right. It's very interesting.'

'Interesting. You are lucky. You should live here. We are trapped here, you know. That's what we are. Trapped.'

Beside him sat his plump, fulfilled wife. She was less interested in our conversation than in me. She studied me whenever I looked away.

'Corruption and nepotism everywhere,' he said. 'Everybody wanting to get out to United Nations jobs. Doctors going abroad. Scientists going to America. The future is totally black. How much, for instance, do you earn in your country?'

'About five thousand rupees a month.'

It was unfair to strike so hard. But he took it well.

'And what do you do for this?' he asked.

'I teach.'

'What do you teach?'

'History.'

He was unimpressed.

I added, 'And a little chemistry.'

'Strange combination. I'm a chemistry teacher myself.'

It happens to every romancer.

I said, 'I teach in a comprehensive school. You have to do a little of everything.'

'I see.' Annoyance was peeping out of his puzzlement; his nose seemed to twitch. 'Strange combination. Chemistry.'

I was worried. Several hours of our journey together still remained. I pretended to be annoyed by a crying child. This couldn't go on. But relief soon came. We stopped among pines in a lay-by above a green wooded valley. We got out to stretch our legs. It was cool. The plains had become like an illness whose exact sensations it is impossible, after recovery, to recall. The woollens were now of service. The holiday had begun to fulfil itself. And when we got back into the bus I found that the chemistry teacher had changed seats with his wife, so that he would not have to continue talking to me.

It was night, clear and cold, when we stopped at Banihal. The rest-house was in darkness; the electric lights had gone. The attendants fussed around with candles; they prepared meals. In the moonlight the terraced rice fields were like leaded panes of old glass. In the morning their character had changed. They were green and muddy. After the Banihal tunnel we began to go down and down, past fairy-tale villages set in willow groves, watered by rivulets with grassy banks, into the Vale of Kashmir.

1964

PAUL THEROUX

THE DELHI MAIL FROM JAIPUR

'What's this?' I asked Mr Gopal, the embassy liaison man, pointing to a kind of fortress.

'That's a kind of fortress.'

He had ridiculed the handbook I had been carrying around: 'You have this big book, but I tell you to close it and leave it at hotel because Jaipur is like open book to me.' Unwisely, I had taken his advice. We were now six miles outside Jaipur, wading ankle-deep through sand drifts towards the wrecked settlement of Galta. Earlier we had passed through a jamboree of some two hundred baboons: 'Act normal,' said Mr Gopal, as they hopped and chattered and showed their teeth, clustering on the road with a curiosity that bordered on menace. The landscape was rocky and very dry, and each rugged hill was capped with a cracked fortress.

'Whose is it?'

'The Maharaja's.'

'No, who built it?'

'You would not know his name.'

'Do *you*?'

Mr Gopal walked on. It was dusk, and the buildings crammed into the Galta gorge were darkening. A monkey

PAUL THEROUX's books include the novels *Waldo*, *Saint Jack*, *Picture Palace* (winner of the 1978 Whitbread Literary Award) and *The Mosquito Coast* (joint winner of the James Tait Black Memorial Prize in 1981); and the travel books *The Old Patagonian Express*, *Sunrise with Seamonsters*, *Riding the Iron Rooster* (winner of the 1988 Thomas Cook Travel Book Award) and *The Pillars of Hercules*. 'The Delhi Mail from Jaipur' is from *The Great Railway Bazaar*.

chattered and leaped to a branch in a banyan tree above Mr Gopal's head, yanking the branch down and making a punkah's *whoosh*. We entered the gate and crossed a courtyard to some ruined buildings, with coloured frescoes of trees and people on their facades. Some had been raked with indecipherable graffiti and painted over; whole panels had been chiselled away.

'What's this?' I asked. I hated him for making me leave my handbook behind.

'Ah,' said Mr Gopal. It was a temple enclosure. Some men dozed in the archways, others squatted on their haunches, and just outside the enclosure were some tea and vegetable stalls whose owners leaned against more frescoes, rubbing them away with their backs. I was struck by the solitude of the place—a few people at sundown, no one speaking, and it was so quiet I could hear the hooves of the goats clattering on the cobblestones, the murmuring of the distant monkeys.

'A temple?'

Mr Gopal thought a moment. 'Yes,' he said finally, 'a kind of temple.'

On the ornate temple walls, stuck with posters, defaced with chisels, pissed on, and scrawled over with huge Devanagari script advertising Jaipur businesses, there was a blue enamel sign, warning visitors in Hindi and English that it was 'forbidden to desecrate, deface, mark, or otherwise abuse the walls'. The sign itself had been defaced: the enamel was chipped—it looked partly eaten.

Farther along, the cobblestone road became a narrow path and then a steep staircase cut into the rock walls of the gorge. At the top of this was a temple facing a still, black pool. Insects swimming in circles on the pool's surface made minuscule ripples, and small clouds of vibrant gnats hovered over the water. The temple was an unambitious niche in the rock face, a shallow cave, lighted with oil lamps and tapers. On either side of its portals were seven-foot marble slabs, the shape of those handed down from Sinai but with a weight that would give the most muscular prophet a hernia. These tablets had numbered instructions cut into them in two languages. In the failing light I copied down the English.

1. The use of soap in the temple and washing clothes is strictly prohibited
2. Please do not bring shoes near the tank
3. It does not suit for women to take bath among male members
4. Spitting while swimming is quite a bad habit
5. Do not spoil others clothes by splitting water while swimming
6. Do not enter the temple with wet clothes
7. Do not spit improperly to make the places dirty

'*Splitting?*' I said to Mr Gopal. 'What is splitting?'

'That does not say splitting.'

'Take a look at number five.'

'It says splashing.'

'It says splitting.'

'It says—'

We walked over to the tablet. The letters, two inches high, were cut deep into the marble.

'—splitting,' said Mr Gopal. 'I've never run across that one before. I think it's a kind of splashing.'

Mr Gapal was doing his best, but he was a hard man to escape from. So far I had been travelling alone with my handbook and my Western Railway timetable; I was happiest finding my own way and did not require a liaison man. It had been my intention to stay on the train, without bothering about arriving anywhere; sightseeing was a way of passing the time, but, as I had concluded in Istanbul, it was activity very largely based on imaginative invention, like rehearsing your own play in stage sets from which all the actors had fled.

Jaipur was a pink princely city of marvels, but the

vandalism and ignorance of those people who herded their goats into the frail ruins, painted over frescoes, and used the palace as a backdrop for filming diminished its attraction. A shouting film crew had occupied the City Palace, and its presence made the place seem a construction of exorbitant fakery. I gave my lecture; I was anxious to catch the train, but the timetable said there would not be a train to Delhi until 12.34 the following morning. It was an awkward time to leave: a day and an entire evening lay before me, and I did not relish the prospect of standing at Jaipur Junction at midnight.

'Today we go to the museum,' said Mr Gopal, the day after Galta.

'Let's give the museum a miss.'

'Very interesting place, and you said you wanted to see Moghul paintings. This is *home* of Moghul paintings!'

Outside the museum I said, 'When was this built?'

'About 1550.'

He hadn't hesitated. But today I had my handbook. The building he had placed in the mid-sixteenth century was the Albert Hall, started in 1878 and finished in 1887. In 1550 Jaipur did not exist, though I didn't have the heart to tell that to Mr Gopal, who had sulked when I contradicted him the previous day. Anyway, a weakness for exaggeration seemed a chronic affliction of some Indians. Inside the museum, another guide was showing a tent-like red robe to a group of tourists. He said, 'This belong to famous Maharaja Madho Singh. A big fat man. Seven feet tall, four feet wide, and weighing five hundred pounds.'

At Jai Singh's observatory, a garden of astronomer's marble instruments that looks at first glance like a children's playground, with slides and ladders and fifty-foot chutes splayed out symmetrically against the sun, Mr Gopal said he had visited the place many times. He showed me a great bronze disk that looked as if it might be a map of the night sky. I asked him if that was so. No, he said, it was to tell the time. He showed me a beacon, a submerged truncated hemisphere, a tower with eighty steps, a series of radiating benches: these were also for telling time. All this delicate apparatus, used by Prince Jai Singh (I read in my handbook) for finding altitudes and azimuths and celestial longitudes, Mr Gopal saw as a collection of oversized clocks.

While Mr Gopal was having lunch I sneaked off and bought my ticket to Delhi. The station at Jaipur Junction is modelled after the lovely buildings in the walled city. It is red sandstone, with cupolas, great arches, and substantial pillars that approach the palatial; inside are murals of lemon-faced women and turbaned men, enlargements of the traditional paintings, with borders of posies.

'I take it I won't be able to catch the train until after midnight,' I said.

'No, no,' said the clerk. 'Sooner than that.'

And he explained. The first-class sleeping car was already on the siding, being cleaned up to join the Delhi Mail. I could board in the early evening, and after midnight the Mail would pull in from Ahmedabad and this sleeping car would be hitched to it. He said I should not be alarmed if I boarded a sleeping car detached from a train: the train would arrive on time.

'Come down here tonight,' he said, 'and ask for two-up first-class ACC bogie. We will show you.'

Later in the day I had a long meal with Mr Gopal in a Jaipur restaurant and afterwards announced that I would be going to the station. Mr Gopal said there was no train: 'You will have hours to wait.' I said I didn't mind. I went to the station and climbed aboard the cosily lighted sleeping car that was parked at the far end of the platform. My compartment was large. The conductor showed me the desk, the shower, the lights. I took a shower, and then in my bathrobe wrote a letter to my wife and copied out the commandments from the temple at Galta into my notebook. It was still early. I sent the conductor out for beer and had a talk with the Indian in the next compartment.

He was a professor at Rajasthan University, and he was interested to learn that I had given a lecture for the English Department. He said he rather disliked university students; they littered the grounds with election posters and hired people to clean up after the election. They were silly, short-sighted, and disorderly; they were always posturing. 'Sometimes,' he said, 'it makes my blood boil.'

I told him about Mr Gopal.

'You see?' he said. 'I'll tell you something. The average Indian knows very little about his religion, or India, or anything else. Some are ignorant of the most simple things, such as Hindu concepts or history. I agree with Naipaul one hundred per cent. They don't like to appear ignorant before a Westerner, but most Indians don't know any more about their temples and writing and what-not than the tourists—many know a lot less.'

'Aren't you exaggerating?'

'I am saying what I know. Of course, when a man gets older he begins to take an interest. So some old men know about Hinduism. They get a bit worried about what is going to happen to them.'

I offered the professor a beer, but he said he had some paperwork to do. He said good night and went into his compartment, and I withdrew into mine. We were still at the siding at Jaipur Junction. I poured myself a beer and lay in my berth reading Forster's *The Longest Journey*. I had been misled: this was no travel book; it was the story of a bad short-story writer and his callow wife and sniping friends. I threw it aside and read a few pages of *The Autobiography of a Yogi*, then fell asleep. I was awakened at half-past twelve by a bump: my bogie's being coupled to the Delhi Mail. All night the train rocked and clicked towards Delhi, while I slumbered in my cool room, and I was so refreshed on arriving that I decided to leave that same evening for Madras to see if, as my map said—though everyone claimed it was impossible—I could take a train to Ceylon.

1975

RUSKIN BOND

FOOTLOOSE IN AGRA

The cycle-rickshaw is the best way of getting about Agra. Its smooth gliding motion and leisurely rate of progress are in keeping with the pace of life in this old-world city. The rickshaw-boy juggles his way through the crowded bazaars, exchanging insults with tonga-drivers, pedestrians and other cyclists; but once on the broad Mall or Taj Road, his curses change to carefree song and he freewheels along the tree-lined avenues. Old colonial-style bungalows still stand in large compounds shaded by peepul, banyan, neem and jamun trees.

Looking up, I notice a number of bright paper kites that flutter, dip and swerve in the cloudless sky. I cannot recall seeing so many kites before.

'Is it a festival today?' I ask.

'No, sahib,' says the rickshaw-boy, 'not even a holiday.'

'Then why so many kites?'

He does not even bother to look up. 'You can see kites every day, sahib.'

'I don't see them in Delhi.'

'But Delhi is a busy place. In Agra, people still fly kites. There are kite-flying competitions every Sunday, and heavy bets

RUSKIN BOND's first novel, *The Room on the Roof*, written when he was seventeen, received the John Llewelyn Rhys Memorial Prize in 1957. Since then he has written over three hundred short stories, essays and novellas (including *Vagrants in the Valley*, *A Flight of Pigeons* and *Delhi is Not Far*) and more than thirty books for children. In 1992 he received the Sahitya Akademi award for English writing in India, and was awarded the Padma Shri in 1999. 'Footloose in Agra' is from a journal he kept in the mid-1960s when he travelled extensively in the small towns of north India.

are sometimes placed on the outcome.'

As we near the city, I notice kites stuck in trees or dangling from electric wires; but there are always others soaring up to take their place. I ask the rickshaw-boy to tell me something about the kite-fliers and the kite-makers, but the subject bores him.

'You had better see the Taj today, sahib.'

'All right, take me to it. I can lunch afterwards.'

It is difficult to view the Taj at noon. The sun strikes the white marble, and there is a great dazzle of reflected light. I stand there with averted eyes, looking at everything—the formal gardens, the surrounding walls of red sandstone, the winding river—everything except the monument I have come to see.

It is there, of course, very solid and real, perfectly preserved, with every jade, jasper or lapis lazuli playing its part in the overall design; and after a while, I can shade my eyes and take in a vision of shimmering white marble. The light rises in waves from the paving-stones, and the squares of black and white marble create an effect of running water. Inside the chamber it is cool and dark but rather musty, and I waste no time in hurrying out again into the sunlight.

I walk the length of a gallery and turn with some relief to the river scene. The sluggish Yamuna winds past Agra on its way to union with the Ganga. I know the Yamuna well. I know it where it emerges from the foothills near Kalsi, cold and blue from the melting snows; I know it as it winds through fields of wheat and sugarcane and mustard, across the flat plains of Uttar Pradesh, sometimes placid, sometimes in flood. I know the river at Delhi, where its muddy banks are a patchwork of clothes spread out by the hundreds of washermen who serve the city, and I know it at Mathura, where it is alive with huge, probably ancient turtles; Mathura, sacred city, whose beginnings are lost in antiquity.

And then the river winds its way to Agra, to this spot by the Taj, where parakeets flash in the sunshine, kingfishers swoop low over the water and a proud peacock struts across the lawns surrounding the monument.

I follow the peacock into a shady grove. It is quite tame and does not fly away. It leads me to a young boy who is sitting in the shade of a tree, feasting on a handful of small green fruits.

I have not seen the fruit before, and I ask the boy to tell me what it is. He offers me what looks like a hard green plum.

'It is the fruit from the Ashoka tree,' says the boy. 'There are many such trees in the garden.'

'Are you allowed to take the fruit?'

'I am allowed,' he says, grinning. 'My father is the head gardener.'

I bite into the fruit. It is hard and sour but not unpleasant.

'Do you live here?' I ask.

'Over the wall,' he says. 'But I come here everyday, to help my father and to eat the fruit.'

'So you see the Taj Mahal every day?'

'I have seen it every day for as long as I can remember.'

'And I am seeing it for the first time . . . you're very lucky.'

He shrugs. 'If you see it once, or a hundred times, it is the same. It doesn't change.'

'Don't you like looking at it, then?'

'I like looking at the people who come here. They are always different. In the evening there will be many people.'

'You must have seen people from almost every country in the world.'

'That is so. They all come here to look at the Taj. Kings and Queens and Presidents and Prime Ministers and film stars and poor people too. And I look at them. In that way it isn't boring.'

'Well, you have the Taj to thank for that.'

He gazes thoughtfully at the shimmering monument. His eyes are accustomed to the sharp sunlight. He sees the Taj every day, but at this moment he is really looking at it, thinking about it, wondering what magic it must possess to attract people from all comers of the earth, to bring them here walking through his father's well-kept garden so that he can have something new and fresh to look at each day.

A cloud—a very small cloud—passes across the face of the sun; and in the softened light I too am able to look at the Taj without screwing up my eyes.

As the boy said, it does not change. Therein lies beauty. For the effect on the traveller is the same today as it was three hundred years ago when Bernier wrote: 'Nothing offends the eye . . . No part can be found that is not skilfully wrought, or that has not its peculiar beauty.'

And so, for a few moments, this poem in marble is on view to two unimportant people—the itinerant writer and the gardener's boy.

We say nothing; there is really nothing to be said. (But now, a few months later, when I try to recapture the essence of that day, it is not the monument that I remember most vividly. The Taj is there of course; I still see it as a mirror for the sun. But what remains with me, more than anything else, is the passage of the river and the sharp flavour of the Ashoka fruit.)

In the afternoon I walk through the old bazaars which lie to the west of Akbar's great red sandstone fort, and I am not surprised to find a small street which is almost entirely taken up by kite-shops. Most of them sell the smaller, cheaper kites, but one small dark shop has in it a variety of odd and fantastic creations. Stepping inside, I find myself face to face with the doyen of Agra's kite-makers, Hosain Ali, a feeble old man whose long beard is dyed red with the juice of mehendi leaves. He has just finished making a new kite from bamboo, paper and thin silk, and it lies outside in the sun, firming up. It is a pale pink kite, with a small green tail.

The old man is soon talking to me, for he likes to talk and is not very busy. He complains that few people buy kites these days (I find this hard to believe), and tells me that I should have visited Agra twenty-five years ago, when kite-flying was the sport of kings and even grown men found time to spend an hour or two every day with these gay, dancing strips of paper. Now, he says, everyone hurries, hurries in a heat of hope, and delicate things like kites and day-dreams are trampled underfoot. 'Once I made a wonderful kite,' says Hosain Ali nostalgically. 'It was unlike any kite seen in Agra. It had a number of small, very light paper discs trailing on a thin bamboo frame. At the end of each disc I fixed a sprig of grass, forming a balance on both sides. On the first and largest disc I painted a face and gave it eyes made of two small mirrors. The discs, which grew smaller from head to tail, gave the kite the appearance of a crawling serpent. It was very difficult to get this great kite off the ground. Only I could manage it.

'Of course, everyone heard of the Dragon Kite I had made, and word went about that there was some magic in its making. A large crowd arrived on the maidan to watch me fly the kite.

'At first the kite would not leave the ground. The discs made a sharp wailing sound, the sun was trapped in the little mirrors. My kite had eyes and tongue and a trailing silver tail. I felt it come alive in my hands. It rose from the ground, rose steeply into the sky, moving farther and farther away, with the sun still glinting in its dragon eyes. And when it went very high, it pulled fiercely on the twine, and my son had to help me with the reel.

'But still the kite pulled, determined to be free—yes, it had become a living thing—and at last the twine snapped, and the wind took the kite, took it over the rooftops and the waving trees and the river and the far hills for ever. No one ever saw where it fell. Sahib, are you listening? The Dragon Kite is lost, but for you I'll make a bright new poem to fly.'

'Make me one,' I say, moved by his tale, or rather by the manner of its telling, for Hosain Ali is a poet. 'I will collect it tomorrow, before I leave Agra. Let it be a beautiful kite. I won't fly it. I'll hang it on my wall, and won't give it a chance to get away.'

It is evening, and the winter sun comes slanting through the intricate branches of a banyan tree, as a cycle-rickshaw—a different one this time—brings me to a forgotten corner of Agra that I have always wanted to visit. This is the old Roman Catholic cemetery where so many early European travellers and adventurers lie buried.

Although it is quite probably the oldest Christian cemetery in northern India, it has none of that overgrown, crumbling look that is common to old cemeteries in monsoon lands. It is a bright, even cheerful place, and the jingle of tonga-bells and other street noises can be heard from any part of the grounds. The grass is cut, the gravestones are kept clean, and most of the inscriptions are still readable.

The caretaker takes me straight to the oldest grave—this is the oldest known European grave in northern India—and it happens to be that of an Englishman, John Mildenhall. The lettering stands cut clearly:

> *Here lies John Mildenhall, Englishman, who left London in 1599 and travelling to India through Persia, reached Agra in 1605 and spoke with the Emperor Akbar. On a second visit in 1614 he fell ill at Lahore, died at Ajmere, and was buried here through the good offices of Thomas Kerridge Merchant.*

During the seventeenth and eighteenth centuries, the Agra cemetery was considered blessed ground by Christians, and the dead were brought here from distant places. Thomas Kerridge must have put himself to considerable expense to bury his friend in Agra. Mildenhall was a romantic, who styled himself an envoy of Queen Elizabeth. Unfortunately he left no account of his travels, although a couple of his letters are quoted in the writings of Purchas, another English merchant, who lies buried in the Protestant cemetery a couple of furlongs away.

Nearby is the grave of the Venetian Jerome Veronio, who died at Lahore. According to some old records, he had a hand in designing the Taj, modelling it on Humayun's tomb in Delhi. There had for long been a belief that this 'architect' of the Taj

lay buried in the cemetery, but no one knew where. Then in
1945, Father Hyacinth, Superior Regular of Agra, scraped the
moss off a tombstone, revealing the simple epitaph: 'Here lies
Jerome Veronio, who died at Lahore.'

Actually, there is no evidence that Veronio designed the Taj,
and even if he had something to do with it, he was only one of a
number of artists and architects who worked on its
construction. The chief architect was Muhammed Sharif of
Samarkhand. Each drew a salary of one thousand rupees per
month. Ismail Khan of Turkey was the dome-maker. A number
of inlay workers, sculptors and masons were Hindus, including
Manohar Singh of Lahore and Mohan Lal of Kanauj, both
famous inlay-workers.

A man of more authentic accomplishments was the Italian
lapidary Horten Bronzoni, whose grave lies at a short distance
from Veronio's. He died on 11 August 1677. According to
Tavernier, it was Bronzoni who cut the Koh-i-noor diamond;
and, says Tavernier, he cut the stone very badly.

Bronzoni is again mentioned as having manufactured a
model ship of war for Aurangzeb, who had been annoyed by the
depredations of Portuguese pirates and was anxious to create a
navy. The ship was floated in a huge tank and manoeuvred by a
number of European artillery-men. It made a ridiculous sight
and convinced the Emperor that a navy was out of the question.

There are over eighty old Armenian graves in the cemetery,
but the only one that interests me is the tomb of Shah Azar
Khan, an expert in the art of moulding heavy cannon. One of
these, the 14.6-feet-long 'Zamzamah', earned a measure of
immortality in Kipling's *Kim*: Who hold *Zam-Zammah*, that
'fire-breathing dragon', hold the Punjab—for the great
green-bronze piece is always first of the conqueror's loot.

Other historic tombs lie scattered about the cemetery, but
the most striking and curious of them is the grave of Colonel Jon
Hessing, who died in 1803. It is a miniature Taj Mahal, built of
red sandstone. Although small compared to a Mughal tomb, it is

large for a Christian grave, and could easily accommodate a living family of moderate proportions. Hessing came to India from Holland, and was one of a colourful band of freelance soldiers (most of them deserters) who served in Sindhia's Maratha army. Hessing, we are told, was a good, benevolent man and a great soldier. The tomb was built by his wife Alice, who it must be supposed felt as tenderly towards the Colonel as Shah Jahan felt towards his queen. She could not afford marble. Even so, her 'Taj' cost a lakh of rupees.

Outside the cemetery, in the street, people move about with casual unconcern. Street-vendors occupy the pavement, unwilling that their rivals should take advantage of a brief absence. In the banyan tree, the sparrows and bulbuls are settling down for the night. A kite lies entangled in the upper branches.

1965

BRUCE CHATWIN

ON THE ROAD WITH MRS G.

Mrs Gandhi's secretary—her Assistant Private Secretary—
called to say that she would be driving at four-thirty in the
morning to Pantnagar Agricultural University where the riot
police had shot some peasants. Estimates of the numbers dead
varied from thirteen to four hundred.

'If you want to see Madame in action,' he said, 'don't throw
up the chance.'

We left Delhi in the half-light: Mrs Gandhi's air-conditioned
Chevrolet leading a procession of five cars. Our driver had been
to the Doon School with Sanjay Gandhi, and his nickname was
Dumpy. His companion was a tall, dark, graceful girl who had
been a model in New York and wore a painted Rajasthani sari.

'Isn't Mrs G. rather marvellous?' she said.

Later, when the hired claque whizzed by in a minibus, she
said: 'Do look! There go the rowdies!'

At Rundrapur, Congress-Indira workers had put together a
fair-sized, if rather taciturn crowd. But once the Rowdies started
bawling 'Indira Zindabad!' people came running from all

BRUCE CHATWIN launched his writing career in 1977 with *In Patagonia*,
which won the Hawthornden Prize and the E.M. Forster award. His other travel
books include *The Viceroy of Ouidah*, *On the Black Hill* and his most
well-known work, *The Songlines*, about the aborigines of Australia. His novel
Utz was shortlisted for the Booker in 1988. Bruce Chatwin died in 1989. 'On the
Road with Mrs G.' is extracted from *What Am I Doing Here*, a collection of his
essays published posthumously.

directions and jammed the yard outside the Guest House. The police had to bash a way for her to pass upstairs. A man shouted in my ear: 'Everyone is waiting for Indiraji. The people have love for her.'

Mrs Gandhi wore a green-and-white striped sari, and sat down to a breakfast that never came. I introduced myself.

'Oh! *that's* who you are!' she said. 'I can only give you my little finger to shake because there's something the matter with the others.'

She offered round a piece of soap in case anyone wanted to wash. From time to time, she stepped out onto the balcony and glowered at the outstretched palms and betel-stained mouths of the crowd.

Notwithstanding the imperial nose and the great brooding eyes, she seemed small, frail and nervous. She had a tick in her left cheek, and kept rolling her tongue round the right side of her mouth. My immediate impulse was to protect her.

She went into the bedroom, and a hysterical young man in glasses tried to barge past her Sikh bodyguards.

'Let me see her!' he shrieked. 'You're the ones who ruined her reputation during the Emergency.'

The town of Pantnagar lies on a fertile plain of sugar plantations and maize fields. Along the horizon, the foothills of the Himalayas flickered in the heat haze.

The local farmers are Jats. They are a caste of peasant proprietors who have resisted every attempt to make them share their land with the landless. They employ a shifting workforce of Purbias: a poor, landless caste from the eastern half of the state. About 6,000 Purbias are employed on the Agricultural University's farms: only Purbias died in the shooting.

News of the atrocity had filled the Delhi newspapers for five days: the date fell on the fifty-ninth anniversary of the Amritsar Massacre. Worse, the men involved in the shooting were Jats.

Jats had control of the University and were running it as a private fief. The Vice-Chancellor, a Mr D.P. Singh, was a Jat, and he was the nominee of Mrs Gandhi's arch-enemy, the Home Minister of the ruling Janata Government, Charan Singh.

Charan Singh left Mrs Gandhi's cabinet in 1977 with the comment, 'she never speaks the truth, even by mistake!' He is an obdurate seventy-six-year-old, an agricultural economist and a Gandhian. He abhors the city and heavy industry: India is to be saved by its independent peasant farmers. At his prompting, the Janata is channelling investment away from the industrial to the rural sector. The reaction of big business has been to pump money into Mrs Gandhi's campaign.

Charan Singh also heads the movement for her arrest and trial—although he bungled it last October. The police officer turned up with the wrong kind of warrant. (She had fixed this through spies inside the Ministry.) So by the time he returned with the right warrant, she had phoned the entire press corps and was staging a monumental scene in the front garden.

'Handcuff me!' she screamed. 'If I'm a common criminal, I demand to be handcuffed.'

In the kitchen, the cook—whom I managed to interview—was shredding documents with an Italian noddle-cutter belonging to Rajiv Gandhi's wife, Sonia.

Owing to a heart condition, Charan Singh did not show up at Pantnagar in the summer heat. Nor did any member of the Janata Government. But Mrs G. was not going to let the opportunity slip.

At noon, the cars halted by a grain-mill where, half an hour after the main shooting, a police platoon had gunned down five workers as they were having lunch. Dr Pant, a serene, bearded academic, showed us round.

'Pure barbarity!' he muttered. 'How could any civilized government permit such a thing?'

Mrs G. took little notice but strode round the exhibits with a grim face. She peered at a pool of caked blood on the grass. She peered at a lamp post buckled by bullets, and at a bullet-hole through a body's shoulder. Then she met the widows. She gave them no consolation. Instead, she offered her jagged three-quarter profile to them and the photographers. The widows seemed quite pleased.

At the University campus an excitable crowd was waiting. Mrs G. mounted a canopied podium, and the speeches began. Members of the Provincial Armed Constabulary—the PACs—strutted about in perfectly pressed khaki. In one of the buildings some students had begun a 'fast till death'—which they called off the moment she left.

My friend of the afternoon was Sanjay's wife, Maneka—a pretty, freckle-faced girl dressed in scarlet kurta-payjamas. She had not an easy time. Her father, Lt Col Anand, was thought to have siphoned funds away from Sanjay's Maruti car factory and diverted them to Congress-I. Last June he was found shot dead in a field, lying on newspapers full of the scandal. A note at his side read 'Sanjay worry unbearable'. Neither dogs nor vultures had touched the corpse for two days. The gun was missing. The arms were rigid. It was an odd kind of suicide.

'Come on, Brucie.' Maneka took my hand. 'Come and watch me do my fish wife act!'

She led me to the Children's Park where the PACs had pitched camp.

'Show me your rifles,' she screeched at a kind-faced sergeant.

'I can't, Manekaji.'

'You showed them when you murdered people. Why can't you show them to me?'

She raised her camera.

'Please, Manekaji, don't photograph me. I have a wife and a mother. We had nothing to do with the killing. It was the 10th

Battalion from Meerut.'

The 10th Battalion had been transferred.

The speeches ended and Mrs Gandhi went to inspect the scene of the crime: at a crossroads between the student hostel and some staff bungalows.

The trouble began when some non-Jats among the students and staff encouraged the Purbias to strike for higher pay. A local Congress-I politician got in on the act. The Vice-Chancellor panicked and asked for a detachment of police. About a thousand Purbias first prayed in their temple and then set off in a protest march towards the administrative building. The PACs blocked their path—and they sat down.

The students, confined to their hostel, had a grandstand view from the roof. They saw the police officer fire a single shot into the air, and saw his men fire straight into the crowd. Some of the strikers ran for an open drain where we saw their sandals still floating on the surface. Others rushed for the bungalows but were dragged out and bayoneted. There was a list of 81 dead; 160 were missing.

Yet the cheerful crowds milling around Mrs. G. gave the event the air of a race-meeting. A senior student boasted it was he who had persuaded her to come. He knew all along that the Jats had planned the massacre for that morning.

'In which case,' I said, 'why didn't you stop the Purbias from marching to their deaths?'

He shrugged and walked away.

A Janata supporter said the whole thing had been set up by agents-provocateurs.

'And now let me show you something absolutely gruesome,' said a bright-eyed boy from Kerala. He pointed to a bed of zinnias and petunias, in which there was a reddish smear, buzzing with flies.

'The   brains   of   a   murdered   man,'   he   added, melodramatically. 'Pantnagar produces the best seeds in India. Now human seeds have been sown in the cane fields.'

The police, he said, loaded the bodies onto a truck, burned them with gasoline in the cane fields, and ploughed in the remains.

'And even now, sir, in that place you will smell putrefaction and burnt flesh!'

The students dug up the bones and took them to the laboratory, but the verdict passed on to Charan Singh pronounced them the bones of jackals.

'This is a question mark,' Mrs G. said to me in Delhi two days later. 'Whether the bones were jackals' or whether people were burned in the fields, that has not been proved. What the students say is: "Why did they set fire to the fields? They must be hiding *something*." But when we talked to Dr Pant he wasn't sure whether the bones were human or not.'

'So you think the shooting was planned in advance?'

'It's very difficult to say,' she said, 'I mean, it seems so senseless. I always find it very difficult to believe in anything for which you can't find a cause. It all seems so cruel . . .'

COCHIN, KERALA

After a whistle-stop round of speeches at Bombay airport, we have followed Mrs G. to Kerala where she hopes to mend a split within the Congress Party. Her faction here is quite strong: a Kerala MP, Mr C.M. Stephen, is her Leader of the Opposition in Lok Sabha, or Lower House. But she has been a controversial— not to say hated—figure since 1960 when she persuaded her father to boot out the elected Communist State Government.

They put on a good show at the airport. Chanting crowds cheered her and Mr Stephen to a white Mercedes that belonged to a local drink concessionaire. We followed in a taxi.

On the outskirts of town, a lathi-charge was coming down

the street. The anti-Indira demonstrators dropped their black flags and scampered away from the 'hard hats'. We swerved. A man fell close to the taxi and was clubbed in the gutter. At the fourth blow blood spurted over his face. Sixty-one casualties were taken to the General Hospital. No one was killed.

Mrs G. installed herself in the Old Divan's residence: a wooden building wherein, in the ground-floor saloon, there were ferns in a brass jardiniere, watercolours of Venice and a print of *Madonna of the Rocks*.

At sunset black clouds banked up and burst: but the downpour did not prevent about a quarter of a million drenched figures from filing past to pay their respects.

Mrs G. reviewed them from a balcony on the top storey, seated on a chair which had been placed on a table. She jammed a torch between her knees, directing the beam upwards to light her face and arms. She rotated the arms as if performing the mudras of Lakshmi, Goddess of Wealth. One group of marchers carried mock corpses, wrapped in orange cloth and with names in Devanagari script. They were the three old men of the Janata: Morarji Desai, Jagjivan Ram and Charan Singh.

'They'll stop at nothing,' Mrs G. laughed, 'but I suppose it's all right.'

I was sitting on the table.

'Do get me some more of those cashew nuts.' She turned to me. 'You've no idea how tiring it is to be a goddess.'

The rain cleared and I went into the street to join the marchers. Their pupils dilated as they gazed in adoration at the tiny illuminated figure.

An hour later, I was sitting again behind Mrs G. on the podium of the Cochin Stadium: but it really was a dismal performance. She spoke in English, in a thin, whining voice, and listed a catalogue of accusations against the Janata.

'No control . . . strife . . . no law and order . . . atrocities are

commonplace . . . no homes for the homeless . . . Harijans
(Untouchables) burned alive . . . lathi charges . . . Instead of
strengthening the voice of the voiceless they are more interested
in haranguing me . . . But we have something more important,
the love of the people. We can feel the pulse of the masses . . .'

She had not felt the pulse of this mass. Thousands and
thousands turned their backs, and, in the arc lights, we watched
the upper tiers draining, and snaking for the exits.

At the breakfast press conference Mrs G., dressed in a crisp
flower-printed sari, demonstrated her flawless technique for
dealing with a roomful of men. She poured from the teapot in
her best memsahib manner. If anyone presumed to ask an
awkward question, she said, 'Do have another cup of tea!'

One journalist, bolder than the rest, was not to be put off.

'Why,' he asked, 'when you were in power, did you throw
out the foreign press? Why are you now courting the foreign
press?'

She looked hard in my direction: 'I don't see the foreign
press.'

At eight sharp the motorcade set off north for Calicut. Mrs G.
sat on the back seat of the drink concessionaire's Mercedes. We
followed in far greater comfort and style, in the doctor's car: an
immaculate white Humber Super Snipe with the Red Cross flag
fluttering from the bonnet.

'What could go wrong with Mrs Gandhi?' I asked the
doctor.

'She might get stoned,' he said wearily. 'But the worst we
expect is an allergy to flowers.'

The doctor had already surprised us with the bust of Stalin in his
living room. This was his story:

Sometime in the Fifties, he was a house-man at the General
Hospital in Newcastle-on-Tyne. Among his patients was a

Conservative MP who was expected to die of a bloodclot approaching his heart. The MP wanted to die, but wanted to live until Saturday when his racehorse was running at Long-champs. On Friday evening came news that the horse had been kicked and couldn't run.

'Damn it,' said the MP. 'I'd have known what to do. Feed him a couple of pounds of onions.'

The doctor, remembering an ayurvedic cure, asked, 'Do you ever eat onions?'

'Hate onions,' said the MP. 'Always have.'

'Well, I'm going to feed you two pounds of onions.'

They forced the onions down the MP's throat. The clot dissolved—and the man lived.

The doctor took out his album of press-cuttings. *Time* showed a smiling young man in horn-rimmed glasses: the discoverer of carraganen, a chemical contained in onions that was a powerful anti-coagulant and might conceivably transform heart-surgery.

But you couldn't patent an onion: the rest was a sad tale. He came back to India. No one took any notice. He now worked for a private clinic in Cochin owned by a man I felt was completely deranged.

On the way we passed pink-eared elephants, brick-kilns and churches that looked like Chinese pagodas. Most of the slogans were welcoming. But from time to time a string of old shoes was suspended across the road: the worst of all Hindu insults.

One graffito read, 'Indira Gandhi's a notorious fascist witch.'

At every village Mrs G. got out of the car, mounted a platform decked with Congress-I flags, and thanked the crowds for their 'warm and dutiful welcome'. As the morning wore on, more and more garlands of jasmine and marigolds were festooned around her neck: each one had a banknote pinned to it. The heat had the effect of moving her to shriller and shriller rhetoric: 'The force of the Government is on one small woman . . .'

1978

ANDREW HARVEY

LEH

Ahmed knows everything about Leh. He is in league with every dealer, Kashmiri shawl-seller, mok-mok maker, restaurateur, tourist guide, defrocked lama, lamp-fixer, out-of work folk singer in town. He grins, 'Sir, I am not boasting, dear sir. But you name it, I am knowing it very fully. This is truth, sir.

'You see, dear sir, I am a Muslim boy from Delhi. I am working here in summer. Tourist season. I have to make much money. Old father, old mother, sir. Very old. And I only son. So I must know everything, no?'

He grins again and fingers my sleeping-bag. 'How much you want for this?' I say I need my sleeping-bag; and he looks sad.

'Since you know everything, Ahmed, tell me where to eat.'
Leh is no longer imaginary.

'Breakfast? Best place Pamposh. Muslim brothers. To left of main street, wooden. Eggs, chapatis, coffee. All Europeans are going there. Some of them very funny people, sir. You cannot say girl or boy. Lunch? All are going to Tibetan Restaurant. Down street from Pamposh. On the corner. Very good woman,

---

ANDREW HARVEY has written and edited over thirty books. Among his well-known titles are *Burning Houses*, *The Way of the Mother*, *The Way of Passion: A Celebration of Rumi*, *Hidden Journey*, *The Essential Gay Mystics*, *The Tibetan Book of Living and Dying* (co-authored with Sogyal Rinpoche) and *The Direct Path*. 'Leh' is an extract from *A Journey in Ladakh* (Christmas Humphries Award, 1983), both a travel book and a spiritual autobiography.

very pretty lady, sir. I am not liking Tibetan food. It is making
me sick, sir, but you will like. Dinner? I am always saying, go to
Dreamland. It is next to generator. It is good. Tibetan and
Western. Young Tibetan girl, very pretty, with her brother, very
thin. Same food—mok-mok, Lhasa chow-mein. I am sick for
this food. But you are Christian, you will like.'

Pamposh is hardly a café at all. It is a shack, a rickety wooden
shack, open on all three sides to the street. It has coffee so bad,
so old, and so thin, you have to be a caffeine addict to get
through it at all. It has an owner so absent-minded that he
poured salt into my coffee instead of sugar. It is where All Leh
goes, as Ahmed said, toute la cirque of bandana Italians,
Australian sannyasins . . . On one wall there is President Carter,
three smiling portraits of Mohammed Ali, two posters of Donna
Summers (one moustached), and Botticelli's 'Birth of Venus' (no
moustache); on the other are a fat Indian male film-star in gold
lamé trousers walking in the gardens of the Taj Mahal, Indira
Gandhi as Mother Kali, Avalokiteshvara with his thousand
orange, red, and purple arms, Evel Knievel leaping through a
hoop of flame in Colorado on his super-bike, and Cranach's
portrait of Martin Luther with 'Io t'amo Martino', signed
Giovanni Maria Claudio e Pietro in the corner.
    Crazy though this debris of images is, I feel at home, amused
and exhilarated. A German lorry-driver is haranguing me about
Rimbaud; a Kashmiri salesman is trying to squeeze the knee of
the Italian girl with the red bandana, to my left; in the corner an
old, dignified Ladakhi is sipping his tea noisily; a young girl,
slightly pockmarked, in a dark woollen skirt and peaked black
hat, stares in at us all from the street, intently, yet without
malice or fear. Ahmed had said, 'Go to Pamposh, my dear sir,
and everything you will see. You will see girls. You will see
Kashmiris. You will see lamas. You will see foreigners. You will
hear all languages, dear sir. Every smell of the city you will

smell. Everything I am telling you you will see.'

'What do you think of Leh?' the Italian girl asked me.

'I am fascinated . . .'

'You are fascinated. How stupid! There is nothing left in Leh. Look at the Palace. It is ruined. Look at the Gompa. It is modern. Look at the main street. It is the only street. It is ugly. Look at the shops. What do they have? In the Tibetan shops everything is fake; in the Kashmiri shops everything is fake and crazily expensive. Leh is a place where foreigners get fleeced, that's all.'

She stared in front of her bitterly. 'Tomorrow I am going back to Goa. At least there's sea there.'

She was wrong about Leh. It is true that it is no longer the exotic market town with Chinese, Yarkandi, Tibetan and Russian traders that De Vigne described; it is true that there is only one main street with an ugly inefficient post office, an ugly Cultural Academy, and two rows of ugly tumbledown over-expensive under-stocked shops; and there is no graceful order to the streets or houses, that run into each other haphazardly. Yet Leh does have charm.

There is nothing whatever to do. That is Leh's charm. There is a cinema, but it is down the hill, about a mile away, and shows nothing worth seeing; there is a Gompa, but once you've walked round it, making all the prayer-cylinders round its walls shake and whirr, you've seen it—there are no ancient frescoes, no old sculptures to be seen inside; there is a Cultural Academy but nothing happens at it, no Dance Meetings, no Evenings of Ladakhi Songs, no displays of tankas, or half-learned talks on Buddhas and Bodhisatvas; there is a market in the evening of fruit and vegetables along the main street, and another market all day in a side street, where bells and tankas and turquoises are sold, along with cheap sweaters and sleeping-bags and pots and calendars, but neither are so arresting and colourful that you long to return to them. There is nothing to do but to slow down, relax, laze, to become one vast transparent eye.

The solidest joy of Leh is seeing its palace from every angle and in every light; from below, as it stands in the full dazzle of the morning sun; from the side, in the afternoon from the roof of my hotel, as one of its sheer sides ignites slowly in the dusk; from behind, on the road to Leh from Sankar, as it rears, ghostly in the moonlight, hardly distinguishable from the massy dark rock it is built on. You are haggling for vegetables in the market at sundown, and suddenly you look up and see the last sun catch the top of one of its balconies; you are talking to a friend in the evening, walking up the main street, and as you talk you see that the moon has risen above the palace, and seems to be wearing it like a vast earring; you turn a corner of one of Leh's innumerable labyrinthine streets and for a moment a whole flank of the palace stands in front of you, bare and stark as the mountains that surround it. The Queen and her family now live in the smaller palace at Stok, ten miles away; the Palace of Leh is empty and crumbling. When you walk through its large vacant rooms, fat tame mice come out of the dark corners to be fed .

Every morning I pass the slaughterers at work under the bridge.
    There are four young slaughterers, young Muslim Ladakhis with red faces and big arms, and two older ones, one of whom wears a filthy red bandana and has only one eye. They whistle, and chatter, and sing. This morning the youngest slaughterer was singing a ghazal—a slow, melancholy love-song. I remembered some years back rowing on the lake of Pokhara in Nepal with a young Iranian. He had been tortured under the Shah, kept in a room where he could not stand up, had horse hairs shoved up his penis. He stooped, had terrible insomnia. And he sang as beautifully as the young slaughterer. The

slaughterer and the tortured boy sang together in the morning.
The Iranian had sung me a ghazal by Rumi:

Sufi, why are you standing before the door?
What are you looking for?
I am looking, my friend,
For what is impossible to find:
I am looking for a man.

And he had wept as he sang.

The odour of blood is in everything. In the flowers by the
river, in the current of the river, in the wind blowing down-river
from the mountains.

The sheep wait huddled by a small stone shack on the other
side of the bridge. They make no noise. They look at their killers
with hollow eyes. They hardly even twitch as their throats are
cut.

There are always spectators. There is an old woman or two;
a few ragged children; an old man smoking and contemplating,
whirring his prayer wheel round and round.

'Every object in the light of Ladakh seems to have something
infinite behind it; every object, even the most humble, seems to
abide in its real place.'

Francois's words and his voice came back to me as I walked,
in the early evening light, to the stupa at the edge of town and sat
down in its warm shadow. A stupa is a building of plaster and
brick that has four stages: a large cubic foundation, rising
diminishing cubes that support a wide, empty, bun-like middle
portion, which supports in its turn a long spire that comes to a
point in the symbol of a crescent moon cradling a sun. It is a
building in which relics are kept, the relics of saints or kings or
very holy teachers, and each stage of the building symbolizes a
different state of consciousness. All over Ladakh, there are

stupas of every shape and size; in mountain passes, on the long slopes up to monasteries, along the banks of rivers, at the entrance to secluded villages, sometimes with small shrines attached to them, as in the stupa at the entrance to Sankar, where a few badly painted smiling Bodhisatvas raise their hands in blessing. Wherever you walk in the lower parts of this landscape, you are never far from the softly rising brick-red spire of the stupa, from the flash of its crescent moon and sun in the light, from the eye, the Bindu, at the centre of that union of sun and moon, that is an ancient symbol of Universal Consciousness, of the Awareness that is Nirvana. Wherever you walk, you are reminded, in the carefully calculated shape of the stupa, of the different stages of illumination that end in the experience of liberation; each of its different parts is dedicated to a different element, a different Buddha, a different ecstasy. It is a simple building, but its shape represents a whole philosophy, *is* that philosophy in one of its purest statements, crumbling white plaster and brick, against rock and sky.

The stupa at the edge of Leh stands separately on a small raised hill. I noticed as I walked up to it, seeing it against the wide spread of the Karakorams, that its shape was a meditation on the wild forms of the mountains behind it. The stupa echoes the mountains and the mountains are stupas also. Everything in this world is linked.

Everything is dark by ten. Leh is given over to the night, vast, cloudless, soaked in moonlight and starlight, the Milky Way lustrous in this high mountain air, each cluster of stars, each swirling nebula, precise and dazzling . . .

You walk into the main street and look up at the palace, that by day looks so dilapidated. At first you can hardly tell it from the rock it stands on. Then slowly its walls emerge; night gives them back some of their old grandeur. Starlight salts them brightly . . .

Hardly anyone in the street. A few Kashmiris sitting under an extinguished street-lamp talking in low voices and smoking. An old woman who passes and stares at you, her face mysterious and sibylline in that light, until she smiles. A dog you cannot see, that brushes past you suddenly and barks in fear.

There is one café that is always the last to close. It is at the beginning of the main street. At the time I go there, usually about nine, there is no one else there except the young Sikh who is sitting on a table in his dirty yellow turban, making samosas for the next day. We are friends. He has taught me how to make samosas, how to mould the batter, how to fill them with vegetables. But I am ashamed of my slowness, my lack of expertise. He can sit and talk and laugh and his hands move instinctively, shaping, filling, conjuring samosa after samosa out of the chipped white bowls of batter and vegetable . . . I have to watch all my movements. My samosas are lumpy. He laughs at me gently.

Sometimes when I come back to Leh late I pass him sitting alone in the window of his café, making samosas by lamplight. His fine, sad face shines in the yellow light; his hands, pianist's hands, move with an almost magical delicacy and precision . . . He looks up, calls me in, and we talk. An hour or two later, I walk back to my hotel. I can never sleep at once; my mind is too full to read. I lie on the roof and look up at the night, breathing in its mist of stars.

You see and hear water everywhere in Leh. Under all talk, every silence, all slow, sensuous watching runs the murmur and flash of water. Every street glitters with snow water, racing from the mountains into the ragged stone channels that lead it through the town into the fields below.

I wake up and walk to town. The first thing I see is the morning river, leaping in the light over its smooth rocks. I walk up to Pamposh; water, noisy and brilliant, runs down the hill on both sides of the street. I sit in Pamposh and look out at the old lama passing, or the woman sitting on the corner selling cabbages, or a young Kashmiri squatting outside his shop and singing, and in everything I see there is a flash of running water. I walk in the late afternoon to the Tibetan Restaurant, just down the street from Pamposh, and wait for friends, and try to write; every time I look out of its wooden windows on to the street I see the small turbulent stream outside with a child dabbling in it, or a dog wading through it, or two old Muslims sitting by it under a tree and smoking their evening hookah. And when at night I am walking, alone or with friends, through Leh, up the small streets behind and round the main street, or outside to Sankar or Changspa, the villages that are only a few hundred yards away, it is always to the noise of water, shaking in moonlight and starlight, coursing in untidy channels through darkening corn, between moon-washed poplars and willows, bringing a flickering life to paths lined by shrines and small stupas that in the moonlight seem hardly more solid than the stream that runs by chem.

Surrounded by so much water, the mind itself becomes water, hindered by nothing, abandoned, happy.

On the way to Stok, the village ten miles outside Leh, there is a suspension bridge that spans the Indus. From the distance, it looks like a circus tent, it is so covered with prayer flags of every colour. I am sitting on the seat next to the driver, a young Ladakhi, and I ask him, 'Why are there so many prayer flags?' He looks at me as if I am mad. 'If there were no prayer flags, the river would get angry.' Then he adds, 'The bridge is nearly at the middle of the valley. The wind there is very strong. The prayers can be carried down the wind on the back of the river all over this country.' It is such a festive and exuberant gesture, covering the steel lines of the bridge with scarves and mantras and holy dragons, that I want to sing. As the bus crosses the bridge, the prayer flags flap against it. The driver turns to me and smiles. 'Every time I am crossing this bridge I am saying my prayers. It is holy, this bridge.' How old is the bridge? He does not know. It is as if it had always been there like the piles of stones in the mountains, like the stupas, like the small wayside shrines. The spirit of Ladakh has changed it into a shrine, an object of worship. Does the bridge have its guardian Buddha? The driver smiled and did not answer.

I have come to Stok to see the Palace of the Rani of Stok, but as soon as I am standing in front of it I do not want to go in. To be out here, in this light, with all the day before me, and to go into those small rooms . . . I want to walk, to walk up the trail in the mountains, to be alone with the mountains and the summer streams in the valley.

I walked all day higher and higher into the mountains. It is strange no longer to be looking at them across the shifting lights of the valley, against the brilliant emptiness of the sky, but to be walking in them, at last, surrounded by them, travelling their inner paths. The rocks on the sides of the paths are sprinkled with small blue flowers; a fierce wild green grass grows between the boulders; with every quarter of an hour the heat increases and the rocks change, growing more and more fantastical, wings of cathedrals, falling into the river below, large fluted columns, like the hermit perches of Cappadocia, with golden moss spilling over from their height . . . and yet it is not the rocks and their dazzling forms that move me most; it is the signs everywhere, in this wilderness, of human companionship. Two men pass me on the path with donkeys laden with brushwood; they smile at me broadly and pass on. They have been working high in the mountains, getting wood for winter from the small tough bushes that grow in the ravines just below the tree-line. Everywhere along the track there are mantra-stones, stones with the letters OM MANI PADME HUM carved on them, breathing their sacred words silently between rocks, or at the side of a stream, or in a bed of flower-sprinkled moss. There are latos, shrines to the spirits of the rock and air, with dzo horns and bones in large whitening piles on them, shrines to the gods of this landscape that are older than the Buddhist gods but have been reconciled to Buddhism, gods of tempest and avalanche, gods of the streams that carry wealth to the valley. There are prayer flags, lonely, ragged but enduring, high on pinnacles of rock above me; they flap in the wind, breathing everywhere the words of the Buddha. This wilderness of rock and light has not been tamed; it remains exalted, and sometimes frightening. But it does not have the inhuman solitariness of Antarctica or the Sahara; everywhere there are small marks of human love and prayer. Resting on the top of a mountain pass, I found that the rock I was sitting on was ringed by white stones, heaped there by travellers over many years; walking on and on into the highest part of the pass, I found, just as I was too tired to go any further, that there was a deserted shepherd's hut, with its roof torn off by the wind, and a small rose-bush growing in the shelter of one of its walls. I sat in it and ate my bread and cheese. On the wall the shepherd had written with charcoal from the fire, OM, just the one letter, again and again. And under each letter, he had sketched a rough Buddha's face.

1983

SALMAN RUSHDIE

THE RIDDLE OF MIDNIGHT
INDIA, AUGUST 1987

Forty years ago, the independent nation of India and I were born within eight weeks of one another. I came first. This gave rise to a family joke—that the departure of the British was occasioned by my arrival on the scene—and the joke, in turn, became the germ of a novel, *Midnight's Children,* in which not just one child, but one thousand and one children born in the midnight hour of freedom, the first hour of 15 August 1947, were comically and tragically connected to the birth of a nation.

(I worked out, by the way, that the Indian birth rate in August 1947 was approximately two babies per second, so my fictional figure of 1,001 per hour was, if anything, a little on the low side.)

The chain reaction continued. The novel's title became, for many Indians, a familiar catch-phrase defining that generation which was too young to remember the Empire or the liberation struggle; and when Rajiv Gandhi became Prime Minister, I found his administration being welcomed in the newspapers by such headlines as: 'Enter midnight's children'.

So when forty came around, it occurred to me to take a look at the state of the Indian nation that was, like me, entering its

SALMAN RUSHDIE is the author of seven novels—*Grimus, Midnight's Children* (winner of the Booker Prize in 1981), *Shame, The Satanic Verses, Haroun and the Sea of Stories, The Moor's Last Sigh* and *The Ground Beneath Her Feet.* He is also the author of *The Jaguar Smile: A Nicaraguan Journey.* 'The Riddle of Midnight' is from *Imaginary Homelands,* a collection of his essays and criticism.

fifth decade; and to look, in particular, through the eyes of the class of '47, the country's citizen-twins, my generation. I flew to the subcontinent in search of the real-life counterparts of the imaginary beings I once made up. Midnight's real children: to meet them would be like closing a circle.

There was a riddle I wanted to try and answer, with their help: *Does India exist?* A strange, redundant sort of inquiry, on the face of it. After all, there the gigantic place manifestly is, a rough diamond two thousand miles long and more or less as wide, as large as Europe though you'd never guess it from the Mercator projection, populated by around a sixth of the human race, home of the largest film industry on earth, spawning Festivals the world over, famous as the 'world's biggest democracy'. Does India exist? If it doesn't, what's keeping Pakistan and Bangladesh apart?

It's when you start thinking about the political entity, the nation of India, the thing whose fortieth anniversary it is, that the question starts making sense. After all, in all the thousands of years of Indian history, there never was such a creature as a united India. Nobody ever managed to rule the whole place, not the Mughals, not the British. And then, that midnight, the thing that had never existed was suddenly 'free'. But what on earth was it? On what common ground (if any) did it, does it, stand?

Some countries are united by a common language; India has around fifteen major languages and numberless minor ones. Nor are its people united by race, religion or culture. These days, you can even hear some voices suggesting that the preservation of the union is not in the common interest. J. K. Galbraith's description of India as 'functioning anarchy' still fits, but the stresses on the country have never been so great. Does India exist? If it doesn't, the explanation is to be found in a single word: communalism. The politics of religious hatred.

There is a medium-sized town called Ayodhya in the state of Uttar Pradesh, and in this town there is a fairly commonplace mosque named Babri Masjid. According to the *Ramayana,* however, Ayodhya was the home town of Rama himself, and according to a local legend the spot where he was born—the *Ramjanmabhoomi*—is the one on which the Muslim place of worship stands today. The site has been disputed territory ever since independence, but for most of the forty years the lid has been kept on the problem by the very Indian method of shelving the case, locking the mosque's gates, and allowing neither Hindus nor Muslims to enter.

Last year, however, the case finally came to court, and the judgement seemed to favour the Hindus. Babri Masjid became the target of the extremist Hindu fundamentalist organization, the Vishwa Hindu Parishad. Since then, Hindus and Muslims all over north India have been clashing, and in every outbreak of communal violence the Babri Masjid affair is cited as a primary cause.

When I arrived in Delhi the old Walled City was under heavy curfew because of just such an outbreak of communal violence. In the little alleys of Chandni Chowk I met a Hindu tailor, Harbans Lal, born in 1947 and as mild and gentle a man as you could wish to find. The violence terrified him. 'When it started,' he said, 'I shut up the shop and ran away.' But in spite of all his mildness, Harbans Lal was a firm supporter of the Hindu nationalist party that used to be called the Jan Sangh and is now the BJP. 'I voted for Rajiv Gandhi in the election after Mrs Gandhi died,' he said. 'It was a big mistake. I won't do it again.' I asked him what should be done about the Babri Masjid issue. Should it be locked up again as it had been for so many years? Should it be a place where both Hindus and Muslims could go to worship? 'It's a Hindu shrine,' he said. 'It should be for the Hindus.' There was no possibility, in his mind, of a compromise.

A couple of days later the Walled City was still bubbling with tension. The curfew was lifted for an hour or two every day to enable people to go out and buy food. The rest of the time, security was very tight. It was Eid, the great Muslim festival celebrating the end of the month of fasting, but the city's leading imams had said that Eid should not be celebrated. In Meerut, the mutilated corpses of Muslims floated in the river. The city's predominantly Hindu police force, the PAC, had run amok. Once again, Babri Masjid was one of the bones of contention.

I met Abdul Ghani, a Delhi Muslim who worked in a sari shop, and who, like Harbans Lal, India and me, was 1947-born. I was struck by how much like Harbans Lal he was. They were both slightly built, mild-mannered men with low, courteous voices and attractive smiles. They each earned about 1,000 rupees (100 dollars) a month, and dreamed of owning their own shops, knowing they never would. And when it came to the Hindu-Muslim communal divide, Abdul Ghani was just as unyielding as Harbans Lal had been. 'What belongs to the Muslims,' he said when I asked about Babri Masjid, 'should be given back to the Muslims. There is nothing else to be done.'

The gentleness of Harbans Lal and Abdul Ghani made their religious divisions especially telling. Nor was Babri Masjid the only issue between the faiths. At Ahmedabad, in the state of Gujarat, Hindu-Muslim violence was again centred in the old walled-city area of Manek Chowk, and had long ago acquired its own internal logic: so many families had lost members in the fighting that the cycle of revenge was unstoppable. Political forces were at work, too. At Ahmedabad hospital the doctors found that many of the knife wounds they treated were professionally inflicted. Somebody was sending trained killers into town.

All over India—Meerut, Delhi, Ahmedabad, Bombay— tension between Hindus and Muslims was rising. In Bombay, a (1947-born) journalist told me that many communal incidents took place in areas where Muslims had begun to prosper and move up the economic scale. Behind the flash-points like Ayodhya, she suggested, was the Hindus' resentment of Muslim prosperity.

The Vishwa Hindu Parishad has a list of over a hundred

disputed sites of the Babri Masjid type. Two are especially important. In Mathura, a Muslim shrine stands on the supposed birthplace of the god Krishna; and in Benares, a site allegedly sacred to Shiva is also in Muslim hands . . .

In Bombay, I found a 'midnight child', a clerical worker in the docks, a Muslim named Mukadam who was such a super-citizen that he was almost too good to be true. Mukadam was absolutely dedicated to the unity of India. He believed in small families. He thought all Indians had a duty to educate themselves, and he had put himself through many evening courses. He had been named Best Worker at his dock. In his village, he claimed proudly, people of all faiths lived together in complete harmony. 'That is how it should be,' he said. 'After all, these religions are only words. What is behind them is the same, whichever faith it is.'

But when communal violence came to the Bombay docks in 1985, Mukadam's super-citizenship wasn't of much use. On the day the mob came to his dock, he was saved because he happened to be away. He didn't dare to return to work for weeks. And now, he says, he worries that it may come again at any time.

Like Mukadam, many members of Indian minority groups started out as devotees of the old, secular definition of India, and there were no Indians as patriotic as the Sikhs. Until 1984, you could say that the Sikhs were *the* Indian nationalists. Then came the storming of the Golden Temple, and the assassination of Mrs Gandhi; and everything changed.

The group of Sikh radicals led by Sant Jarnail Singh Bhindranwale, the religious leader who died in the Golden Temple storming, could not be said to represent more than a small minority of all Sikhs. The campaign for a separate Sikh state, Khalistan, had similarly found few takers among India's Sikhs until November 1984, when Indira Gandhi died, and it became known that her assassins were Sikhs.

In Delhi, angry Hindu mobs—among whom party workers

of Mrs Gandhi's Congress-I were everywhere observed—
decided to hold all Sikhs responsible for the deeds of the
assassins. Thus an entirely new form of communal violence—
Hindu-Sikh riots—came into being, and in the next ten days the
Sikh community suffered a series of traumatizing attacks from
which it has not recovered, and perhaps never will.

In Block 32 of the Delhi suburb called Trilokpuri, perhaps
350 Sikhs were burned alive. I walked past streets of charred,
gutted houses in some of which you could still see the bones of
the dead. It was the worst place I have ever seen, not least
because, in the surrounding streets, children played normally,
the neighbours went on with their lives. Yet some of these
neighbours were the very people who perpetrated the crime of
32 Trilokpuri, which was only one of the many massacres of
Sikhs that took place that November. Many Sikh 'midnight
children' never reached forty at all.

I heard about many of these deaths, and will let one story
stand for all. When the mob came for Hari Singh, a taxi-driver
like so many Delhi Sikhs, his son fled into a nearby patch of
overgrown waste land. His wife was obliged to watch as the
mob literally ripped her husband's beard off his face. (This
beard-ripping ritual was a feature of many of the November
killings.) She managed to get hold of the beard, thinking that it
was, at least, a part of him that she could keep for herself, and
she ran into their house to hide it. Some members of the mob
followed her in, found the beard and removed it. Then they
poured kerosene over Hari Singh and set fire to him. They also
chased his teenage son, found him, beat him unconscious, and
burned him, too. They knew he was a Sikh even though he had
cut his hair, because when they found his father's beard they
found his cut hair as well. His mother had preserved the sacred
locks that identified her son.

Another taxi-driver, Pal Singh (born November 1947), told
me that he had never had time for the Khalistan movement, but
after 1984 he had changed his mind. 'Now it will come,' he said,

'maybe within ten years.' Sikhs were selling their property in Delhi and buying land in the Punjab, so that if the time came when they had to flee back to the Sikh heartland they wouldn't have to leave their assets behind. 'I'm doing it, too,' Pal Singh said.

Almost three years after the 1984 massacres, not one person has been charged with murdering a Sikh in those fearsome days. The Congress-I, Rajiv Gandhi's party, increasingly relies on the Hindu vote, and is reluctant to alienate it.

The new element in Indian communalism is the emergence of a collective Hindu consciousness that transcends caste, and that believes Hinduism to be under threat from other Indian minorities. There is evidence that Rajiv's Congress-I is trying to ride that tiger. In Bombay, the tiger is actually in power. The ruling Shiv Sena Party, whose symbol is the tiger, is the most overtly Hindu-fundamentalist grouping ever to achieve office anywhere in India.

Its leader, Bal Thackeray, a former cartoonist, speaks openly of his belief that democracy has failed in India. He makes no secret of his open hostility towards Muslims. In the Bhiwandi riots of 1985, a few months before the Shiv Sena won the Bombay municipal elections, Shiv Sena activists were deeply involved in the anti-Muslim violence. And today, as the Sena seeks to spread its influence into the rural areas of Maharashtra (the state of which Bombay is the capital), incidents of communal violence are being reported from villages in which nothing of the sort has ever happened before.

I come from Bombay, and from a Muslim family, too. 'My' India has always been based on ideas of multiplicity, pluralism, hybridity: ideas to which the ideologies of the communalists are diametrically opposed. To my mind, the defining image of India is the crowd, and a crowd is by its very nature superabundant, heterogeneous, many things at once. But the India of the communalists is none of these things.

I spent one long evening in the company of a ('47-born)

Bengali intellectual, Robi Chatterjee, for whom the inadequacies of society are a cause for deep, permanent, operatic anguish. 'Does India exist?' I asked him.

'What do you mean?' he cried. 'Where the hell do you think this is?' I told him that I meant the idea of the nation. Forty years after a nationalist revolution, where could it be said to reside?

He said, 'To the devil with all that nationalism. I am an Indian because I am born here and I live here. So is everyone else of whom that is true. What's the need for any more definitions?'

I asked, 'If you do without the idea of nationalism, then what's the glue holding the country together?'

'We don't need glue,' he said. 'India isn't going to fall apart. All that balkanization stuff. I reject it completely. We are simply here and we will remain here. It's this nationalism business that is the danger.'

According to Robi, the idea of nationalism in India had grown more and more chauvinistic, had become narrower and narrower. The ideas of Hindu nationalism had infected it. I was struck by a remarkable paradox: that, in a country created by the Congress's nationalist campaign, the well-being of the people might now require that all nationalist rhetoric be abandoned.

Unfortunately for India, the linkage between Hindu fundamentalism and the idea of the nation shows no signs of weakening. India is increasingly defined as Hindu India, and Sikh and Muslim fundamentalism grows ever fiercer and entrenched in response. 'These days,' a young Hindu woman said to me, 'one's religion is worn on one's sleeve.' She was corrected by a Sikh friend. 'It is worn,' he said, 'in a scabbard at the hip.'

I remember that when *Midnight's Children* was first published in 1981, the most common Indian criticism of it was that it was too pessimistic about the future. It's a sad truth that nobody finds the novel's ending pessimistic any more, because what has happened in India since 1981 is so much darker than I had imagined. If anything, the book's last pages with their suggestion of a new, more pragmatic generation rising up to take over from the midnight children now seem absurdly, romantically optimistic.

But India regularly confounds its critics by its resilience, its survival in spite of everything. I don't believe in the balkanization of India any more than Robi Chatterjee does. It's my guess that the old functioning anarchy will, somehow or other, keep on functioning, for another forty years, and no doubt another forty after that. But don't ask me how.

1987

JERRY PINTO

DEATH LIVES IN VARANASI

'*Burrning* is *lurrning*,' says Suresh Boatman as he pulls on the
oars past Manikarnika Ghat in Varanasi where boatloads of
tourists stop to watch as the bodies of the dead are consumed by
fire. It is a catchphrase that has yielded results before and Stu
Mills, a twenty-three-year-old Australian computer nerd, puts
down his copy of *The Tibetan Book of Living and Dying* and
grins.

'Yeah,' he says, face reddened by the fires, sweat beading his
brow. 'I hope it will be.'

Like many other westerners, Stu did not come to Varanasi
because it merited four pages in his *Lonely Planet* guide to India.
With a slight trace of embarrassment, he describes his journey as
a spiritual quest.

'Someone very close to me died. Of AIDS. And I realized that
death was not something that would come at some indistinct
point in the future. I realized it was going to happen to me.
Nothing in our civilization prepares us for it, or even encourages
us to prepare for it. Death is negative and we are taught, trained,
forced almost, to focus on the positive. And yet I could die
tomorrow; it was time to confront it.' He looks around and then
says, 'And if anywhere, death lives in Banaras.'

Indians have always had a special place for the Ganga in
their traditions and mythology. Along her banks are some of the
most sacred sites of Hinduism: Gangotri, where the river starts

JERRY PINTO is a journalist, poet and travel writer. He is the author of
Surviving Women. A version of 'Death Lives in Varanasi' appeared in the
Sunday Times of India (15 June 1997).

as a stream and where the devotions of the gods keep a single diya burning for the six months of the year that snow closes the temple doors; Haridwar, where the temples of Har-ki-Pauri enshrine the sacred footprint of Vishnu; Rishikesh, where the river was crossed by the Ramjhoola made of Lakshman's arrows; Varanasi, where those whose ashes are immersed are assured of heaven; Allahabad, where three rivers meet and the Kumbh mela takes over the world's imagination for three weeks.

But what's in it for Stu and those like him who come to Varanasi and Rishikesh in search of something more than the ability to say 'Been there, done that' with the oft-heard codicil, 'It was reely reelly intense'?

'Earlier they would ask where they could get ganja,' smiles Minto Panjwani of Hotel Midtown near Haridwar. 'Now they ask where they can get lessons in yoga.'

I had come to Varanasi to look for a story that wasn't happening. *Time* magazine had reported that thousands of young Western people were flooding India carrying the ashes of their dead to the Ganga. They were following in the footsteps of Jerry Garcia's wife who had brought his ashes to the Ganga for immersion. The last bits and bobs of the star of Grateful Dead, a rock group with cult status, were floating down the river. That much had happened.

Nothing else had. The hotel owner in Rishikesh who had so willingly claimed to *Time* that they were all here with their urns, suddenly clammed up. And as for the foreign faithful, their knee-jerk response was, 'No.' It did not matter that I was not a tout, had nothing to sell, that I just wanted to talk. They saw a brown skin and said 'No'.

The story was not happening because nothing was happening.

Then two days before I was about to leave, I met Raju Boatman.
He had followed me across four ghats, urging me to try his boat,
and finally, disheartened by another five 'No's, I gave in.

'Why are you chasing the phirangis?' he asked when we
were ensconced in a boat of considerable vintage and suspect
river-worthiness.

I explained.

He sighed and tucked his chin into his shirt.

'Why are you called Raju Boatman?' I asked in turn.

'There are no surnames on the Ganga,' he replied.

Only philosophers, I thought. A long silence. And then
suddenly: 'How much will you pay to meet one of these
phirangis?'

We haggled for a while and settled on a price.

That was how I met Yvette.

Yvette had come to Varanasi to die. When the sixty-five-year-
old Belgian had a section of her intestine cut out of her and a bag
took over the functions of excretions, she decided it was time to
admit that she was terminally ill.

'Only, no one else seemed prepared to admit it. I don't
know whether it was my imagination, but everyone around me
seemed to want me to say that I was getting better, feeling better.
All their solicitous enquiries began to ring false. Eventually, it
got to the point where I would say that I was feeling better even
if I was feeling terrible, simply because there seemed to be such a
premium placed on putting on a brave face, on a denial of death.
I wanted to shout, "I'm dying, I'm not getting better." When I
couldn't bear it any more—this persistent negation of what was
inevitable—I left.'

And Satyajit Ray brought her to Varanasi. 'A few years ago
there was a retrospective of his work in Paris where I was living
and I saw the Apu trilogy. One of the many images that stayed
with me was those solid geometric steps leading down to the

river, and the flight of pigeons. And I decided that like Sarbojaya I would die in Banaras.'

Each night she comes to the empty western bank, across from Manikarnika Ghat, and takes up a lonely vigil under the stars. Around her there is nothing; in front of her a city that turns its face to the rising sun, Diana Eck's city of light.

Like so many things in her life, she muses, this is not what she expected.

'I thought I would find the black-and-white beauty of Ray's Banaras. Now I watch the bodies come down and come down and I watch some of them borne away in boats and some burn for hours and it is nothing like what I expected . . . but there is something more here for me than just beauty. This is the way I want to die: with people around me, and singing, and the fire burning all night and—see there, how that man is drying his clothes against the flames? And those boys wrestling in the mud? And those women washing their clothes and the men taking dips near the place where the dead bodies are also immersed before they are burned? I want that continuity, that pageant around me . . .'

In the end she hopes that her ashes will end up in the river. 'I hear it's a direct route to heaven,' she smiles. 'I've never had any firm religious beliefs but sometimes I find it consoling.'

She may find it even more consoling that according to Sudanshu Shastry, the principal of the School of Sanskrit Studies and Theology, Banaras Hindu University, 'It does not matter whether she was a Hindu or not while she was living. If her ashes are immersed in the Ganga she will attain heaven.'

Raju Boatman is not so sure.

Pocketing his money, he rows me away from Yvette's vigil.

'This is not good,' he sighs. 'I have told her and told her but she will not listen to me.'

I try to explain that she has chosen not to undergo any

further medical treatment.

He looks at me strangely. He understands *that*. What he doesn't understand is why she crosses the river.

'If she dies on that side of the river [the west bank] she will be reborn a donkey. I have told her and told her . . .'

On the right bank, he tries to make me pay for the ride as well. Shanti, the Bengali owner of Kumiko Guest House ('specialist in Japanese food') drives him away with a few choice abuses.

'You see how it is? This is what makes Banaras so bad, so bad.'

He leads me into the eccentric building that balances on the edge of the ghats. And I begin to see where the refusal to speak begins. An entire wall of the reception area is covered with photographs of missing persons, none of them Indian, each with its tragedy rendered in terse phrases:

> 'Noriko, 23, Japanese, last seen going towards Dasashwamedha Ghat with a local boy . . .'
> 'Tarmezi, 19, Indonesian, last seen in the company of three men in a boat . . .'
> 'Shoji, 27, Malaysian, last seen taking a train to Haridwar . . .'

'I tell them,' says Shanti, 'I tell them the Ganga can take you to heaven or to hell. But they do not listen. Why should they? The gods have promised them mukti . . .'

Perhaps it is this promise that has brought Yuki to Rishikesh with its thirteen-storey Godmall, where the top of the pops is *'Vishnu ke charnon mein Gangaji ka vaas hai'* sung to the tune of *'Gore gore mukhade pe kaala kaala chashma'* (from the popular Hindi film *Suhaag*). Yuki ignores the music, the fake tribals with their real snakes, and the innumerable offers of everything from rooms to let and shilajit to rudraksha beads, and crosses the Lakshman jhoola with a small bundle containing a few of her mother's effects.

Her mother died suddenly of a coronary embolism at the age of fifty-seven. 'Most of her stuff I gave to charity,' says the twenty-seven-year-old graphics designer who left Japan to work in Singapore. 'But there were some things I couldn't let other people have, but which I couldn't bear to keep either. I had planned this trip to India really as a tourist. But now I suppose I'm here as a pilgrim.'

She steps into the river, quiet here and shallow in the summer, with an underbelly of richly coloured stones. Hitching up her loose trousers, she puts the bundle down into this conduit of corpses and other offerings just as peculiar. Almost immediately, barely a few metres away a little boy swims out into the stream and snags the bundle. Bobbing furiously in the water, he opens it and checks the contents. Then he's off, shrill in triumph. He gains the shore and hotfoots it up the steps and vanishes.

Yuki sighs. 'I don't know what I expected. I thought perhaps the Ganga would miraculously wash my grief away.'

I pick up a purple stone, lined with the white of several Gangetic tides. Yuki looks too and finds a red stone dappled with grey. In a few minutes, we have a collection of riverine oddities and an audience. A wet little boy squirms his way through the crowd. He is wearing Yuki's mother's spectacles.

Yuki sighs again and climbs the steps away from the river and folds her hands in a namaste to the pandas trying to lure her into a temple. Later, sipping a soft drink, she tries to put reality into her vision of the river.

'I suppose it's about letting go, isn't it?'

The wet little boy interrupts with an engaging smile and an offer. For five rupees a stone, he is willing to get us as many as we want.

Yuki abandons her drink and gets up to go. Her feet are

clumsy with grief and anger.

The boy grabs the drink, throws away the straw and slurps what's left. Then he offers to find us stones for four rupees, three rupees, two . . . one?

The Ganga is now an international phenomenon. Every great river is, in its own way. And it could equally be argued that every great river has its own offer of spirituality, its own metaphors for our lives. The only difference is that the Ganga has spirituality on direct wholesale offer. At Varanasi, you can do a four-day course in yoga to 'rise up your Kundalini' as the Scientific School of Yoga offers. Or you can learn Hindi in a one-day course at Haridwar with 'special attention to scripture-reading'. All geared to the spiritual day-tripper like Gabriel, the catering college student from Sweden who wants to 'get all there is from this intense experience and get back in time for term'. Or to those who want a quick escape from reality via ganja which to the consternation of the locals is freely available around Har-ki-Pauri. The newspapers are full of a campaign to eliminate 'anti-socials' who sell these drugs.

This could also be a resurfacing of the '60s, the Mystic East Made Easy by the ubiquitous sadhus and the availability of mineral water and tissue paper. The Beatles may have disbanded, the Maharishi is no longer the force he was, the Beat guru Ginsberg may be dead, but quietly flows the Ganga. Is Karma Cola on sale again?

Stu rejects the idea vociferously: 'I am *not* a hippie. I'm not looking for a way out, I'm not trying to evade responsibility. I'm trying to face it. I'm trying to look life full in the face.'

For him the quest is real. As it is for some of the young people from the West at the Centre for Tibetan Studies at Sarnath—where the Buddha attained enlightenment—who have spent years of intense concentrated work there. And at various places, there is evidence of a genuine interest in mythology and religion. At Kankhal, three kilometres outside Haridwar for instance, Cathy from London and Sreela from Birmingham discuss the possibility of recasting the Sati story as a fable for misdirected feminine anger which according to Sreela, 'is too often turned against the self instead of the offender'.

As Ram Chandra Pathak, also of the School of Theology at BHU warns, 'How can we judge with what intention they come to the Ganga? The quest is as much internal as it is external and that is something that we should leave to the gods to decide.'

And to the Ganga.

1997

ANITA NAIR

THE ELEPHANTS ARE COMING

Christmas morning. I wake up tired of tinsel and the spirit of the season—fairy lights, shopping mall Santas and fifty per cent off sales . . . There is a state-owned bus to Wayanad at eight in the morning. It's a day bus; semi-deluxe, non-air-conditioned—and besides, who would travel on Christmas Day, except someone seriously considering escape.

On the other side of the aisle is a couple. She in her twenties. He in his forties. Nicely dressed; surreptitious glances. A quick dekko as soon as they get in to check if there are any familiar faces . . . and relief when they realize they needn't worry about being spotted.

I grin to myself. They are running away from the reality of their lives too!

The countryside flees past. But I concentrate on the couple. He with his *India Today*. She with her *Femina*. Two headphones, one walkman. Hands linked, cheeks nestled against each other, they have about them the contained smugness of new love. When she falls asleep on his shoulder, he turns his face towards her and presses little kisses down. I turn my eyes away feeling like an intruder and meet the eyes of the lady conductor.

She has had a busy morning; a child threw up and the parents pretended not to notice. When they wouldn't listen to her quiet entreaties to clean up the mess, she did so

ANITA NAIR is the author of the novels *The Better Man* and *Ladies Coupé*. She also writes a fortnightly literary column for the *Sunday Express*.

herself—both the seat and the child. Another couple behind me grumble in Hinglish on her behalf: indignation at the parents' callousness, their lack of manners. But the father peels an orange and the mother shakes her jhumkies and both stare resolutely into the distance. And the lady conductor smiles. I wonder if a male conductor would have been so forgiving.

At lunchtime, the man across the aisle wants the bus to stop at a new restaurant after Nanjangud. The bus driver refuses. He pulls up at a little shack after Gundulpet. There is smoke and grime on its walls but it is packed with passengers from another bus.

The couple and I have to sit at the same table. They share a plate and feed each other little flakes of fried fish. I settle for egg curry, parotas and watching them. The egg curry resembles in colour, texture and aroma the fish curry and mutton curry that is being eaten at the next table. But I say nothing. Besides, the meal, with a cup of strong coffee thrown in, cost me less than twenty rupees.

It is early evening when we cross the Karnataka-Kerala border. The lady conductor wakes me up. 'One hour more,' she says.

Coming along the mountain roads, I don't notice the electric fences. Perhaps there is nothing about it that suggests the extraordinary. At least in the beginning. But gradually, kilometres of barbed wire hovering constantly in the periphery of vision create a new atmosphere. A darkness, a weight in the air, a feeling of presence; everything seems to suggest there is an elephant, a single rogue male, lurking behind this thicket of trees, that clump of bamboo.

In Wayanad, I encounter Andy Warhol's theory of fifteen minutes of fame. Here, the road to celebrityville begins with the elephant. Everyone, almost everyone has an elephant tale to tell; elephant wisdom to disseminate; elephant theories to propound; and an I-don't-know-how-I-lived-to-tell-you-this encounter-with-an-elephant story.

Bathery town [or Sultan's Battery, the last outpost of the
district] is just another small town in Kerala. Its uniqueness
doesn't extend beyond the kinnath appam. A steamed pudding
made of rice flour, jaggery and coconut milk, the kinnath appam
is available in just two of the many shops that flank either side of
the main street which also is the highway. However Bathery has
plenty of everything else: plastic buckets, duck eggs, jewellery,
cast iron skillets and purple seedless grapes from Sangli. Add to
this the knowledge that the shops are just a façade. Behind them
is the jungle, a dark slumbering beast. During the day, monkeys
dart through its leafy limbs. At night, it comes alive with a
stealthiness. Branches splinter under its heavy feet. A jackal
yowls.

A report comes in of a lone tusker sighted at Anjham Miles
[literally, the fifth milestone].

In the clear light of the day, courage surfaces easily. I coerce
my hosts, a veterinary surgeon and his wife whom I call Mad
Mama and Amayi, into a day trip. There is much to choose
from. All the 344.44 kms of Wayanad is a forest sanctuary.
Twenty-five kilometres away is Pulpalli, a place whose claim to
fame, even if dubious, is distinct. In the forest surrounding the
region, Che Guevara and Castro once reigned through
disillusioned and angry young rebels. In 1969, Ajitha, one of the
demi-goddesses of the Naxalite movement in Kerala, massacred
several policemen and left the impression of her bloodied palm
on the walls of the Pulpalli Police Station.

We settle for the Chethalayam range. At Anjham Miles, the
road curves around a thick bamboo copse. On either side, the
wooded slopes lead to more dense forests. Though it is noon, a
thin mist hangs in the air. Mad Mama points out fresh elephant
dung. And suddenly I am spooked into consciousness of the
tusker's presence.

The air begins to throb. The hairs behind my neck begin to
prickle. 'What is that noise?' I ask.

'That is the sound of my cattle shaking their heads!' A man

sitting a little away explains.

Pebbles are inserted into bamboo cylinders and hung around the cattle's necks, he says. When the animal moves, it causes a sound that will linger long after the note is struck. 'It scares the panthers and tells me where they are,' he adds.

The man, Ravunni Chetty, is wearing a paint-splattered shirt, faded khaki shorts and a pair of scuffed plastic shoes. But there is to him a dignity, an aura of quiet strength. This is a man who has faced death many times over and knows that the only way to escape it is to deceive it by stepping into the shadows. 'No abrupt movements; that's what scares the elephant and prompts it to attack!'

He has his share of hunting narratives. I sit on a stump and listen while Ravunni leans against a tree, exhaling bidi smoke and memories. Of those times when he could walk into the forest with a gun early in the afternoon and return only after he had meat for the entire village. 'These days, these forest chaps are so strict that you can't even aim at the moon,' his mouth splits into a wry grin.

'See that?' he says pointing to a giant anthill. 'You'll find the finest honey inside that. Why don't you come back next week for the temple festival in my village? I'll keep some honey for you and if you want I'll take you deep into the forest.' The promises come one after the other. The last bid of a man to pass on to the world his understanding and love for the forest; a father who can't hide his disappointment, or understand why his sons, a drawing teacher, a barber and a bus cleaner, turned their backs to the forest.

Ravunni Chetty belongs to one of the original inhabitants of Wayanad—the Chettys. The other being the Adivasis. But it is difficult to get a sense of the native population. Everywhere are the plantations and migrants. Yet there is, unseen, this overshadowed mountain population lodged on the slopes and in the crevices. In the wider valleys are the specially created Adivasi colonies where, tamed and shackled, Adivasis thrive on handouts.

Malayalam newspapers burgeon with reports of atrocities committed against the Adivasis. Young girls raped; men beaten up; land seized by bourgeois estate 'mothalalis' . . . In Wayanad you hear another version. 'They know they are a large vote bank and exploit it ruthlessly. They shirk work and hang around expecting us to feed them for doing nothing. Even the police won't interfere if they get into a brawl with you. Look at that,' an acquaintance says, pointing to an Adivasi woman lying on the side of the road in a drunken stupor. 'Even if all I did was to help her to her feet, tomorrow I'll be hauled up for molesting her!'

I have been here almost three days and I still haven't seen an elephant. A friend of Mad Mama's, Dr J, appoints himself our tour guide and we set out to explore the Muthanga range. Dr J has fey brown eyes that'll mesmerize until you realize he's cracked yet another joke. We drive into the forest. A herd of deer crosses the road. Peacocks, wild fowl, more deer . . . 'Where are the elephants?' I demand.

'Don't tempt fate,' Dr J says. 'The last time I did, I ran for my life. Two days ago, I was at the watchtower watching the elephants. On our way back, the jeep's engine shut off. So the driver began raising the throttle. That must have irritated an elephant that had wandered away from the herd and he began running towards us.' He paused. 'I've never run like that in my life. And then he . . .' he added scathingly, pointing to the grinning armed guard, 'wanted me to climb a tree. I said I'd rather let the elephant gore me than try climbing a tree!'

Dr J drives towards a watering hole. We don't have to wait for long. Twigs snap and branches part. All we have between the elephants and us is water and a few feet of marshy slush. Thirteen elephants. One bull, seven cows and five calves. The cows flank the lone bull like elephant folklore claims they would. They stand knee deep in water causing giant ripples. One of the cows stares at us and charges a few feet forward only to brake abruptly. Some minutes later, the herd leaves. 'They'll return once we are gone,' Dr J says, hastening me to the jeep. 'How would you like it if a bunch of people stared at you as you bathed?'

Night comes quickly to Wayanad. There is a strange clear beauty of form about the mountains of Wayanad. They are large, imposing and grimly handsome. They stand set back, shrouded in a clear frosty air, as if each one of them would isolate itself further and for ever from the landscape. Giant shadows hold the damp blue mountains in their grip.

The moon has a devilish cast to it. There is a sense of momentariness and expectation.

It seems as though some dramatic occurrence is about to take place. An upheaval, an explosion, a furrowing of the horizon . . . All I know is I am glad I would be a part of it.

2001

DOM MORAES

THE FOREST

*In 1981 I travelled in the wilder parts of Central India.
I stayed in the Abhujmarh area for some days. The
Abhujmarh is a plateau, where primitive tribes lived. At
least they were primitive then.*

Sitting by the roadside on a rock, with the sullen sunfire, for it
was now noon, making my body incandescent, I looked up to
see a tribal youth riding past on a bicycle. He sat very erect and
stiff in the saddle, holding the handles with his arms at full
stretch, as though fending off some hostile animal. He wore a
turban and loincloth, and his axe hung from his shoulder.
However, from the handlebars dangled, on one side, a furled
umbrella, and on the other a small transistor radio. He had
affixed a small mirror, covered in pink plastic, to the pivot of the
handlebars. Into this mirror, as he pedalled onward, lifting his
knees high, he stared with a look of intense admiration.

Detach the boy from the bicycle, and he would have his own
dignity. On the bicycle, with its appurtenances, he seemed both
laughable and pathetic. Yet the bicycle was necessary to the boy
now that he had found out that it existed: it assisted him in his
life. This was the process of change now taking place amidst the

DOM MORAES published his first collection of poems, *A Beginning*, when he
was nineteen. He won the Hawthornden Prize for the book in 1958, and
remains the youngest person to win the prestigious prize. His other books of
poetry include *Poems* (Autumn Choice of the Poetry Book Society, 1960), *John
Nobody*, *Absences* and *Serendip*. He has also written twenty-three prose books,
including a biography, *Mrs. Gandhi*. 'The Forest' is an excerpt from *Answered
by Flutes*, his book on Madhya Pradesh published in 1981.

tribals, crystallized into a symbol. Greatly cheered for some reason, I went back up to the rest-house. The verandah was covered in blood and feathers, and the chowkidar, his unattractive face embossed with a broad smile, held up the freckled, mollescent, and naked corpse of the chicken, and inquired politely what I intended to do with it.

I was cooking the chicken, a difficult process for one unaccustomed to charcoal stoves, when the others returned, the jeep refuelled and loaded with food and water. We lunched late, and then headed back up the Orchha road. It was a long, wild, bumpy ride to Orchha, and the scenery changed considerably as we neared it. Mountains rose around us. The road, already bad, became steadily worse: twice we stranded ourselves in rocky riverbeds and had to push. The General had not come: with Shukul Saheb and myself were two guides, both of whom, by some weird coincidence, were lame. Across the Marhi river we entered the Marh.

Orchha, once a hamlet, had become Block Headquarters, and was full of nissen huts, officers, and tribesmen of discontented appearance. More mountains rose directly ahead, wrinkled and hairy. Mist covered their summits, and Orchha lay at their feet. Shukul Saheb inquired from an officer how we could get up. 'You cannot get up,' the officer replied. 'Not like that. It is impossible without a four-wheel drive.' The jeep was put into four-wheel drive, but the officer who had been watching closely, shook his head. 'It is very dangerous,' he said, 'without two vehicles. If you wanted to climb really far up, the arrangements should have been made a week ahead. Now you can only climb up a short way, not too far.'

Very soon, I saw what he meant. Even on four-wheel drive, the road was next to impossible. It was muddy and strewn with rocks, and veered this way and that amidst dense forest. At one point Shukul Saheb pulled up, since a tree had fallen across the road. As we climbed out to survey the situation, he placed a bundle wrapped in newspaper on the bonnet. 'We must be very

careful with that,' he said. 'What's in it?' I inquired. 'Gold?"
Shukul Saheb did not appreciate this weak effort at humour.
'Bidis,' he said. 'We have to take presents to them, and bidis are
what they most appreciate.' Then we started, with no little
effort, to move the tree. It took us approximately half an hour.

About a quarter of a mile further up the tortuous trail,
Shukul Sahib suddenly said, 'Where are the bidis?' I replied that
I did not know. One of the guides then volunteered the
information that they had fallen off the bonnet while we were
moving the fallen tree. Why he had not picked them up it was
difficult to say. 'They are most important,' said Shukul Saheb,
and sent the guides back to find them. Another half hour passed
in this fashion, while dusk approached. Shukul Saheb honked
the horn irritably. Some minutes later I saw the searchers
returning at an approximation to a run up the steep path. I had
forgotten they were lame. Their hirpling approach brought a
touch of black comedy to the scene.

We struggled onward and upward, and presently came to a
very large flattened piece of land, a plateau in itself. Patches of
blackened earth and charred treestumps showed where the
penda (forest) had been. Huge tracts of land were surrounded by
rickety picket fences. 'Those could be called cooperatives,'
Shukul Saheb said. He is a slight, intent bespectacled man, and
he seemed to evoke a plangency from the pickets as he ran a long
finger through the air to indicate the length of the fence. 'A
number of cultivators work this area together. There should be
some kind of village further on.' The quality of the road had not
improved with its incursion into cooperative civilization. We
bumped on.

Then, ahead of us, we saw a hamlet. It consisted of huts of
straw and hatch, which seemed to be set down at random over a
cleared area. Some children and women, all in an advanced state
of nudity, stared curiously at us, then, gracefully as antelopes,
ran or floated in the opposite direction. We climbed out of the
vehicle, and stood about, and presently they returned, shyly,

with huge eyes. About this time a muscular young man with an axe turned up. He spoke broken Hindustani and proved to be friendly. Everyone, including some very small children, took bidis, and, having lit them, became very helpful. They showed us around the hamlet, which I gathered had a population of about eighty people.

The houses were small and dark, and unfurnished apart from the odd charpoy. Each had a kind of hearth inside, in which utensils, usually of clay but in a couple of instances of metal, were kept. An outer extension behind each house was apparently reserved for women during their menstrual periods. In front of the hamlet, with no houses beyond, was a pigsty, full of animals which resembled wild boar, in an excessively filthy state: there were also curious little patches of turned earth, which I was told were vegetable plots, though no vegetables were visible. Since the tribals have their own names for plants, it was difficult to ascertain what vegetables they cultivated.

By this time more people had started to turn up: naked women with pots on their heads, who had been down to a nearby stream for water; naked men with axes. They all took bidis and lit them, sucking the smoke down avidly through cupped hands, letting it trickle out between their fingers: it was exactly as though they were drinking water. A granary, mounted on stilts, stood between two houses, looking a little empty. There was also the *ghotul.* This was a small, dark hut, cluttered with charpoys, with drums and flutes hanging on the straw walls. The *ghotul,* in the Marhia way of life, is a dormitory shared by adolescents of both sexes: part of the activity is sexual.

Among the Hill Marhia, however, which these people were, the *ghotul* is only for boys, though girls may visit it from time to time. The youths sing and dance, or ask one another riddles. An example: 'When I am not yet born they beat me as hard as they can. After I am born, nobody dares to touch me without respect. What am I?' The answer is an earthern utensil, pounded into shape by the potter, but thereafter treated carefully lest it break. The youths also simply talk: the idea is that they will learn from one another. It is very much a community idea. Since these boys will shape the future of the village, they should establish close ties between themselves in adolescence.

We talked on for a while. But dusk had now fallen, and the trip back would be hazardous in the dark. The tribals, puffing at the bidis we had left them, faded away into mist: as we descended the mountain the misted sky seemed lightly drenched in a pinkish colour. 'They are burning the forest to clear space, to cultivate,' said Shukul Saheb. What neither he nor I realized was that they were burning miles of forest, all down the road from Orchha towards Chhote Dongar. When we started down this road we seemed to plunge into the incandescent heart of all fire, its source, distilled from the earth, a burning liquid that filled the crannies of the night. All round us the flames rose till the mountains seemed made of fire.

The outline of the ridges ahead was stencilled in fire on the sky. Flames made immense arabesques down the faces of the cliffs: they formed pools on the flatlands, which flowed one into the other. The hunched shapes of the flames on one mountain created the illusion of a lighted city at its crest. There were eidola of fire above us and all around us in the darkness, and fire seemed to float from the mountaintops. No smoke could be seen, so that the flames seemed to have assumed a life of their own, without cause or effect, eddying from the slopes and valleys, forming circles on the flatland. Sometimes, when on the mountains they stayed static, they looked like solidified sunlight.

Unwieldy and ugly though it was, the jeep, bathed in this radiance, became in my mind a chariot, and Virgil rather than Shukul Saheb sat beside me on the flaming road. The shadows between the oceans of fire had that 'deep but daz'ling darkness' of which Vaughan writes; I had never been able to visualize the line clearly before. We ran on between the fires till in the lee of the burning mountains we came back to Chhote Dongar. All round the little rest-house the hills were rimmed with flame, like dormant volcanoes: but seen from the rest-house, this was not the unquiet liquid flame through which we had passed, but the orange roses I had seen before, silhouetted on the summits.

The air whirred with mosquitoes next day as we reloaded for the trip back to Raipur. The chowkidar looked very distressed, and was not cheered by a tip. At last the General asked him what the matter was. He uncaulked his bosom in a free flow of speech. Would the sahebs not stay one more day? It was very lonely here. We understood his emotions, but couldn't help him. We had our own commitments. I reflected that perhaps the last people in the world to retain a sense of human community are the tribals, and even they are preoccupied with their own community, not with others. People act for reasons unconnected with humanity, as we now did. The chowkidar said there would soon be a *madai* (tribal fair) at Orchha.

If his intention was to persuade us to return, he succeeded. The General hastily took down notes in his diary and started to peruse the schedule so he could rearrange it. The chowkidar stood in the verandah looking triumphant as we slowly moved off. As we drove towards Raipur and away from Abhujmarh I had a terrible sense of returning to civilization, to transistor radios and cinema halls, barbers and tailors, knives and forks, people with furniture and theories. It was a very long hot drive and I had plenty of time to think about all this. The General took another papaya from a tree presumably belonging to some innocent cultivator. It tasted warmly of the forest.

About a week later we were coming back down the same road, headed for Orchha once more. The weather had now suffered a dramatic translation: rain whipped at the car, first in occasional showers, then, as we neared Chhote Dongar, in a downpour so terrific it seemed the whole sky, a sac of waters, had collapsed. The windshield bleared over like an old man's eye. The tyres swished and hissed as the wind swept the surface water up in deep ripples from the flooded road. There were explosions of thunder like stage thunder. Javelins of lightning stabbed into the clouds, and seemed to puncture them. More and more water came down, and at last we had to stop at the first rest-house we could find.

Next day the rain had stopped, and the sun was out. The *mahua* was in flower: waxy white petals strewed the earth around every tree: barebreasted young women with baskets were busy picking up the petals: the bright primary colours of their skimpy saris streaked the brown earth like paint. At Chhote Dongar the rest-house was full of officers who had come for the *madai*: there was no room for us; but the chowkidar was happy with all this company. We wound up at a very primitive rest-house at a place called Dhodai, with no indication of human habitation in the vicinity. It came on to rain once more as we started around midday towards Orchha, down the now familiar road.

There were great black patches on the mountains, memorials of the night of the fires. Charred treestumps lay about the slopes, pathetic, like toys the tribals had used and then destroyed. After the rain, the riverbeds flowed thickly with brown water, and in this we were twice becalmed, the engine whirring and roaring as it strove with the current and the rocks. Eventually we arrived at Orchha, and encountered the same officer who had warned us about the mountains on the previous trip. 'You aren't late,' he said. 'The tribals couldn't come yesterday because of the rain. They are coming now. By nightfall there will be hundreds, some of them from the deep interior of the Marh.'

They were coming in, trickles of them like brown water down the hirsute slopes. The women were often in white, and

carried pots on their heads and baskets in their hands. The pots
contained liquor and the baskets forest produce to barter with at
the bazaar. Their firm dark breasts were bare, their pectorals
covered in dark blue tattoo marks which were repeated on their
arms and faces. They wore hibiscus in their hair. They were
nearly all young women: I supposed they would have to be for
the trek over the mountains. They looked towards the dozens of
stalls that had been set up in the open space at the foot of the
mountain with awed but covetous eyes.

The men wore headcloths in heavy colours, and *langotis*.
Their muscular brown bodies were not usually tattooed. Axes
hung from their shoulders. Often their thick raven hair was
done up in a bun, and adorned with a comb. They also had small
knives sheathed in their coiffures. Some had flowers in their
hair, some the exotically brilliant feathers of wild birds. They
wore coloured bead necklaces, shining on their dark chests,
armlets and headbands. At each man's waist was a
bottle-shaped yellow gourd containing liquor, quite literally a
hipflask. Most also carried, tied to their waists, a cloth pouch
containing a supply of homecured tobacco, and had green leaves
for cigar-making rolled up and tucked behind their ears.

There were two quite separate physical types among these
people. The main type had complexions that were more or less
black, and regular features like Dravidians, but there were some
with blunt features and curly hair. There is also, I was told,
another physical type in Abhujmarh, people with a lighter
complexion than the others, and somewhat taller, but none of
them was around, or if they were I didn't see them. R.P.
Noronha, a former Chief Secretary of the state, has the theory
that the negrito type of tribals were the first inhabitants of the
Marh, and were driven deep into it by the incursions of the other
two racial types.

If so, no hostility seemed now to exist, though the negrito
parties and the Dravidian parties squatted down separately.
Both groups made the same automatic motions: the women

started to build cookfires, the men, with deep sighs of
anticipation and contentment after their long march, rolled and
lit leaf cigars, and started to drink deeply from their gourd
hipflasks. 'They will all be drunk by nightfall,' said the friendly
officer in sepulchral tones. 'Then there may be trouble.'
Meanwhile I strolled over to inspect the shops. Not many tribals
had yet arrived, but the shopkeepers waited patiently. 'By the end
of the day,' one of them assured me, 'our stock will all be sold.'

The stalls sold a number of things which, it seemed to me,
would be a little useless in Abhujmarh: synthetic cloth, plastic
ware of all kinds, cheap ornaments. They also sold aluminium
utensils, and in one stall I noticed with surprise several sets of tin
spoons, knives and forks. Other stalls sold toiletry: tawdry
cosmetics and scent, soaps and powder. There were stalls selling
paan and bidis, and food stalls with cauldrons sizzling over fires.
Most of the tribals, however, seemed to have brought their own
food. The piles of salt common to all *madais* lay about on mats
or blankets. More tribals came.

With their coming the usual sort of encampment started to
form at the opposite end of the open space from the shops. By
the afternoon there were hundreds of tribals all over the area,
numbers of them leaving the *madai* to look around Orchha.
Hundreds, however, stayed at the *madai*: crusts of dry tamarind
bark piled up as they deposited their forest produce, and
quantities of dry fish of different shapes and sizes squinted up
from the spread mats. Garlic and onions were on sale.
Eggplants, okra and yams appeared to be popular. Middlemen
bought produce from the tribals, who promptly went and spent
the money in the stalls. They seemed dubious of the small notes
and coins and surprised when they produced results.

Meanwhile men, women, and children alike drank *mahua*
and *salfi* in prodigious quantities, sucked at leaf cigars or bidis,
and ate. The cookfires spat and smoked under iron pots, which
appeared principally to contain millet and salt. The tribals
scooped the porridge out of the pot with broad leaves, in which

they then buried their faces, lapping the mixture up from the leaves. Some also ate dry fish. They were happy: there was liquor; there was food; there were strange sights to see; things to buy, money to buy them with; they had one another. The stallkeepers were doing the roaring trade they had prophesied, the goods, cheap and flimsy, melting from the kiosks and off the tattered mats and blankets.

I saw a very drunk tribal with a bar of soap in his hands. He caressed it in wonder, pressed it to his breast, raised it to his nostrils to inhale the smell. He obviously didn't know what it was for. Presently, tentatively, he licked it. He didn't like the taste, from his expression, and ceased his investigations in that direction. The more sophisticated visitors, tribals in lungis from Chhote Dongar area, who had arrived on bicycles, brandishing umbrellas, laughed heartily at him. The girls who had come off the mountains with hibiscus in their hair had replaced it with plastic flowers acquired from a stall. They had fastened the raven hair to the sides of their heads with red plastic hairpins.

A very old man in a *langoti*, wearing ornaments in his ears, told me he had bought vegetables and millet which was what he normally ate. This was not available to him in his village, though I couldn't work out why not. In the past, he said, he had supplemented his food supply by hunting, but he was now too old to hunt. He had also bought himself an embroidered waistcoat, because it was very cold in the high place where he lived. I noticed traces of ash on his upper body and legs. Noronha, who went up Abhujmarh in 1950[*], notes that elderly people and children were covered in ash, as a protection from the cold. He also notes that the tribal villages communicated with one another by means of drums.

When I was in the Dani valley in West Irian[+] in 1972, the cannibals there used to cover themselves in pigfat and ashes to keep warm. The communication between villages was by means

---

[*] R.P. Noronha: *A Tale Told By An Idiot*, Vikas, 1976.

[+] Indonesia, New Guines.

of drums, and the cannibal's main weapon, which he always carried slung from his shoulder, was an axe: an axe with a stone-head, but it is not many years since the Abhujmarh tribals started to blade their axes with steel. Like the Abhujmarhias, the Danis kept pigs, and maintained small vegetable plots; like the Abhujmarhias, they cultivated yams, and slaughtered the pigs for special feasts. Noronha also describes an Abhujmarhia funeral, where the corpse 'was wrapped in bamboo matting and red cloth and lashed to a pole.'

I witnessed a Dani funeral. The corpse was wrapped in a net made of bamboo twine, and lashed not to a pole but to a chair made of banana trunks. It was not buried like the corpse Noronha saw, but burned. But the correspondences between the two tribes, divided by thousands of miles, are more remarkable than the divergences. Both tribes live in high forested country, the Dani much higher than the Abhujmarhias, yet the concept of clothing seems not to have evolved among either, despite the dampness and the cold of their habitats. The Dani also have the curious habit, when absorbed in thought or deep in conversation, of standing on one leg with their arms crossed. I noticed that several of the Abhujmarhias did the same. The Abhujmarhias are, of course, so far as is known, not cannibals.

A desultory dance with drums started up as dusk fell. The cookfires continued to fume around the camp. The tribals were now really drunk. The stalls were empty and the summit of the mountain above us completely wrapped in clouds and mist. It was clearly about to rain. A wind approached delicately as though on stilts, then rasped the embers out of the cookfires and sent them racing round the camp like a thousand fire-flies. Leaf cups and plates whirled myriad through the air, dropped to earth and skidded on out of sight, a crazy version of an English autumn: blankets and mats were blown away, their twisted shapes borne skyward and silhouetted on the moon, a coven of air-borne witches on their way to an unholy tryst.

A giggling girl, who was trying to prevent a drunk boy from

pulling her sari off, screamed suddenly. People ran towards the couple: an axehead flashed in the darkness. A man stooped and came up with a long writhing shape in his hand. The girl, about to surrender her sari and herself, had seen a cobra. One of the men who had run up when she screamed had decapitated it with his axe. He now, leaving the head behind, carried the body, squirming still with the unspent reflexes of life, triumphantly back to his family by their cookfire. 'They will eat it. They like to eat snakes. Rats also. So far as food is concerned they have few taboos.' A sigh in the darkness: the sigh of civilization.

The question of malnutrition among the Abhujmarhias, when they have so varied a diet, was now explained to me by an officer. 'It starts in childhood. The children are breastfed. But after five or six months, the mother has little milk. The tribals have a taboo about animal milk, they will not drink it, so the mother's milk is not supplemented, nor does the child receive any other form of protein food. If it survives all this till it is ten or so, it will be all right, probably. The tribals lead very hard lives: they usually have to walk anything between five to ten miles a day. They have plenty of carbohydrates in their diet to sustain them, so they keep fit. But the food supply is irregular. They lack minerals and vitamins.

'So from childhood there are deficiencies in their diet. The vegetables they cultivate are mainly carbohydrate crops, yams, roots, and tubers of various sorts. If they could be taught to accept milk, and to cultivate and consume vegetables with a mineral and vitamin content, many problems would be solved. But then, can you teach a Brahmin to eat beef?' His voice died away. The drums and the dance restarted, and those who did not dance pushed forward to watch. I found myself standing next to the old man with the waistcoat. The dancers shuffled and stamped in the flare of the fires. The girl who saw the cobra and her clumsy courtier slipped past into the dark. He cackled hoarsely. 'She has gone to see another kind of snake.'

1981

MARK TULLY

KUMBH MELA

The Kumbh Mela is billed as the biggest religious festival in the world, but no one knows exactly how big it is. Perhaps the gods keep records of the devotees who wash away their sins in the rivers Ganges and Jamuna at Allahabad during the festival. As far as mortals are concerned, satellite photographs, computers and the other paraphernalia of modern technology might give a reasonably accurate estimate, but they have not so far been used for this purpose. So all one can say is that the official guesstimate was that about ten million people bathed on the most sacred day of the 1977 Kumbh Mela. There was every reason to believe that even more would come in 1989. As the official description of the preparation for the Kumbh Mela said, 'Due to increase in the population and also due to increasing interest towards religion it is expected that on the main bathing day about fifteen million people will take bath near the Sangam.' The Sangam is the point where the Jamuna and the Ganges meet. A third river, the Saraswati, is also said to have flowed into the Sangam, but there is no sign of it today, nor is there any record of when or how it disappeared . . .

DIG Mishra helped me to find my way through the maze of religious organizations attending the Mela—more than 800.

MARK TULLY joined the BBC in 1964 and in 1972 became the Chief of the Bureau in Delhi, where he still lives and works. 'The Kumbh Mela' is extracted from *No Full Stops in India*. His other books include *Heart of India* and *Amritsar: Mrs Gandhi's Last Battle*.

'The akharas,' he told me, 'are the focal point of the Kumbh
Mela—the big draw, with their naked sadhus. They are the
gymnosophists, the warriors of the faith. They have the right to
march in processions to the central point of the Sangam to bathe
on the big days, and they guard that right jealously.'

That is not surprising, because the Allahabad Mela is the
most important gathering of Hindu holy men. The akharas are
monastic orders of militant sadhus. Historians are not entirely
clear about their origins, but they are related to the ascetic
orders founded by the great Hindu reformer, the
Sankaracharya. He lived in the eighth or ninth century and is
often credited with the final defeat of Buddhism in India,
although some scholars argue that Buddhism was already on the
way out. The Sankaracharya learnt from his enemies and
introduced the Buddhist tradition of monasticism to strengthen
the sinews of Hinduism.

The akharas are said to have defended Hindu ascetics
against attacks from militant Muslim fakirs, or holy men. Some
of them also hired out their services as mercenaries. As with all
good soldiers, there was considerable rivalry between the
different regiments, which often led to fights. The British
administration put strict restrictions on the movement of the
akharas' naked sadhus, or Nagas, but even Victorian prudery
could not prevent them marching at Kumbh Melas. The
administrator of the 1906 Kumbh Mela had had to order a
cavalry charge to break up a battle between the Nagas. DIG
Mishra was to have his own difficulties with these
quick-tempered ascetics, although he had taken the precaution
of separating the camps of the akharas who followed the god
Shiva from those of their long-standing enemies who followed
Vishnu.

The akharas were now changing, as Mishra explained to
me. 'Most of the sadhus now wear clothes. They are also out to
recruit a better class of person. For many years now there has
been intense rivalry between them to attract good scholars,

because they realize now that faith must be tempered with reason. They are also anxious to get older people with influence. Everyone has to deal with government—even sadhus—and for that you need influence.'

'But do many influential people take sannyas [renounce all worldly ties] nowadays? Surely they don't want to give up their modern lifestyle.'

'Oh yes, plenty do. I think I will take the robe when I have finished with the police.'

'Will you join an akhara?'

'I think I will go for one of the modern organizations.'

The great reformer the Sankaracharya formed four monasteries—one in the north, one in the south, one in the east and one in the west—to be bastions of the faith. Each is still headed by a Sankaracharya, and three of them had come with their followers to the Mela. A fifth Sankaracharya, whose claim to enjoy the Hindu equivalent of apostolic succession is disputed, was also there.

There were hundreds of other holy men and organizations whose pedigrees were not as good as the akharas' and Sankaracharyas' but who all had their disciples. Gurus known in the West, like the Maharishi Yogi, were well represented at this Mela, and so was the Hare Krishna movement. One thousand seven hundred other religious organizations applied for places at the Mela for the first time. Mishra said, 'We decided the best way to deal with them was to say we would charge for all the facilities they got. We didn't hear from them again.' The Mela is, of course, a wonderful opportunity for religious organizations to recruit and raise funds, but the competition is very stiff.

Mishra also had to deal with the wandering sadhus, the mendicants who were not attached to any akhara or other religious group. They camped near the free kitchens set up by some of the organizations. Mishra was rather dismissive of the mendicants: 'They normally become viraktas or wandering sadhus,' he said, 'because they have lost their families or are frustrated with life But there are some genuinely spiritual people among them.'

According to Mishra most of the pilgrims came for only one of the big days, but he estimated there were also some 100,000 kalpvasis, pilgrims who came for a longer stay and who took a vow to bathe three times a day in the Ganges, to eat just one meal a day—and that uncooked, or cooked by their own hands—and to spend their time meditating and reflecting on the state of their soul.

Mishra told me that he was about to umpire a dispute between the three akharas which followed the god Vishnu. They were arguing with each other over the election of their leader. Two of the akharas had chosen one sadhu and the third another. The dispute had to be resolved quickly, because the leader would be surrounded by special pomp and splendour during the procession of the akharas on the big day. I left the deputy inspector general to judge this spiritual contest and set off to find out more about the Mela for myself.

Hindu sages have said that to learn you have to be like a honeybee, flying from flower to flower to extract the nectar which will eventually make up the honey of knowledge. DIG Mishra had given my nectar-gathering a good start, but as a civil servant he could not talk about the politics of the Mela and of Hinduism.

The Vishwa Hindu Parishad, or World Council of Hindus, which coordinates the activities of many organizations, was present in strength at the Mela. It was leading controversial campaigns to convert Muslims and Christians, and to pull down mosques which it claims were built by Muslim rulers on the sites of Hindu temples they had destroyed. I went to see its president, Shivnath Katju, a retired judge of the Allahabad High Court. His father had been a leading member of Pandit Nehru's secular government.

Katju was small and frail and looked every one of his

seventy-nine years. He told me, 'The Council was formed twenty-six years ago to defend Hinduism. In spite of our independence, Hindus are still under serious attack. The government is always out to appease the minorities, especially the Muslims. We suffered during the Muslim days and we are still suffering now.'

'But you have freedom to practise your religion. You are not persecuted in any way.'

'Well, I don't think you are right. There is this issue of the temple in Ayodhya, where our god Lord Ram was born. The Mughals built a mosque there, and it's clear they did so by destroying a Hindu temple, because there are Hindu columns inside the mosque. Images of Ram and Sita, his wife, have sprung up there. We can only peep at them through locked doors. Ram is under house arrest. If the government doesn't let us build a temple on this site, it will become a very serious political issue.'

I said, 'The government has suggested compromises which could defuse the issue. Wouldn't it be better to accept one of them rather than risk communal riots?'

'That,' replied the retired judge firmly, 'is the problem. Because we are the majority, we are always being asked to make sacrifices to placate the minorities. We can't go on like that.'

Although its president insisted that the Vishwa Hindu Parishad was not inciting religious hatred, the sadhus and saints who gathered for a special meeting under the Parishad's banner did just that. The stage in the vast tented pavilion on Kumbhnagar's main road was crowded with holy men wearing saffron, lemon-yellow, dark-red or white robes. Some were old and frail; some young, sleek-skinned and prosperous. Some were lean and intense, and some rather stout and somnolent. Thousands of people sat shoulder to shoulder on straw strewn on the floor of the pavilion, and thousands more stood outside listening to the speeches on loudspeakers. They shouted, 'Long live Mother India. Long live the holy place where Ram was born. Long live our mother the cow!' and many other Hindu slogans. Women stuffed notes into collection boxes tied to posts supporting the pavilion; the men seemed less generous. A thin sadhu with a greying beard ranted over the loudspeaker system: 'The Muslims stole all our temples. They stole our land. There is Inglistan for the English, Pakistan for the Muslims, there should be Hindustan for the Hindus. Now is the time to fight back. We should undo partition and make our beloved Bharat Mata, Mother India, one again. We will make every sacrifice to achieve our sacred end, to defend Hinduism, and to restore Bharat Mata. Raise your hands if you are ready to sacrifice your lives for Lord Ram!'

Thousands of hands were raised and thousands of voices shouted 'Bhagwan Ram ki jai!'—'Victory to our god Ram!'

A portly white-bearded sadhu bellowed hoarsely, 'This holy place where we have gathered was known to Hindus as "Prayag". It was the Muslims who called it "Allahabad". It's our misfortune that after independence our governments, out of their greed for Muslim votes, have refused to restore the name "Prayag". We must stand and fight for Hindustan.'

Suddenly the crowd became restless. A murmur went round the pavilion: 'The baba is coming.' The sadhus on the platform tried to recapture the crowd's attention by shouting slogans. Marshals ordered people to sit down, but no one heeded them. All eyes were on a wooden platform built just above the right side of the stage. A young man wearing just a white loincloth and a sacred thread, his hair matted and his forehead marked with the tilak of Vishnu, came through the curtains, dusted the platform and spread a white sheet. The sadhus on the stage gave up: the legendary Devraha Baba was about to make his entrance.

It was said—although inevitably some disputed it—that this would be the first time that the hermit had appeared on a public platform. Silence descended on the vast audience as we all excitedly awaited the sage, who was reputed to be 300 years old.

The curtains were drawn back slightly and an old man, bent double, shuffled to the front of the platform. The crowd exploded with shouts of *'Devraha Baba ki jai!'*—'Long live Devraha Baba!' The holy man was naked except for a deerskin he held loosely round his waist. His thighs were emaciated, his skin was blackened by the sun, his eyes were rheumy with age, his hair was matted; but, surprisingly, his beard was quite neatly trimmed. He sat down hurriedly and raised both his hands in blessing. A woman near me stood up and folded her hands in devotion, ignoring the tugs at her sari and the cries of 'Sit down, we can't see.'

When the crowd had quietened, a former head of the state police force who had turned sadhu—it seems to be a tradition in Uttar Pradesh—read out a statement on behalf of the baba. That, I thought, would be that. But the crowd was not satisfied. They shouted, 'We want Baba's blessing. Baba, speak to us.' A model of the temple of Ram which the Vishwa Hindu Parishad planned to build if it succeeded in getting that mosque destroyed was brought to the baba, who laid hands on it. The baba, still sitting, pulled himself to the edge of his platform, clasped a microphone and started speaking in a quiet but remarkably clear voice. He told the now silent crowd, 'Protecting this temple of Ram is holy work. You protect your religion and it protects you. My platform from which I give my blessing every day is the platform of the Vishwa Hindu Parishad. They have my blessings. I want everyone to cooperate with their work.'

Then he turned to his young disciple and said in a whisper caught by the microphone, *'Bahut hai?'*—'Is that enough?' The disciple's reply was inaudible, but apparently he thought not because the baba started to talk again, this time about the need to protect cows. After a few brief sentences he again turned to the disciple and asked, *'Bahut hai?'* He was told to exhort the crowd to worship Ram by reciting his name. After a few sentences on that theme, the baba again lifted his hands in blessing. Every woman there seemed to be standing with folded hands. The baba scurried off his platform, and the crowd started to melt away—much to the disappointment of the other saints, many of whom still had plenty of fire and brimstone in their bellies.

There is nothing that Hindus respect more than austerity in others, no matter how much difficulty they may find in practising it themselves. Austerity was one of the keys to Mahatma Gandhi's success. The Vishwa Hindu Parishad knew the value of Devraha Baba's support for their cause. I hoped it might be possible to gather some more nectar by learning about the life of the legendary ascetic, but, when I reached the baba's camp, I found that it was not only the Parishad that was taking advantage of his austerity.

The baba had established his camp about a quarter of a mile from the nearest tents, right on the edge of the Mela. Inside the gateway, a ruffianly guard with a ferocious black moustache told me that, until the great man emerged from the Ganges and began his daily audience, I could not meet any of his associates. I waited with some 300 devotees in front of the baba's small thatched hut standing on stilts about six feet above the ground. After half an hour, the aged hermit, again covered only by his deerskin, scuttled like a crab out of the door of his hut on to the edge of the platform. He lifted his hands in blessing while his henchmen urged the crowd to buy copies of a commentary on the Bhagvat Purana, a scripture dedicated to Vishnu, on sale in one corner of the camp. The baba obligingly touched the books and blessed them. This greatly encouraged the sale of the commentary, to the considerable profit of the publisher, as the book was expensive by Indian standards. Inevitably an impious thought crossed my mind: I wondered what was in it for the baba's disciples.

One villager had the impudence to light up a bidi in the presence of the baba. It was snatched from his mouth by one of the baba's guards. Another guard, seeing a man wearing shoes, pointed to me and said, 'Look, that Englishman has taken his shoes off and you, an Indian, show such disrespect to the baba.'

While the devotees were thronging around the saint's platform, I found two of his disciples. I asked them to tell me about the baba's routine. One who was a printer—not, apparently, the printer of that commentary—said, 'The baba lives and is everywhere. He has no fixed place, but always stays by river-banks. He is an ageless man who has travelled all over India on foot. Everyone claims that the baba comes from this area. Some say that he was born of water. He takes bath in the river four or five times every day.'

'Why does he live on a platform?'

'Because he says that the public are infected with worms which he will get if he stays on their level. The baba's memory is like a computer—people will tell you that he remembers what they told him thirty years ago.'

'Some people say he's 300 years old. How old is he really?'

'No one knows exactly what exercises he does, but he has mastered age and will die only when he wants to. He is a sidh yogi [an ascetic whose mastery of the yogic arts is so great that he has attained supernatural powers and transcended them] all the time he is practising the yoga position of Udyan Band, which means his stomach touches his back.'

'What does he eat?'

'Air. He doesn't even eat fruit. You see, any great yogi can extend his tongue from inside until it touches the top of his head. That's where the nectar is situated, and one drop of nectar is all you need to live for a very long time.'

I couldn't help wondering what happened to all the baskets of fruit which were being given to the baba as offerings.

'Is it true,' I asked, 'that Indira Gandhi used to come to see the baba?'

'Yes, she came several times.'

'What about Rajiv?'

'No. He will come when his heart is cleaner.'

When I returned to my jeep, the battery was flat. There were plenty of volunteers to help push it, but the clutch wouldn't engage and I had to abandon it. Until then it had been running perfectly. As I started on the long and dusty walk back, I was reminded of a friend of Sant Bax Singh's. He had told me that all those who travelled to the baba in good faith had a safe journey. Was I being given a reminder about the dangers of cynicism?

1991

JOE ROBERTS

ENCOUNTERS IN SOUTH INDIA

Pondicherry, at least the part that's called Ville Blanche, was laid out exactly like a small French town; the street signs were in French and the buildings were more vernacular French than colonial. The remaining British buildings to be found in cities like Bangalore would certainly look strange in England—a distinct colonial style had developed very early on in domestic architecture and even the offices and government buildings were different in scale and material—whereas the French buildings of Pondicherry seemed practically identical to buildings in France. It was a strikingly clean city, I didn't see any cows or pye-dogs. The cycle-rickshaw-walas wore straw hats like the Vietnamese. There were a few elderly French people, obviously residents, sitting outside, their little dogs, also elderly, poodles or dachshunds, on leads. Tree-lined squares, benches under shade trees. Along the Rue de la Caserne to the sea front. An expanse of beach, a long pier; out on the horizon, big white tankers. I went to the Integral Guest House at the end of Avenue Goubert, opposite the Alliance Française where a painted board advertised a season of classic French films and language courses at different levels. The guest house belonged to the Sri Aurobindo Ashram but anyone could stay there. My room overlooked the beach. There was a balcony and a good breeze,

JOE ROBERTS has worked as a bookseller, baker and cook, and has also written for the *Times* and *Harper's & Queen*. In addition to *Three Quarters of a Footprint*, his book about South India from which this piece has been extracted, he has written *The House of Blue Lights*, about coastal Texas, and *Abdul's Taxi to Kalighat*, about Calcutta.

away from which it was baking. There was a portrait of Sri Aurobindo on the wall; he looked like an Old Testament prophet. I walked down to the refectory, a room that was built right onto the sea wall. A languid woman in a white smock served me, she had stepped out of a Gauguin painting. The other guests were mostly Europeans, lots of French people; quite a few were followers of Aurobindo, wearing white Indian clothes, bourgeois couples who'd been young in the 1960s, one or two children. A black American wearing crimson and orange clothes, a follower of Sri Bhagwan Rajneesh, was chatting in English with a Nordic couple, both flaxen-haired and pinkly sunburned. The Nordic man had a crewcut and one thick rope, a single yellow dreadlock like a battered corn-dolly, growing at the back. The American had a singsong voice. I heard him saying, 'You take in all the protein you need from pulses, let the cows be.' It was like the dining-room of a school and the menu was a blend of Southern Indian and European wholemeal. The coffee was good, no doubt due to the French influence. On every table, next to the salt and pepper, was a quotation from either the Mother or Aurobindo. I was reminded of Kahlil Gibran, Alan Watts, the Desiderata: that same quasi-mystical high-faluting tone and the tang, however faint, of charlatanry. Or perhaps it was my reaction, not quite cynicism but a wariness that sprang up like an electronic fence whenever I felt that the great infathomable mysteries (that are *meant*, after all, to take a lifetime to solve) were being brushed off with a set of platitudes. If you can tell a man by his friends, you can tell a prophet by his followers; I didn't get the impression from the devotees in the refectory that much intellectual vigour was required nor any adjustment of lifestyle. Whatever makes them happy, I thought, let them get on with it; they think they've got the answers, I'm still confused . . .

Villupuram, Kiranur, Veppur, Ranjangudi, then mountains of

piled boulders to the west of us as we passed through Padalur and approached Trichy. Viralimalai, Valanadu, Tovarankurichi, then the foothills of the Palanis, Melur, at last Madurai. A teeming temple town, cows and bicycles and huge film posters. Narrow streets, paan stalls, money-changers, sadhus. Fly-blown sweet stalls, fruit and vegetables. Downtown was an enormous bazaar, peeling pale-blue paint, unfinished advertisements on the sides of buildings; all the chaos that was missing in Pondicherry. I saw the vast gopuras of the Sri Meenakshi temple, writhing with thousands of carvings. A cycle-rickshaw took me into what I presume had been the cantonment, to a government-run hotel.

As we approached the gates there was a naked man face-down on the ground, twitching and jerking, having some kind of fit. I told the rickshaw-wala to stop, I wanted to make sure the man was all right. He laughed at me. 'No, no, sir. He is a liar.'

As I was checking in, a coach drew up. The receptionist said, 'Please you will excuse me one moment,' and notified the manager; then he signed me in and gave me the keys. The manager of the hotel came into the lobby to greet the coach party; taciturn elderly Spaniards, bad-tempered, hot, bored by temples and palaces, longing for familiar surroundings and decent food. 'Welcome, one and all,' he said—trembling like a whippet—but the Spaniards ignored him. They were followed by their courier, a Junoesque woman in a tight blue uniform, aviator sunglasses pushed up like a hairband, small green irritated eyes. She barked some instructions in Spanish. Everyone's nerves, it was clear, were frayed. When the last of her charges had been led along the corridor, she slumped on to one of the sofas and lit a cigarette. The manager quivered.

'Gabriella, how sweet to see you again.' His eyes flashed from her cross puffy face to her knees.

'Yeah, yeah, yeah,' grunted Gabriella who spoke English with an American inflection.

'You will dine with me tonight? It will be my pleasure?'

'Let me see how I feel, OK? Don't hassle me, Nilesh.'

'You misunderstand me . . .'

'I will wash and rest, then let you know, OK? Calm down.'

Nilesh (still a-quiver) walked over to a mirrored panel and combed his hair with his fingers. In a soft voice, he spoke to the courier's reflection. 'Eight months since I have seen you. Eight months I have waited.'

The Spaniards occupied two long tables. They had ordered Western food which seemed to disappoint them. They ate gloomily and drank Indian lager. I sat in a corner next to an American couple. I assumed at first that they were tourists but, listening to their conversation, worked out that they were missionaries. They weren't as crass as the missionaries I'd overheard in the Connemara Hotel, they seemed more assimilated to Indian life. The man was very pale and thin with a ginger crewcut and a close beard that was much darker than the hair on his head. The woman was obese with short mousy hair and oversized glasses that gave her a cartoonish appearance, she looked like Garfield. She wore a salwar-kamiz that didn't conceal the enormity of her bottom. They were discussing a convention to be held in Madras. They were planning to attend and to take a party of teenagers. 'I ask myself if they're ready. Most of them haven't been away from home before. It's easy to forget how immature these kids are. You've got to take their parents into consideration. Screw up this one time and that's that.' Arnold had a pleading voice. 'Lindy, lighten up, why don't you?'

'I'm sorry, Arnold. It's just, oh I dunno, kids like Vikram. I mean, he's a pain in the butt. None of this is serious for him, he's got no responsibility.'

'Hey, Lindy. Just breathe out slowly. Relax. He's just a dumb kid. You're doing fine. Just breathe out slowly.'

'Sure, Arnold. You don't see how obnoxious he can be

sometimes. You know why they come at all?'

'They hear the true word and that's what I believe with all my heart, Lindy.'

'Some of them maybe, but Vikram and, well, I gotta say, Apu, they're not listening, Arnold. I ask them questions and they haven't been listening.'

'Lindy, come on. You mustn't think that way. That's Satan talking to you. Relax now, won't you? Hey, you've done real good.' Tears were rolling down Lindy's cheeks and welling up where her glasses rested on her cheeks. 'I'm sorry. I'm sorry, Arnold. I just get so uptight. I just wanna, I just wanna . . .' She made a funny growling noise that caused some of the Spaniards to turn around. 'Baby, relax, relax,' cooed Arnold soothingly.

I ordered palak paneer and naan. For some reason the naan, when it arrived, was soaking wet. My guess was that it had been cooked earlier in the day and the water was to revive it before heating it under a grill—the waiter had picked it up before it had been reheated. '*Naan*, sir.'

'I know it's naan but it's all wet.'

'Sir, I get you rice instead.'

'Could you get me another naan please?'

'Two naan, *achha*, sir.'

'No, just one, please.'

'This is one naan, sir.' Another victory for the Indian catering industry. 'OK, I'll have some rice.'

Two well-dressed Indian businessmen came into the dining-room. Arnold stood up (he was very short) and greeted them in fluent Tamil. He pressed his palms together in salutation and even wagged his head when he answered their questions. For some reason, no doubt jealousy, I found his linguistic skill intensely annoying. The head-wagging was a particularly silly affectation. He sat down again and said, 'There you are, Lindy, you know who that was? Apu's father.' I found it strange that the father was so friendly to a man attempting to steer his son away from his ancestral beliefs. Maybe the arrangement wasn't as simple as I suspected, perhaps they hadn't let on that they were missionaries—that seemed unlikely—maybe they weren't missionaries, just born-again types. I certainly didn't intend to ask. The rice arrived long after I'd finished the palak paneer so I ate it on its own. Just as I was finishing it, Nilesh and Gabriella entered the dining-room. Nilesh was wearing a dress shirt made out of satin chintz and high-waisted slacks. He was in a very excited state. Gabriella was very drunk. She was still wearing her blue uniform but it was unbuttoned at the front, revealing considerable cleavage and a lacy black bra. She could have been an air-hostess strip-o-gram. Her charges, who'd finished eating by now, stared at one another solemnly, then filed out of the room. Nilesh helped Gabriella, who could barely stand, to a table. As soon as she sat down, she kicked her shoes off and lit a cigarette. Lindy was horrified. 'Arnold, do you think that woman has a chemical dependency problem?'

'Sssh, now, sssh.' His tone was emollient. 'She'll find her Higher Power.' Apu's father and his friend were riveted. Gabriella was ordering whisky. Nilesh was trembling so much that he could hardly hold a glass to his lips. He made a sudden furtive darting movement, his hand shooting up Gabriella's skirt. She removed the thin little hand and shouted at him. 'No quiero. Understand? I don't want it. Understand? Tell me you understand. Say it, OK?' Nilesh grovelled. 'Please, please, forgive me. I remember last time.'

'That was now, this is then, I mean, that was then . . .'

Lindy hissed frantically, 'You gotta do something Arnold, that lady's heading for a date-rape situation.'

'Oh, Lindy, you can't make such allegations.'

'Arnold!' Arnold walked over to their table and, pressing his palms together, addressed Nilesh, quietly and politely, in Tamil. Nilesh, bristling, stood up and declared that he was a native of Calcutta. 'Tamil is not a language I speak. Why not, pray, English?'

'My colleague and I are concerned for the lady's welfare.'

'You will find, I think, that she is a Roman Catholic. She does not seek conversion.'

Lindy waddled over. 'I'll take you to your room. Come on, honey, tell me the number.' Gabriella took Lindy's arm and stood up, retrieved her shoes with some difficulty, grabbed her drink and downed it in one gulp before leaving the dining-room with the two Americans. I heard Lindy saying, 'Turn, honey, turn to the Lord,' and Gabriella muttering back in Spanish . . .

At sunset I was joined by a girl from Wolverhampton. Her name was Rachel and she was a stout dark girl in her late teens. She had a vaguely ursine manner (perhaps more badger than bear) that was accentuated by her muscular hairy limbs and quick black eyes. She was going to study fashion design at Brighton. That surprised me because her whole appearance suggested a more down-to-earth career; I'd have guessed that she was a chemistry student. She had been travelling around India with her boyfriend Matthew and another traveller that they'd teamed up with in Rajasthan. When she told me that I realized how much of a loner I'd become. I'd never have considered 'teaming up' with anyone. It wasn't unfriendliness, it just hadn't occurred to me. Rachel, in turn, was amazed to hear that I'd been staying with Indian families. Matthew had decided that India was fine, the problem was the people. She tended to agree. They were so dishonest. Eric, their friend, got on better with them than they did. He was older than Matthew and Rachel and had been to India before.

We arrived at Alleppey in the dark. Saint George's Lodging was supposed to be good value. A single room with an attached bathroom was only twenty-five rupees a night. The three of them decided to stay there as well. Matthew was tall with a chubby smiley face. He was dressed in surfer fashion (at least an English fashion chain's notion of surfer fashion): a T-shirt with

the logo 'Fat Willy' on it, gaudy baggy shorts and checked
'vans'. Eric was my age, a sunburnt Scot. He had red hair tied in
a neat pony tail and carried his luggage about on a foldable
trolley. He was an actor and drama therapist. We set off
towards the lodge, using the map in the *Lonely Planet*. As we
approached the town centre, we discovered that a parade to
celebrate Onam was about to take place. Saint George's
Lodging was the top three floors of a large city block. There was
a sign at the top of the stairs: *Your Home Away From Sweet
Home*. We signed in and were told that dinner was unavailable
so we decided to find somewhere to eat in town after we'd
dumped our bags. I was just being shown to my room when
there was a powercut. The bearer went back to reception to get a
candle. What I saw of the room appealed to me, a monk's cell.

Outside, the whole city had blacked out. People had
gathered along the pavements to watch the parade. The only
available lighting came from torches and candles but it went
ahead anyway, a ghostly procession that ought to have been
merry, with bright yellow flags waving. The marchers, most of
whom seemed to be from trade unions, trooped cautiously
along, like a jungle platoon behind enemy lines. Very few of the
banners that one could read were in English but the whole thing
appeared to typify the Keralan mélange of left-wing politics and
religion. Eric thought that there might be power nearer the jetty
so we went back the way that we came. The streets got more and
more crowded.

There were several drunks. By and large, a drunken Indian
is nothing to worry about; alcohol brings out a floppy silliness,
that's all—one rarely comes across the confused and pent-up
fury that can make a Northern-European drunk so threatening.
But, as we pushed our way through, one young man lurched
forward to put his hand on Rachel's breast. It looked to me as if
he was trying to steady himself more than molest her but it was
hard to tell. Rachel's immediate reaction was to strike him
across the face; the man was so plastered that her slap knocked

him over.

As he lay on the ground, Matthew kicked him in the mouth, repeatedly, until blood spouted from his lip and ran down his neck and soaked into the collar of his white shirt. I was shocked. It seemed excessively violent and sickening, out of all proportion to the man's offence. His companions pulled back, as horrified as I was. I muttered to Matthew that he could have just told him off. 'Bollocks I could have,' he snapped back. Rachel, trembling, said that it was always happening. They had both reached boiling point 'They don't treat their own women that way. They're such fucking lechers with white women.'

It surprised me that she persisted in wearing a thin cotton singlet without a bra. Rachel could have worked out what was acceptable, or unlikely to draw attention, by observing the way Indian women dress. One wouldn't expect her to wear a sari but she should have realized that what might be all right to wear on a beach was unwise to wear on a busy city street at night. That isn't to excuse the behaviour of the men who'd grabbed her—but if such confrontations had become a problem for Rachel, it seemed to me that the situation was avoidable. We walked on without talking, numbed by Matthew's outburst. It was all the more disturbing to me because, to be honest, there'd been times when I'd wanted to hit people myself. Rickshaw-walas who'd drive me miles out of my way (in Bangalore where I knew the routes well) to bump up their meters; the persistent money-changers, hustlers, all the hopelessly transparent con men who plagued one at every corner. So often I'd felt that the last recourse, the only way to say 'stop bothering me' would be violence (even threatened violence) but I'd always managed to keep my cool. Now I felt guilt by association, as if I myself had broken a self-imposed rule. I wanted to get away from Matthew, not to be seen with him. Rachel's and Matthew's circumstances were such that all the Indians they had met were people who looked at them as Europeans instead of as individuals. Insulated by one another's company, their only encounters had been small business transactions; there were no Trivedi families in their experience of India; they must have felt as if they were running a gauntlet of petty entrepreneurs and low-lifers. Something, that had been about to snap, had snapped.

We eventually found a café with its own generator. All the proprietor could offer were dosas or idlis. Most of the staff, he explained, had left to watch the parade; if we hadn't just walked in, he would have closed for the night. Matthew didn't know what dosas or idlis were and didn't like the sound of them when Eric told him. He was in the middle of protesting when the lights of Alleppey came back. So we moved on to another restaurant where he could get egg and chips; he needed comfort food . . .

We left the sprawl of Madras and headed down a wide dusty road, fine sand on either side. Sometimes the Bay of Bengal was to the right; sometimes it became an islet and the road a bridge. Sometimes the road curved quite far inland, away from the coast, through coconut plantations. We passed a white modern church of the kind that Texan television evangelists build with viewers' donations.

I asked the driver to let me know when we reached Mahabalipuram. 'Not yet, not yet, not yet,' he barked. All his concentration was on the road ahead. 'Soon now,' a passenger informed me, 'one half hour.' There were painted advertisements for beach resorts. One, the Silver Fish, depicted a leaping marlin. I was just wondering if there was deep-sea fishing off this coast when we came to the resort itself. I asked the driver to stop and he scowled at me.

The gates of the Silver Fish Holiday Centre were open. I walked down a drive, stretching ahead at least half a mile, towards the beach and the office. Dhobis had spread sheets on the ground to dry. An incinerator puffed black smoke. Cabins were set up among the palm trees. Two obese white men in bikini swimming-trunks waddled past me. An old woman with long plaits wore a batik kaftan; she looked like a very old squaw. I tried to work out what nationality she was. In the office was a portly young Indian who offered his hand and told me his name was Johnny Boy—later I saw it was spelt Jhalibhoi. He had a Stewart hairstyle, layered spikes on top and long rats' tails at the back. He wore a snow-bleached denim beach suit; a short-sleeved (what Mr Prakash called 'half arm') shirt and very short, obscenely tight shorts. On his feet were multicoloured flip-flops. The office was decorated with bamboo furniture and potted palms and a mural of a Polynesian island with a smoking volcano. A blown-up black-and-white photograph of, I assumed from the kurta and garland, a local politician, turned out to be a portrait of Johnny's father: Mr P.K. Jhalibhoi, the proprietor. I asked if it was possible to rent a cabin for the night. 'No way,' replied Johnny with a grin. He was trying to see his profile in a cane-edged mirror.

'You're full?'

'That's right!'

I asked if I could walk down the beach to another resort instead of going all the way back to the main road. Johnny made a gesture that looked rehearsed, stretching his arms and raising his shoulders. 'Hey, hey, man! Whatever you like!'

As I turned around, in through the door came a familiar but none the less extraordinary figure. Elvis Presley was alive and walking about in Mahabalipuram! Petrol-blue oiled hair, sideburns, the great paunch like a bay window above the narrow hips. Elvis wore dark glasses, a black velour track suit. Around his neck was a red towel. 'Welcome to Silver Fish Holiday Centre. I am Berjiz Jhalibhoi.'

'Thank you but I'm afraid I'm not staying.'

'Why is that?'

'No room is available,' said Johnny.

'You would take a budget cabin?' Berjiz asked me.

'I'd prefer a budget cabin.'

'Budget cabin there is,' said Berjiz.

'Daddy says not for Western visitors.'

'That is an only peak-season ruling. Also Daddy says—always—an occupied cabin is better than empty.'

'I'm quite happy with a budget cabin.'

'Happy is what we aim at,' said Berjiz, exuding largesse. Johnny looked in the mirror and patted the sides of his hair while his brother signed me in. 'Daddy stayed in England five years,' Berjiz told me when he looked at my passport.

'One Englishman is here. Otherwise all Russians.'

'Tonight is disco night,' Johnny said.

The budget cabin, I felt sure, was not intended for commercial use by either Western or Indian guests. My guess was that it was used for putting up sales representatives. For a start, it was the whole drive's distance away from everything else, the nearest building was the chowkidars' shelter. It was very basic indeed: no ceiling fan, a hole-in-the-floor lavatory. Having said that, it wasn't uncomfortable at all. It was clean. There was a strong smell of disinfectant. I washed in the sink, then arranged my mosquito net over the hospital bed.

I walked back down the drive towards the beach. A narrow wooden bridge crossed a drainage ditch. A stout Russian woman elbowed past me. She was wearing a blue-and-yellow floral swimsuit and a white cellophane hat, woven like straw and decorated with plastic flowers; a Jamaican grandmother's 'Sunday-go-to-meeting' hat.

An expanse of fine, slightly grey sand; green wooden sun-loungers; a thatch-sheltered restaurant area. There were Russians everywhere in the weirdest clothes: swimming trunks made from unevenly cut-off track suit bottoms, string-vest T-shirts, ivory satin pyjamas. One red-haired man wore a brown shirt with an orange tie tucked into a pair of crimson Y-fronts, lace-up brown shoes and crumpled black socks; he looked as if he'd mislaid his trousers. Their faces, the strange mixture of Central European and Asiatic feature, intrigued me.

One or two of the younger Russians swam. The rest paced the beach in broad circles, stopping to talk to one another like prisoners in an exercise yard. Only the oldest ones sat down at all, the rest kept moving.

To the south I could see the shore temple, considerably further away than I'd expected. I drank a small pot of coffee, then set off towards it. There were hundreds of tiny crabs scurrying about. The beach was dirty and deserted. The sun started to go down, as quickly as it always does in India: a fleeting twilight, then semi-darkness, the blue half-light of the shining moon and the stars. The brightest light was the edge of the surf, a white string winding out ahead of me. I could still see the bulk of the shore temple, still some way off, and I could hear the waves pounding against its walls. It was the most romantic building I'd seen in India. The temple—a cluster of three shrines—was built at the beginning of the eighth century by Rajasimha, who also built the Kailasanatha Temple at Kanchipuram. The sea, I am told, has eroded much of the carved detail but it is still an elegant building. The temple was there for the sea to worship. I stood on the beach below the processional road for about ten minutes, listening to the waves booming their mantras. I turned around and walked back along the beach. Halfway back to the resort a pack of six dogs surrounded me. One was a bitch in season and the others were prospective mates, squabbling with each other, sometimes fighting quite viciously. The dogs took no notice of me but followed me, squabbling and panting, all the way back to the Silver Fish Resort where some Russian men pelted them with handfuls of sand.

The Russians ate, en masse, at long tables. There was a pile of sliced white bread in front of each place setting. I was seated at a small table and handed a menu. It was a big laminated card, like a menu in an American family restaurant. The spelling was rather wild.

Each section was given a heading: 'Soups and Such' (I decided against the 'Coromandel crap soup'), 'A Visit to China Town', 'Meat You Must Eat', 'Fried Corner'. I chose 'specal' fried fish and spinach, a lime soda to drink, 'fruity platter' from the 'Time for Pudding' section. The waiter came back with a flat serving dish. On the dish were round slices of white radish, trimmed to form letters that spelt WELL COME JOSEPH. A tall thin man with very thick glasses, whom I recognized as Mr P.K. Jhalibhoi, was talking to the Russians, in Russian. There were cheers and claps. Mr Jhalibhoi had a funny snuffling laugh. He slapped some of the Russians' backs then came over to my table, stretching to shake my hand. 'Please, don't get up. Relax . . .' he checked the radishes, 'Mr Joseph!'

He was quiet for a moment. 'Why did you come to Silver Fish Holiday Centre?' Because the bus had passed the gate. My answer seemed to disappoint him 'So you had not heard of us in UK?'

I shook my head.

'That is bad. There is supposed to be advertising in the *Daily Worker*.'

'I think it's called the *Morning* Star now.'

'Yes, yes. You're quite right. In my day we called it *Daily Worker*. *Morning* Star now.'

'Not many people read it, that's the problem.'

Mr Jhalibhoi made a pained expression. 'You are wrong. Working classes are reading this paper.' This was clearly a belief that it would be unfair to shatter. I asked Mr Jhalibhoi about his time in England.

'Do you know Butlin's, Minehead? There I worked. Billy Butlin I would name as inspiration. He started out with hoopla stall. A man with visions.'

'You don't hear much about Butlin's any more. The Minehead one is called Somerwest World now.'

It was another shock, absorbed with dignity by Mr Jhalibhoi. He shuffled his feet.

'This cannot be right. What of Butlin's Beavers coming year after year? What of the space-age monorail?'

'You see, holidays abroad are more widely affordable now than they were when Butlin's was thriving. People can be sure of sunshine in places like Majorca.' Mr Jhalibhoi winced as I spoke but, I could tell, refused to believe my heresies.

'You have met Geoffrey?' he asked. 'Geoffrey's father I knew thirty years ago. Now he has a restaurant in Cromer, The Jolly Friar. You will know it.' Geoffrey was sitting between two elderly Russian women. The women were talking loudly to each other. He was a dim-looking teenager with a band of acne running across his forehead, a crucifix ear-ring and peroxide yellow hair.

Mr Jhalibhoi called over to him. 'Geoffrey! Here is another from Merry England. Mr Joseph!'

Geoffrey glanced over. 'All right then?'

'Second time Geoffrey comes here,' Mr Jhalibhoi told me proudly. 'Two weeks he spends, then home again.'

'Is this the only place he visits in India?'

'It is complete holiday break.'

'I'm sure it is . . .'

'It is.'

'It's just that, I'd have thought, coming all the way to India, he'd want to see more.'

'Mahabalipuram is world-famous heritage site, is that not enough?'

'Does Geoffrey speak Russian as well?'

'No, no, no. I don't think he speaks Russian.'

Johnny, who had changed into a shiny black shirt and green pegged slacks, asked his father if he should start the music soon. 'Yes, yes, start the music any time soon. First clear these unused tables.' Mr Jhalibhoi asked me if I had disco fever. 'My sons, they go disco crazy.' He snuffled. 'If you ask me, it is a fever.'

Johnny created sufficient space for a dance floor then went into

a glass DJ's booth. He played three Madonna songs, sung in
Hindi by Alisha. 'All right! Lovely Alisha, India's Lady
Madonna! Ladies, you too are so lovely, please, come on!' By
the third song four Russian women had taken to the floor. They
danced by rocking from side to side on their heels, pointing their
elbows outwards. Mr Jhalibhoi and several Russian men
clapped to the beat. I wondered why the dancing women looked
so strange. It was the constant bright lighting; most disco
dancers are seen under flashing colours. Here was a steady
operating-table glare. The next song was Stevie Wonder's
'Living for the City', followed by a sequence of film songs, some
of which I recognized. In the middle of one of the film songs
Johnny called out. 'You all know him well! Please, here he is,
coming to you direct! My very own brother!' Berjiz (in dark
glasses, a white satin cap with a matching scarf, a tight denim
cowboy shirt and shiny red flares) appeared on the dance floor.
He looked less like Elvis than he had 'offstage', more like a
Bombay film star. There was a round of applause. Berjiz
shimmied among the swaying women, working his hips like a
belly-dancer. He took his scarf off and waved it gracefully. The
dancing women started to clap. The song changed and Berjiz
entered his stride. His hips continued to shake but, with the
upper part of his body, he appeared to be miming the lyrics.
Dabbing his eyes with the scarf, he signified sorrow. Then,
looking upwards, he dropped to one knee and clutched his
heart. Soon he was lying on the ground, to great applause, his
hips still shaking. A dramatic expression, as stylized (and
incomprehensible) as the *rasa* of a Kathakali dancer, played
across his features. One arm lifted. He started to get up again.
Now he was back on one knee and picking imaginary flowers.
Soon his arms were full of flowers. Then he rose and presented
the invisible bouquet to one of the women. Great applause.
After this set piece, the ice was broken. Several Russian men
joined in. Within ten minutes the dance floor was full. Even the
gormless Geoffrey was dancing: his thumbs in his belt-loops, his

torso bending forward at the waist, the classic Status Quo boogie. Berjiz remained the most accomplished dancer. He swirled through the mass of other dancers like Scheherazade.

But his thunder was soon to be stolen. A short Russian man in a white T-shirt and black trousers, a cigarette dangling from his lip, took to the floor. His dark hair was swept back, his muscular torso rippled under the white cotton, he was rather like James Dean. When he danced he emphasized, not his hips like Berjiz, but his small bottom. His sense of rhythm was stronger than Berjiz's. There was no need for him to mime. And, whereas Berjiz performed in front of, rather than with, his nearest partner, this Russian seemed to transform the lumpen women he danced with into beings as graceful and sleekly sexual as he was. One in particular, a tall fair girl, responded magnetically to each move he made, thrust for thrust, shimmy for shimmy, until the floor cleared around them. Fred Astaire was dancing with Cyd Charisse. Berjiz, hopelessly upstaged, holding his white scarf in his teeth, stopped dancing and stared Byronically out to sea.

1994

R.K. NARAYAN

THE EMERALD ROUTE

The term occurred to me when we started out on the first phase
of a tour of Karnataka, from Mysore, through Hunsur and
Hassan, and returned to Mysore nearly one week later, having
continuously journeyed up and down the ghats, the Konkan
coast and Coorg, and never seeing a dry patch anywhere. Green
of several shades we saw, mountain-sides lightly coated with
verdure and fern, the dark foliage of trees rising hundreds of feet
from the valley, light green, dark green, pale green, evergreen,
and every kind of green shade were offered for our delectation
all through our circular tour of approximately a thousand
kilometres.

The road to Hassan passes through rice fields on both sides,
across the course of both Kaveri and Hemavathi rivers. This is
the most unwearisome part of the journey by car since there is so
much to watch—tiled farmhouses, or little shrines set amidst
transluscent, waving paddy fields, and the roadside villages
consisting of no more than a dozen houses along the highway,
displaying signboards of tailor shops, restaurants and hair-
cutting saloons and hoardings advocating two-children families
on all their walls. I used to live in Hassan over half a century

R.K. NARAYAN's first novel, *Swami and Friends*, was published in 1935. Since
then he has written several novels and collections of short stories and essays,
including *The Bachelor of Arts*, *The Dark Room*, *The English Teacher*, *A Tiger
for Malgudi*, *The Guide* (winner of the Sahitya Akademi Award, 1958), *A Horse
and Two Goats*, *Malgudi Days* and *A Writer's Nightmare*. This piece is an
extract from *The Emerald Route*, a travel book on Karnataka. R.K. Narayan
died in May 2001.

ago, long before the railway was laid, when we had to reach it by bullock cart from Arsikere—an all-night caravan journey to cover twenty-seven miles. Hassan had only one main road, flanked by lantana hedges, and the homes of the district officials were set far back, beyond a drive of murmuring casuarina trees. My father's official residence, for a Headmaster, was a colonial style house, with a trellised porch covered with purple flowers and guarded by a huge gold mohur tree, set in a three-acre ground amidst grass fields where cobras also lived, but at peace with us. Now on arrival, I searched for this landmark. I was told that our old house was now a hospital behind the Taluk Office signboard. Brick compound walls having replaced the lantana hedges, it was difficult to identify places, and I could not locate our old house.

Although the town is much changed today with new buildings and shops and a Town Square from where the roads radiate, its inherent charm (which for some reason I cannot understand made people name it 'Poor Man's Ooty') is still there. Its grassy downs, vista, and stately trees on the roadside are still there. From our window at the motel built amidst evergreen trees, we noticed thousands of bats hanging topsy-turvy from their high branches and squealing and squeaking. Banyan, gold mohur, and casuarina are still there in abundance; the town has not grown at the expense of its tree population.

Hassan, apart from its own charms, is a portal through which one could pass into an ancient culture at the temples in Belur and Halebid. Belur, 32 km from Hassan, on the Yagachi river, is a small town. At a turning beyond a row of shops, one suddenly faces a temple, which is unprepossessing at first sight; but passing in, one finds oneself entering a paved corridor so wide and spacious that a whole town's population could be accommodated in it comfortably.

The Hoysala ruler Bittiga, who had come under the influence of Ramanujacharya (whom he had sheltered from his

Chola persecutors) and changed his name to Vishnuvardhana, marched against the Cholas, captured their capital at Talkad in 1116, and built a number of temples to commemorate his victory, the foremost among them being the one at Belur. It was designed by Jakanachari, although on the walls appear signatures of other sculptors such as Dasoja of Belgaum, Chavana, Nagoga of Gadag, Masana of Lakkundi, etc. Here we have the finest example of what has come to be known as the Hoysala style. The actual temple is mounted on a star-shaped basement, which you climb by a short flight of steps. All around the base are carved 650 elephant figures, each one in a different pose. On the rows above, you find a variety of themes depicted. The *Ramayana* and the *Mahabharata* and all the legendary characters or episodes are represented in minute detail, on every available inch of space, from bottom to top. Every nook and corner and angle is filled with figures and decorations. Moving along the circumference of the star-shaped pedestal, if you could spare about ten hours a day for examining each section of the wall methodically day by day, you could complete the viewing of the figures in fifteen days. The profusion seems superhuman. If you are in a group, you will be distracted by excited calls:

'Come here, and see this; here is a marvellous composition of Vishnu's ten avatars, as Vamana, Varaha, Narasimha, Rama, Krishna and so on. Nothing like it anywhere.'

'Tell me, is this not Arjuna rescuing Virata's cows?'

'Did you notice the dancer at this angle? You must not miss this. Note the folds of her drapery!'

At the same moment the seasoned guide will be flourishing his baton while explaining: 'Note that jack fruit, the fly settling on it, and the wall lizard poised to attack the fly.' You will be looking up and down all the time in consonance with the motion of his baton; he doesn't pause for breath while explaining; he doesn't even look at what he is pointing out, being familiar with every inch of the wall. 'The lady is distressed while that monkey is tugging at her sari . . . Notice the overcoat on this figure with

buttons, which proves that there were buttons in those days . . .
And this woman has done up her hair in pony-tail fashion,
which is again popular today . . .' His jokes are seasoned to
appeal to the tourists who come in waves all day long.

Inside the temple, the elaborate amount of work done on
the inner wall of the central dome is to be seen by flood-light.
(Formerly, they were illuminated by a mirror reflecting the
sunlight.) The pillars in the hall are smooth, glass-like with
polish, and lathe-turned, displaying a variety of designs. In the
sanctum   sanctorum   you   see   the   seven-foot   figure   of
Chennakesava, to whom all this artistry is dedicated, a god who
imparts grace and protection when you watch Him by the
lamp-light in the inner shrine.

CHIKMAGALUR

Fifty-five kilometres from Hassan is our next halt in the Emerald
Circuit. Chikmagalur nestles in a valley south of the Baba Budan
range, and looking about one sees the mountain ranges
stretching away in serried ranks. An attractive hill town with its
bright buildings, vast open spaces, tree-covered slopes and
parks, Chikmagalur is also the centre for many coffee estates.
The first generation of coffee plants in India was cultivated in
this area. The Muslim saint Baba Budan, after whom the range
of mountains is named, arrived from Arabia and settled in this
mountainous country, bringing with him a handful of coffee
seeds; he planted them for his own use around his tabernacle,
and this was the beginning of coffee cultivation in India, and one
has to salute the memory of this saint for the lasting gift he
brought us. The cave containing his tomb is at a deviation on the
ghat road to Kemmangundi, sacred both to Muslims and
Hindus, and known as Dattatreya Peeta. It is believed that
Dattatreya disappeared into this cave and will reappear when
Vishnu incarnates next as Kalki avatar to redeem the world.

Kemmangundi (64 km from Chikmagalur) is reached

through a winding ghat section after a four-hour drive from Chikmagalur, the road passing through coffee estates, over the edge of deep valleys and at the base of towering precipices. Kemmangundi captures a traveller's heart at first sight, with its neat red road, hedged by luscious plants and ferns, foot tracks mysteriously cutting through them leading to grassy uplands, valleys and forests. Here live officials and workers connected with the Mysore Iron and Steel Works (now called Visvesvaraya Iron & Steel Works) and officials of the Forest and Horticulture Department who tend the gardens and are in charge of the guest houses. The main activity here is the mining of iron ore by blasting the red mountainsides and loading them in trolleys which roll down on cables to Bhadravathi Iron Works, seventy-two kilometers below.

A co-operative store, a couple of shops, a dispensary and a row of workmen's quarters, beyond a sloping down, are the ingredients of this little mountain habitation (which is what I would prefer to call it, instead of a 'town'). People who live here seem to be happy in this isolation, which is now and then enlivened with the presence of weekend revellers who arrive in bus-loads from the coffee estates and the industrial establishments in Shimoga and Bhadravathi, and who sometimes make the local citizens nervous as they knock on doors and carry on their revelry uninhibited. An old resident confessed rather ruefully, 'It is frightening sometimes as they come in great numbers and we have no police protection, unless we call them from Chikmagalur. It must be especially discouraging for those who come for a quiet holiday at the guest house, Dattatri Bhavan, which used to be the residence of the Maharaja of Mysore in old days.' According to this person, film-shooting companies are coming in greater numbers and cause much distraction to the local population. 'They also take up all the available space at the guest house, and normal tourists who may want a quiet holiday are likely to be turned away.'

The great event in their day is the arrival of a bus from

Chikmagalur at noon going to Tarikere, which is the nearest
town for shopping or to enjoy a movie at a couple of theatres
there. Their attuned ears catch the arrival of a bus a mile away:
the passengers waiting at the bus stand with godly patience stir
themselves, happy to escape the isolation for a few hours, and
return by the same bus in the evening.

Our guest house is a new one built on the topmost hill, a
spacious, well-furnished building. We are in a room, one side
walled with sheet glass, through which a full moon can be seen
almost as if within touching distance, shining on a rock face
looming up in the shadows. At dawn one observes that the
looming shape is a reddish mountain wall. As the sun rises the
fleecy, white mist, filling the valley to the brim, at first looking
like ocean waves stilled in calm air, melts gradually, revealing
glimpses of fields far below in the valley as through a rent in the
veil; gardens and undulating fields are revealed inch by inch as
the mist melts; and one notices the presence of a family far off,
husband and wife, and their child in a red sweater, perched on a
promontory jutting out; the lady in her purple sari looks like a
flower bed herself at this distance; the child seems to be in
ecstasy as he waves to a red bus, toy-size, crawling down the
winding road far below. Little farmsteads dotting the fields in
the valley, moss-covered rocks and tree tops, shimmer and
glisten in the sun.

SRINGERI

Twelve centuries ago Sankaracharya was born at Kaladi (in
Cochin) of parents who had been childless, but praying night
and day for an issue. In answer to their prayer Shiva appeared in
the guise of an old man, in a dream, and asked, 'Do you want
numerous children who live to be a hundred but are dullards
and evil-doers or only one who is exceptionally gifted, but will
live with you only for a short time?' They chose the latter. And
Sankaracharya was born, with only sixteen years as his allotted

span of life. In his fifth year he underwent spiritual and other disciplines; in his eighth year he mastered the Vedas, Shastras and Puranas. And in his tenth year he renounced all worldly interests and became a Sanyasi. The rest of his life is the record of a World Teacher. Through his writings, debates, and talks, he propagated his Advaita philosophy—a doctrine which says that all that exists is a particle of a Universal Soul and merges in the end in that Soul. 'His was the task of ending the nightmare of separateness,' says one of his commentators.

After travelling extensively from Kashmir to Cape Comorin, he arrived in Sringeri, which had already been sanctified by the presence of sages like Vasishta, Viswamitra, Vibhandaka, Kasyapa and others, who had had their ashrams in its forests, and spent their days in meditation in this tranquil setting of wooded mountains watered by River Tunga, which is considered holier than any other river in the world.

Sankara was carrying with him the golden image of Sharada, or Saraswathi, the Goddess of Knowledge, and had been in search of the right place for installing the image. He stood on the right bank of the river absorbing the scene before him. At his feet Tunga was flowing, its water radiant in the midday sun. He beheld now a spectacle on the opposite bank which was significant; he felt convinced that he was at the end of his quest. A cobra had spread its hood and held it like an umbrella over a spawning frog, to protect it from the sun. 'This is the place!' Sankara said. 'Here is harmony, an absence of hatred even among creatures which are natural enemies.'*

Sankara crossed the river, deciding to establish his mission

---

* This sounds more a symbolic statement than a fact. I have heard similar reports at other temples in the course of my travel, with occasional variations. If it was not a cobra and frog, it would be a tiger protecting a lonely calf. Even at Sringeri, when I visited it some years ago, the spot on the river was marked by a niche made of a couple of rough stones; this niche was covered with mud and sand but a slight excavation with one's finger revealed a stone surface on which a cobra and frog were faintly etched. Now the spot is marked by a properly built mini-shrine with a realistic statue of a cobra with its hood raised.

at this little village. First he proceeded to build four guardian temples on the surrounding hillocks, which were to protect the village from dangers, diseases, and the forces of evil. On the eastern hillock he built a temple for Kalabhairava, on the west for Anjaneya, on the south for Durga, and on the northern for Kali. Poojas are still being continued at these temples.

There is a repose and tranquillity in the air. The river flows softly. Strolling along its edge I notice a group of young men with an elderly companion in their midst. They are bathing in the river, washing their clothes, and at the same time listening to the lecture their elderly companion is giving them and answering questions put to them. When they get up to go, muttering their lessons, I follow them through the narrow passage behind the consecrated tombs of ancient saints.

I follow them into a large hall where groups of students are squatting in shady corners, quietly chanting their lessons and memorizing. A few scholars, wrapped in shawls, move about softly, absorbed in their own discussion.

In the upper storey there is a library containing over four thousand manuscripts and books, neatly classified, labelled and arranged in glass shelves. In an adjoining room pundits are seated before heaps of manuscripts and books, examining a vast store of literary material that has accumulated in the *math* from time immemorial.

In the central courtyard there is a shrine, fittingly enough, of Sankaracharya. This is a college run by the *math*, providing a course of studies that extends over ten years; and here young men are being trained for a religious and priestly life. Once a year the pupils are examined and the successful candidates are led by their masters across the river to the presence of the chief guru, the apostolic head who lives on the other side of the river. He is a man of deep learning and austerity, whose hours are occupied in meditation, prayer, worship and studies. He tests the candidates himself, and distributes to them clothes and money.

There is a Sanyasi sweeping the temple of Anjaneya and decorating the image with flowers, completely absorbed in his work, and indifferent to those passing by him. To my inquiry my guide answers: 'He is one of the four of five Sanyasis here. He speaks to no one. He came here some years ago. We don't know where he has come from. He spends most of his time in yoga; occasionally when he is free, he sweeps the temples. Since he is here he is our guest.' I observe two Sanyasis, sitting on the river-steps, in the shadow of a banyan tree, with their eyes closed. They look disembodied souls in the pink glare of the setting sun. Their purpose is also unknown. One of them, it was vaguely understood, came all the way from the Himalayas in order to discuss certain metaphysical questions with the chief guru. But he never met the guru, but just stayed on, dividing his time between meditation and service. He voluntarily teaches certain subjects in the college, where another Sanyasi is a pupil. No one questions who they are or why they are here, but treats them as honoured guests. Sringeri acts as host to whoever visits it. The moment you arrive, you are freed from all concerns of food and shelter. You are shown a room in the Guest House, and then your hot water is ready for your bath, and as soon as you have bathed, your food is brought to you. There is an old cook, bent with age, who gets up every morning at four o'clock, and goes to bed at eleven in the night, spending his waking hours in serving guests. Every day hundreds of visitors are fed by the *math*, not counting the pupils in the university, the Sanyasis, and others. This hospitality is not confined to human beings. In the niches of the temple towers live thousands of pigeons. From the stores of the *math*, large quantities of corn are scattered in the courtyard; it is fascinating to watch the birds sweep down to feed at their hour. Rice is cooked and dumped in the river for the fish also. Numerous fish of all sizes, mostly dark blue in colour, sporting and splashing about, come to the surface expectantly whenever a human being approaches the river-step.

There are numerous temples in Sringeri besides the chief one of Sharada. The temple of Vibhandaka in Sringeri itself and of his son Rishyasringa, which is at Kigga, six miles from Sringeri, built on a high hill, are two of the oldest temples here. Both are of the same type with an inner shrine in the middle, an open corridor around, and a roofed platform on the edge of the corridor. The platform can accommodate thousands of persons at a time. It is believed that by praying at these temples rain can be called or stopped. Vibhandaka and his son are famous sages mentioned in the early portions of the *Ramayana*. Rishyasringa, like his father, was a man of great attainment, but he had grown up without ever having seen a woman. At that time there was a severe drought in Anga; the king was told that the drought would cease if Rishyasringa could be brought to his country and married to the princess. A bevy of young women disguised as hermits were sent in order to entice this sage. They arrived, stopped at Narve, a village near Sringeri, waited for an opportunity and came before the young man when his father was away. He felt such a deep interest in these strange hermits that it was not very difficult for them to decoy him. His approach to Anga brought rain. He married the princess and became the priest of King Dasaratha of Ayodhya, and officiated at the great sacrifice which resulted in the birth of Rama, the hero of Ramayana. There is a carving on a pillar in the Rishyasringa temple at Kigga in which the young sage is shown as he is being carried off happily on a palanquin made of the intertwined arms of fair women.

1977

CHARLIE PYE-SMITH

IN THE MIDST OF LIFE

I have forgotten her name, but I shall not forget her face, nor what she said, nor the manner in which she said it. She was thirteen, though she looked somewhat older, and she had jet-black hair, the darkest of eyes, a powerful nose and a fleshy and expressive mouth. She wore a pink dress the same colour as the bindi on her forehead and she spoke Bengali in a rasping voice, more like a boy's at puberty than a girl's. There were thirty other children crammed into the small upstairs room in Bowbazar—pictures of Ramakrishna, Tagore, Gandhi and Nehru on the walls—and to escape their screams and chatter we went out on to a narrow wooden balcony with one of her teachers. We closed the door on her classmates and from where we stood we could observe the restless stream of life in the ill-lit alley below. I was reminded of Gustave Dore's lithographs of the poorer districts of Victorian London. A tall building with crumbling balconies and sagging lintels loomed above a fruit stall like the stern of a rotting galleon. Smoke drifted up from charcoal braziers and women waited as still as statues for the early-evening trade, while cyclists and pedestrians swirled around them like shoals of passing fish.

The girl told me first about her daily routine, using the teacher as an interpreter. In the morning she went to school,

---

CHARLIE PYE-SMITH first spent time in India when he researched and wrote *In Search of Wild India*, which accompanied a Channel Four television series. 'In The Midst of Life' is from *Rebels and Outcasts: A Journey through Christian India*. He is also the author of *The Other Nile* and *Travels in Nepal: The Sequestered Kingdom*.

then at midday she returned home, cooked lunch for her brother and sister and helped her mother with domestic chores. In the afternoon she did her school homework and then around four-thirty she came to this class: she liked painting and drawing and playing with the other children, but most of all she loved the drama lessons. When the class finished, around seven o'clock, she would return home, watch television and go to bed. She didn't say what her mother would be doing when she got there: working, presumably, for the evenings were a busy time for Bowbazar's prostitutes.

Her teacher had told me when we stepped out on to the balcony that Calcutta's pimps liked to get hold of children when they were twelve or thirteen. He and his colleagues had arranged for this particular girl to stay at a hostel some distance from the red-light district, largely to protect her from the pimps, but she had missed her mother and her mother had missed her, so she had come back home again. He said they realized now that she was a headstrong girl and that she was in no danger of being inveigled into prostitution. So what did she hope to do with her life? I asked.

'I'd like to be a doctor,' she replied in a confident voice. 'I can't stand seeing all the poor lying around in the streets and dying without medical treatment. When I'm a doctor I'll open a hospital for the poor. I'll look after them.' All the children in this evening class were the offspring of prostitutes, but their economic situations varied greatly: some of them had relatively wealthy mothers, but many were very poor. Doctors carried out regular check-ups, but they had to be paid for their services. 'When I'm a doctor,' said the girl emphatically, 'I'll take care of them all for free.'

Even in the days when Calcutta was known as the City of Palaces, and long before Kipling more tellingly described it as the City of Dreadful Night, most visitors were shocked by its poverty. 'Find, if you can, a more uninviting stop than Calcutta,' wrote Sir George Trevelyan in 1863. 'It unites every condition of a perfectly unhealthy situation ... The place is so bad by nature that human effort could do little to make it worse; but that has been done faithfully and assiduously.' Kipling put similar sentiments into awkward verse. Calcutta, in his view, was:

Chance-directed, chance-erected, laid and built
On the silt
Palace, byre, hovel—poverty and pride—
Side by side

This was my third visit to Calcutta and I found myself, as always, in the grip of conflicting emotions. When I wandered among the early-evening crowds on Chowringhee as a red sun sank behind the angular bulk of Eden Gardens; when I walked across the Maidan in the early morning and saw a trail of cattle egrets flap slowly past the great white bulk of the Victoria Memorial; when I watched the gangs of children with their broken bats and battered balls playing cricket among the imperial graves of South Park Street cemetery: on these and many other occasions I was utterly beguiled by the city and by the exuberance of her people. But just as frequently I was overcome with disgust. I recall, offhand, walking down Park Street to meet a pastor at the offices of the Assembly of God. Shortly before I reached there I passed a man sprawling face down on the pavement. He was naked and a swarm of flies buzzed around his buttocks, which were smeared with excrement. There was an appalling stench and passers-by covered their faces with hands and handkerchiefs. No one, myself included, stopped to help him—I suspect he was already dead—and I suppose we all comforted ourselves with the knowledge that Mother Teresa's Sisters of Charity would eventually lift him from the pavement and take him to a home for the destitute or, more probably, to a crematorium ...

Calcutta is said to be India's most cultured city, and I suppose I should have spent my evenings in smoke-filled rooms listening to discussions about Tagore or Satyajit Ray, or watching the latest offerings of the Bengali theatre, or rubbing shoulders with bearded intellectuals in galleries specializing in the avant-garde. I did not do any of these things, and even if I had, I doubt whether I would have been any better entertained than I invariably was when I called in for a drink at the Fairlawn Hotel.

The Fairlawn was tucked away behind high walls midway along Sudder Street, whose pavements appeared to have been cleaned up since my last visit, presumably for the Wills Cricket World Cup, which had concluded a few days before my arrival in the city. A bald-headed man in a dhoti used to occupy the pavement opposite the Indian Museum, lolling about like a dejected Caesar among a motley platoon of dogs which he loved deeply and who loved him in return. They ate together on the pavement, slept on the pavement and appeared as much a fixture of Sudder Street as the chapel a little further on. However, he and the dogs had gone, and so too had the squabbling, procreating families who once lived below a faded sign which read 'Mass Feeding of the Poor on Sundays'. But beggars and taxi-drivers still milled about outside the gates of the Fairlawn and I was relieved to see that nothing else had changed in my absence. The green columns of the portico and the trees in the garden were still slung with coloured fairy lights, the waiters were still dressed like the sepoys in *Carry On up the Khyber* and the walls were still hung with portraits of Queen Elizabeth and Prince Philip, Diana and Charles and other prominent members of the royal family. Most important of all, Mrs Violet Smith was still there, sitting in a chair behind the small reception desk and gazing imperiously around her domain, while Fifi, a white poodle of great antiquity, sat obediently at her feet. She seemed to remember my face but I had to remind her who I was. She slapped me affectionately on the forearm and shouted over her shoulder to a waiter: 'It's an old friend! Bring him a beer.' Then, turning to me: 'Now you don't expect me to call you Charlie, do you? What sort of a name is that, for heaven's sake?'

While I waited for the beer to arrive we had a conversation, or rather Mrs Smith talked while I listened; her monologue, as far as I could recall, was almost an exact replica of the one she had offered two years earlier when I also dropped in at the Fairlawn, unannounced but dimly recognized. Mrs Smith was an Armenian, born in Dacca, but everything about her manner and aspirations seemed English, although she spoke scathingly of the snobberies of the old expatriate community, now long since gone. She reminded me that she had a grandson who had been to Charterhouse, that she and her husband spent several months in Europe each year and that she was seventy-something years old. She always looked the same: younger than her years, with clear skin, lovely brown eyes, beautifully manicured hands and a magnificent hair-do which was carefully tended, like a piece of exotic topiary, by someone who came in each morning. She also reminded me, waving a hand towards the framed pictures and newspaper cuttings on the stairs, that many famous people had stayed in her small hotel.

'Eric Newby, Tom Stoppard, Felicity Kendall,' she said, wagging a finger. 'And just the other month Clive Anderson of the BBC came to see me. He had me interviewing Jyoti Basu outside the gates. Very slippery.'

Who was slippery? The Chief Minister?

'No, darling. Clive Anderson. When I interviewed him he was very tricky, very devious. I found it very stressful.'

The beer came and I drank it standing at the desk.

'And just today,' continued Mrs Smith, 'a girl came to see me here. Indian. Very pretty. Asked me to act opposite Richard Attenborough.' She looked hard into my eyes, nodding her head and tossing her eyebrows about, which was a habit of hers, while she waited for me to react to this astonishing piece of news.

'Well?' I said.

'The girl said: "You'll have to go to Ootacamund to do the acting." Well, I couldn't possibly, and I told her I couldn't!'

By now the small garden had filled up with evening drinkers and Mr Smith, a former major in the British Army, had come downstairs from the family living quarters to take Fifi for a walk. The dog's hair had been primped up as lovingly as Mrs Smith's, although it was going bald in places along the spine. Last summer, when the Smiths had taken their annual holiday in Europe—'We always stay in the best hotels,' said Mrs Smith—they took the dog to Amsterdam to have her eyes done.

'She spent the whole holiday with you?' I asked.

'No, darling, she flew back with KLM. First-class.'

Mr Smith and the dog tottered out of the gates to take some air among the beggars and drug addicts and ne'er-do-wells of Sudder Street. It was an improbable sight, even by Calcutta's improbable standards.

'Why aren't you staying with us?' asked Mrs Smith.

I told her that I was staying at a guest house in Middleton Street; it was far cheaper than the Fairlawn and I could choose where to eat, which the Fairlawn's guests could not.

'Well, we've modernized everything,' she continued. 'A/c in all the rooms. Music in the garden every night. You know, pop music. Loudspeakers, that sort of thing. We're very modern now.'

The following evening I came again and when Mrs Smith saw me chatting to a couple who were sitting in wicker chairs in the foyer, she said, without so much as a glance at me: 'How do you know Charlie?'

They replied that we had only just met.

'If I'd known he was here,' she said as she turned to leave, 'I'd have thrown the bastard out!'

Later that week she suggested to a waiter that he should sprinkle arsenic in my beer, then led me to a table to meet a man whom she introduced as one of her dearest friends. He was about my age, with short hair and jeans and an aggressive air about him, and he was sitting with a group of people whom he had presumably been foisted upon by Mrs Smith. They were from Australia, though the younger of the two couples were Armenians who had been brought up in Calcutta. Mrs Smith's dear friend said that he was a narcotics agent and that he had been working in Calcutta and the Far East for the past twenty-three years. He looked and sounded English. I happened to mention that I had just come from the evening class for prostitutes' children in Bowbazar and I asked him if he knew the area.

'You're raping them,' he said.

'I beg your pardon?'

'You're raping them, I said.'

At most, I replied, I might be writing about the children and the people that were helping them. He ignored what I said and embarked on a lengthy diatribe in which he accused organizations which help Calcutta's poor of imposing the liberal values of the West on people who were struggling to avoid starvation. In Calcutta, he said, you could have sex with a two-year-old girl if you wanted or with a cripple. People had to make a living, and if a mother could sell her child for 300 rupees for sex, then that could feed the family for a week. Life was cheap in Calcutta, he continued, and there were people outside the gate at the Fairlawn who would blow him away for twenty bucks. That, he said, was why he never went anywhere without his gun. Later I overheard him telling the elderly Australian couple that he had helped a great many people in Calcutta. For all I know, he may have had a saintly streak in him, but he certainly did his utmost to hide it.

I had not intended to visit Calcutta's dwindling Armenian community, but the Armenian couple I met that evening invited me to accompany them to Park Circus early the following morning and there I met Charles Sarkies, vice-president of the Armenian Association and superintendent of the Sir Catchick Paul Charter Home, in which resided, at present, fifteen elderly

Armenians. He came over to greet me while I was studying the small chapel in the grounds and led me up to his residence on the second floor of the old people's home. He was a man of great warmth and charisma and his looks suited his character: he was attractive in a rugged way with a large nose, humorous, hooded eyes and the complexion of a man who had spent much of his life outdoors. We sat at a table in his study and drank Kingfisher beer, into which he sprinkled some salt.

'In this weather,' he explained, 'you must always have salt in your beer. You know we were the first race in the world to embrace Christianity? When Archbishop Fisher came to Calcutta for the 250th anniversary of the Holy Church of Nazareth—that's on the other side of town—he said: "Armenia is a bastion of Christianity. You should be proud to be the first Christian nation in the world."'

Mr Sarkies had spent his childhood in Persia, but at the age of thirteen his parents had sent him to Calcutta to take advantage of the free education which could be had at the Armenian College. 'I arrived by ship in January 1935,' he recalled in a deep, gravelly voice. 'The only English I knew was "good morning" and "good evening", but I didn't know which one to use when. Next I learned to say "thank you".'

I asked him whether he used to return to Persia in the school holidays and he laughed. 'I never saw my mother again,' he said, 'and the next time I saw my father was in 1960, when I brought him out here for three months.' Financial considerations, he implied, had made the separation inevitable; many other Armenians who had been dispatched to Calcutta as children had had a similar experience. Anyway, Mr Sarkies completed his studies in Calcutta and became a mining engineer. In 1942, at the age of twenty, he began work in a British-owned coal mine in Bihar and he continued to work in the mines, which were nationalized after Independence, until his retirement forty years later.

When Mr Sarkies arrived in Calcutta there were over 3,000

Armenians in and around the city. Some worked on the railways; others were involved in the coal, jute and shellac industries and in the hotel trade. 'Now,' he said, 'there are just 103 adult Armenians left here—that's excluding the students who come from Iran—and in the last twenty-five years we have only had two Armenian weddings.'

There had been plenty of deaths, though, and Mr Sarkies had recently helped to establish the Christian Burial Board Funeral Service. 'You know, there's only one undertaker in Calcutta to look after all the Christians and they've got a hearse that won't even go five miles,' he said, his lips curling in disapproval. 'Even when a person dies they've got no peace. There's no one to clean them up, dress them properly.' If one of the old ladies died in the home during the night Mr Sarkies put her on blocks of ice and had her buried first thing in the morning in the Armenian plot in the cemetery next to the home. He expected matters to improve now: all the main churches had come together to form the new Burial Board and an architect was presently designing a funeral parlour which was going to be built where the children played cricket in South Park Street cemetery. This was bad luck on the children, but Mr Sarkies thought that Christians could now look forward to a decent burial.

When we had finished our beer he led me through a gate in the garden wall into Lower Circular Road cemetery. It lacked the monumental grandeur of the more famous South Park Street cemetery, but it was an impressive place nonetheless, with over 10,000 graves spread across 350 acres of land. The 300 or so graves in the Armenian section were beautifully tended and Mr Sarkies had recently planted flowering shrubs along the neatly kept paths. 'We don't bother with lead lettering now,' he explained. 'The urchins outside just come and steal it.' Mr Sarkies had taken over responsibility for managing the cemetery a little over a year ago. One of his first acts was to increase the wages of the fifteen workers. 'Now they're expected to work,' he remarked dryly as we wandered down a brickwork path towards the main entrance. During the course of the last year the paths had been cleared, old graves which were buried by scrub and spoil had been unearthed and restored and Mr Sarkies's men had planted over 250 trees and shrubs; this year the target was 500. The brick wall which surrounded the cemetery had been raised by four feet and this had stopped vandals coming in from outside. Mr Sarkies was hoping to get the defunct crematorium back into working order—the Catholic archbishop had agreed that his people could now be cremated—and this would help to lengthen the cemetery's active life. 'If we cremate them,' said Mr Sarkies, 'I'll be able to fit six people into the same space that I need to bury one.' He was a great believer in simple graves and he scoffed at some of the more elaborate affairs near the entrance. One particularly ornate grave with a pretentious canopy would have looked fine in a Californian pet cemetery, but here it looked very out of place. Mr Sarkies put on his glasses to inspect the inscription. 'Anglo-Indians,' he said. 'And I'll tell you something. They never spent any money on the old lady when she was alive, so why spend 10,000 rupees on her now she's dead?' A little further on we came to the section where the British had been buried in the latter years of the last century. Two graves belonged to women who had had eight children each.

'Yes,' mused Mr Sarkies, 'nothing else to do, you see. That was the entertainment in those days.'

1997

STEPHEN ALTER

AMRITSAR: CITY OF NECTAR AND GOLD

The Golden Temple Mail was scheduled to arrive in Amritsar at six o'clock in the morning. The only other passenger in the air-conditioned compartment had been asleep when I boarded the train at Saharanpur. As we got up, the two of us nodded to each other. The man was a few years younger than I, in his mid-thirties, with thinning hair and wire-rimmed glasses pinching his face into a look of bleary-eyed curiosity. Speaking in English, he asked if this was my first visit to Amritsar. I replied that I had been there a couple of times before, but not since the late seventies. He handed me his card: Arjun Mehra, gold merchant. His family owned a small workshop in Amritsar that produced wedding ornaments, mostly for export to Indian communities abroad.

As soon as he learned that I was on my way to Pakistan, Arjun Mehra became intensely interested. He told me that his family was originally from Sialkot, a town across the border. As Hindus they had been forced to leave their home and move to Amritsar at the time of Partition. Arjun Mehra was born long after 1947 and had never been to Sialkot, even though it was less than a hundred kilometres away. He said that he had always been curious to know what it was like in Pakistan. After I explained that my grandparents had once lived in Sialkot, he insisted that I come to his house immediately and meet his

STEPHEN ALTER is the author of the novels *Neglected Lives*, *Silk and Steel*, *The Godchild*, and *Renuka*, and the autobiographical *All the Way to Heaven*, about his childhood in Mussoorie. 'Amritsar: City of Nectar and Gold' is taken from *Amritsar to Lahore: Crossing the Border Between India and Pakistan*.

family. By this time the train was already pulling into Amritsar.

A Maruti car was waiting for Arjun outside the railway station and, waving aside my protests, he had the driver load my suitcase into the boot. All the way home he kept quizzing me about my itinerary, as if the names of each of the towns I planned to visit in Pakistan were answers to a riddle that he had been worrying over for years.

His family seemed bewildered and amused by my arrival. They lived in a modern two-storey house off a narrow lane, barely wide enough for the car. There was a heavy metal gate across the driveway and cast-iron grills on the windows. As with most large middle-class homes in the country, it was a joint family residence, with grandparents, parents, children, and other relatives living under the same roof. Arjun introduced me to his wife Annu and their two sons, Navin and Kapil. The boys had just woken up and were getting ready for school. The grandparents were drinking tea on the veranda, along with an uncle who was staying in the house.

After a few awkward pleasantries I was offered a cup of tea and biscuits. Arjun's father, Randhir Mehra, spoke Punjabi and a little Hindi. He was a short, stocky man, whose face showed his age, though his hair was dyed jet-black. His wife remained silent and after a few minutes disappeared. When Arjun told his father that I was going to Pakistan, Randhir Mehra showed no interest at all and asked me instead about Mussoorie. He said that he had just returned from there a week ago. Being retired he enjoyed the chance to go up to the hills every summer and escape the oppressive heat and humidity of Punjab.

Though his father seemed reluctant to talk about their former home in Pakistan, Arjun kept pestering him to tell me details. Randhir Mehra said that they had owned a gold business in Sialkot but that everything had been lost in 1947.

'Have you ever gone back?'

'Only once,' he said. 'I got a temporary visa to watch a cricket match between India and Pakistan in the early fifties. We were supposed to stay in Lahore but a couple of us caught a bus and went back to visit Sialkot.'

'Did anyone recognize you there?'

'A few people remembered us but we didn't stay very long. Things had changed.'

At this point one of the boys switched on the television. A woman announcer, with her head covered, appeared on the screen and Arjun pointed to the TV.

'We get all of the Pakistani programmes here, from across the border,' he said. 'Sometimes it's interesting to watch.'

His father nodded.

'I enjoy listening to the Urdu ghazals and we follow some of the serial dramas,' he said. 'But their news is always slanted against India. You can never be sure what's true or not.'

Growing impatient, the boys flipped to another channel that was playing songs from Hindi films, costumed dancers squirming to a disco beat.

After we had talked for about an hour, I asked to be excused so that I could check into a hotel. Arjun tried to persuade me to stay at his house but I could see that it would have been an imposition on the family. As I was about to leave, his father told me to wait a moment. He got up slowly and went across to a bookcase on the opposite side of the room. Pulling out a file he flipped through the contents, then handed me an old document, printed on heavy paper and torn at the creases. Most of the writing was in Urdu, with scribbled dates and numbers. The smeared patterns of ink from rubber stamps looked like purple bruises.

'That's my old ration card,' he said, with a hesitant smile. 'From Sialkot. Don't ask me why I've kept it.'

The yellowed paper seemed ready to fall apart in my hands. A column of cryptic numerals tallied up the monthly quotas of flour, rice, and cooking oil — the basic staples of life — which had been bought more than fifty years before. Yet for Randhir Mehra the ration card had a much greater significance; it was a record of the past, a faded symbol of identity, proof of his name, his family, his origins. His reluctance to speak about Partition came from a private sense of loss, and this document I held in my hands was probably the only tangible evidence he possessed of his former home. When I returned the ration card, Randhir Mehra slipped it back into his file and carefully tucked the papers away inside the bookcase . . .

The Golden Temple, holiest of Sikh shrines, lies at the heart of the walled city of Amritsar. In the narrow, congested streets bicycle rickshaws remain the most convenient form of transport, and the drivers weave through swarms of pedestrians, ringing their bells to clear the way. I entered the walled city through Gandhi Gate, which was decorated for the arrival of the Congress Party President, Sita Ram Kesri, who was coming to Amritsar as part of the Jubilee celebrations. Streamers of gold and silver tinsel had been strung from the balconies overhead and banners had been erected every fifty feet, offering felicitations from local members of the Congress Party. But the crowds in the bazaar seemed to ignore these decorations and the market was alive with commercial activity. There were dozens of 'Pugri shops' selling turbans, and I saw a sign for the 'Guru Nanak Computer School (for girls only)'. Further on we passed a 'Spiritual Museum for Character Development', hemmed in by dozens of fabric stores. Amritsar is well known for its cloth mills and my rickshaw driver assured me that it was the best place to purchase woolen fabrics. With the temperature close to a hundred degrees, however, and humidity pressing in around me like damp felt, the last thing I wanted to buy was a suit-length of heavy tweed or a woolen blanket.

    A square arcade of shops and offices surrounds the Golden Temple. Most of this market caters to Sikh pilgrims and there are shops selling kirpans of every size and shape, from small daggers with a curved blade to ceremonial swords in velvet sheaths. Near the main gate is a visitor's information centre, where I stopped to ask directions. The man behind the desk was a tall, dignified Sikh with an orange turban and free-flowing beard. He explained that I could take my camera inside but that I should leave my shoes and socks in a pigeonhole at the back of the office, along with any tobacco or alcohol that I might be carrying. I was also required to cover my head before entering the sanctuary.

The temple itself, known as the Har Mandir, stands at the centre of a square tank of water, its gilded walls and domes almost blinding in the mid-morning sun. A white marble promenade, the parikrama, surrounds the tank, with shaded galleries on all four sides. Hundreds of pilgrims were circling the temple, most of them Sikhs but many Hindus as well. Some of the men were stripping off their clothes and preparing to bathe. Dressed only in their undershorts they descended the marble steps and plunged into the murky depths of the tank. Women prostrated themselves and dipped their hands into the water to drink. This water is regarded as nectar, or amrit, from which the city of Amritsar gets its name. At several places there were trees growing at the edge of the promenade, their trunks and branches polished smooth by the hands of pilgrims. The sun baked down on the marble floors and jute carpets had been laid out so that visitors wouldn't burn their feet. The walls were covered with memorial plaques and inscriptions, many of them bearing the names of Sikh officers and soldiers who had died in the two world wars and the battles with Pakistan. From the temple a musical recitation of the scripture, or kirtan, was broadcast over loudspeakers. A mood of contemplation and sanctity enveloped the clusters of worshippers circumambulating the tank and bathing in its sacred waters. Even the Nihang Sikhs, members of an ultramartial sect, armed with swords and bows and arrows, their blue turbans decorated with circlets of steel, seemed to be at peace.

At the eastern end of the sanctuary is a langar and

dharamshala, where visitors are given free food and shelter. The kitchens are mostly staffed by volunteers. A steady stream of people were sitting down to eat and when they finished each of them stood up and took their turn helping with the cooking and serving. Mounds of flour were being kneaded by muscular young men, while a group of women rolled the dough into balls which were then flattened between their hands to make rotis. These were tossed onto a giant griddle, almost ten feet in diameter. Another team of volunteers flipped the rotis as they cooked. All the food and fuel in the langar comes from offerings that are donated by pilgrims and wealthy benefactors. Each devotee who visits the temple contributes his or her share of the work. A young boy, six or seven years old, his long hair twisted into an unruly topknot, sat in front of a trough full of ash and sand. He was busy scrubbing stainless-steel bowls and glasses that are used for drinking water and sweetened sherbet. The Sikh religion has always emphasized the importance of community service, and within the temple precincts there is an atmosphere of collective harmony.

Completely covered in gold leaf, the Har Mandir is the focus of devotion. Its gilded walls and dome were built by Maharaja Ranjit Singh, though the foundation stone is said to have been laid by a Muslim Sufi. There are no idols in the temple and worship centres around the *Granth Sahib*, the Sikh scriptures. A continuous singing of Guru Nanak's hymns can be heard over the loudspeakers and the priests, dressed in white robes and wearing dark blue turbans, sit at the heart of the inner sanctum. The gold leaf on the walls has been worked into elaborate floral patterns. The *Granth Sahib* itself is wrapped in embroidered velvet and men with flywhisks stand sentinel. Pilgrims cross a marble bridge that leads to the temple and, shuffling slowly forward, they circle a narrow balcony, peering in at the priests who sit on cushions that cover the floor. As the devotees leave the temple and file back across the bridge, they are given prasad to eat, a sweet halwa made of semolina, sugar, and ghee. Prasad is a symbol of spiritual sustenance and blessing.

Despite the peaceful atmosphere of reverence and devotion the Golden Temple has a violent history. In June 1984 this complex was the scene of an intense gun battle that killed several hundred people and left many of the surrounding buildings destroyed. At the height of the Sikh separatist agitation, Jarnail Singh Bhindranwale, who led a guerrilla war against the Indian government, took refuge in the Golden Temple along with his lieutenants and a large cache of arms. After a prolonged siege Indira Gandhi ordered the Army to enter the temple. For many Sikhs, even those who did not support the separatists, this was an act of sacrilege. Most of the bullet holes on the temple walls have now been patched, and the Akal Takht, a building badly damaged in the fighting, has been completely rebuilt. For the time being the separatist agitations in Punjab have been suppressed, though the temple still evokes an aura of martyrdom.

The roots of the Sikh separatist movement in Punjab can be traced to the aftermath of Partition. It only came to a head during the 1980s, however, when militant members of the Sikh community, supported by expatriates in Canada and England, called for an independent nation of 'Khalistan'. The Indian government's response to this threat was predictably ruthless, but the irony of the situation was that Congress Party politicians were the ones who actually helped fan the flames of separatism. Indira Gandhi's stalwarts, men like Giani Zail Singh, who would later become president, provided support and legitimacy to Sikh militants in an effort to undermine the political power of moderates in the Akali Dal.

Jarnail Singh Bhindranwale, a fiery small-town preacher and activist, was propelled to a position of notoriety and influence through a political power play that went awry. He combined fundamentalist rhetoric with the rustic appeal of grassroots populism. Bhindranwale gave voice to the frustrations of Partition and the desire for an independent Sikh homeland in the Punjab. He advocated the use of violence as a means toward secession and surrounded himself with armed militants, using the martial symbolism of his faith. Adopting the title of Sant, or Saint, he took on the mantle of Guru Gobind Singh. The iconography of Sikh resistance and martyrdom became a central part of Bhindranwale's campaign, even before he took refuge in the Golden Temple.

As Punjab's law-and-order situation deteriorated in the early 1980s, and with growing support for the separatists coming from Sikh communities abroad, a tragic confrontation was set in motion. Bhindranwale's intransigence, combined with the incompetence of government, police, and military officials, allowed the crisis to escalate and erupt. Most commentators agree that until this point the majority of Sikhs did not support Bhindranwale and his fellow separatists. The campaign of terror that the militants launched in Punjab hurt the region economically and caused many people to turn against them, even though they lived in fear of extortion and murder. But the Indian Army's siege and attack on the Golden Temple (code named Operation Bluestar) was a wholesale military assault against the most sacred shrine of the Sikhs. Bhindranwale may have embarrassed and outraged members of his community by holing up in the temple precincts, but the Army's desecration of the shrine led to widespread disillusionment and despair. Newspaper and television images of shattered walls and gutted sanctuaries, tanks and artillery, pools of blood on the marble floors and the bullet-riddled bodies of teenage militants left most Sikhs with a communal sense of violation. Their disillusionment and fear was reaffirmed, six months later, by the anti-Sikh riots that followed Indira Gandhi's death . . .

When I returned from the Golden Temple to my hotel, I found the Mehra's car and driver waiting for me. Arjun had sent word that he was busy but he had asked his wife, Annu, and a friend of hers, Harjit, to show me around the city. The two of them were seated in the Napoli restaurant nearby and, after a cold drink, we set off to see Khalsa College and Guru Nanak University. Harjit had been a student at Khalsa College and her mother was a lecturer in the English department.

Annu and Harjit were in their late twenties, both of them vivacious and attractive young women. One was a Hindu and the other a Sikh. When I asked how long they'd known each other the two of them laughed and said that their families had been close for years. Harjit was unmarried and worked as a nutritionist, though she had taken the day off. Annu lived at home with her in-laws but my arrival had given her an excuse to get out of the house. Looking at the two of them it would have been virtually impossible to tell which was the Hindu and which the Sikh, except that Harjit wore a thin steel kara around her wrist.

Aside from the walled city, with its frenetic bazaars and cluttered lanes, Amritsar is a quiet, provincial town. The tensions which lay over the city for more than a decade, have finally eased, even though police patrols and barricades are in evidence everywhere. Earlier I had asked Arjun Mehra what it was like to live in Punjab during the separatist agitations. He explained that many of the Hindu residents were attacked by Sikh 'extremists' and much of the 'terrorism' was intended to drive them out of the state. As gold traders the Mehra family would have been prime targets for extortion. Arjun told me that during this period his workshop was only open from eleven in the morning until three in the afternoon because of curfews and that nobody dared go outdoors after dark.

Though Annu and Harjit spoke briefly about the 'troubles and disturbances' in Punjab, they were more interested in asking me questions about America. Annu explained that she had a brother who was a doctor in New York and some day she wanted to take her sons to visit him. Harjit told me that she was thinking of emigrating.

'Why would you want to leave Amritsar?' I said.

'It's a nice place. I like it here,' she said, 'but it's very quiet and things have changed.'

Without saying it directly she was hinting at a mood of disillusionment in the Sikh community. Some of her relatives had already emigrated to England, and she was thinking of going there.

The campuses of Khalsa College and Guru Nanak University are situated along the Grand Trunk Road, covering an area of five or six square miles. Guru Nanak University is a much newer institution, with concrete buildings and modern dormitories. The red-brick facade of Khalsa College, however, looked more like a palace than an educational institution, with domes and cupolas, deep verandas and curving balconies. Established by the British at the end of the nineteenth century, Khalsa college was part of a colonial effort to promote the English language and create an educated elite. The official medium of instruction at Khalsa College is now Punjabi, though certain subjects are still taught in English.

The buildings are examples of Orientalia at its most excessive extreme, constructed with a confectioner's eye. As we entered the campus, Harjit explained that the architect who built this college was the same man who designed the Victoria Memorial in Calcutta. The lawns and gardens were well maintained, with spreading Ashoka trees and royal palms, but the classrooms were in disrepair, the wooden desks worn and broken, the lecture halls poorly lit and uninspiring. None of the rooms were air-conditioned and the tiny fans overhead seemed out of proportion with the rest of the building. The main auditorium had ceilings that rose fifty or sixty feet above the floor. On the stage a group of college women were rehearsing a play that would be presented as part of the fiftieth-anniversary celebrations, gesturing defiantly as they re-enacted Gandhi's Salt March.

Harjit led the way up a narrow staircase to the second floor where she showed me the botany and zoology departments. A group of students sat in front of a line of microscopes, glancing up at us with amusement as we passed by. On one of the outer walls was a glasscase, six feet high, containing a crumbling specimen of a tree fern. The delicate fronds had completely disintegrated into dust, and all that remained were a few bleached sections of the stem.

The vast majority of students at Khalsa College were Sikhs; Harjit explained that every year on Guru Nanak's birthday the entire student body marched in procession from the college to the Golden Temple. She had been a student during the eighties, when there were violent protests against the central government following the attack on the Golden Temple.

'I remember watching from this balcony,' said Harjit, pointing in the direction of the main road. 'The police and army were lined up there and students uprooted bricks from the flowerbeds and threw them at the soldiers.'

Annu and Harjit dropped me back at my hotel in the early afternoon but around five-thirty the car returned. This time the Mehra's two sons and their uncle, Mamaji, accompanied me to the border post at Atari to watch the 'Beating Retreat' that is held each evening. Navin, the eldest boy, had recently written a report for school on these ceremonies. He and his brother had been to Atari several times before but their uncle and I had never seen the border. As we drove west from Amritsar, along the Grand Trunk Road, a sprinkling of rain left the asphalt steaming and put a shine on the wheat fields and kikad trees along the margins of the two-lane highway.

The Border Security Force maintains their post at Atari with all of the spit and polish for which the Indian Army is renowned. Flowerbeds of zinnias and marigolds stood at attention beside an archway proclaiming *'Hamara Bharat Mahan'*, and the BSF motto 'Duty unto Death'. A cement sculpture of two hands clasped together in friendship served as a monument of reconciliation. In a curious way, the border post reminded me of the highway rest stops maintained by the Punjab Tourism Department. There were several cold-drinks stands and young boys selling sweets and roasted peanuts. From the parking area I could see the steel gate at the border and beyond it the green and white flag of Pakistan, emblazoned with a crescent moon. On the near side of the gate was the Indian tricolour.

Beating Retreat is an archaic military tradition that symbolizes a cessation of hostilities on the battlefield. In earlier times it was a chance for the opposing armies to collect and bury their dead at sunset. Even though their compatriots continue firing at each other across the disputed line of control in Kashmir, the Indian Border Security Force and the Pakistani Rangers put on a coordinated display of military pageantry that could only have been achieved through complete cooperation and planning on both sides. This daily ritual attracts regular crowds of tourists from Amritsar and Lahore. The BSF soldiers taking part in the parade were uniformed in khaki with starched turbans and pleated coxcombs, jackboots, gold braid, and ribbons.

Close to three hundred spectators had gathered on the Indian side of the border and the sentries kept us back about a hundred metres from the gate. As the sun began to drop behind the neem trees there was a rustle of activity and the BSF soldiers let us move forward to a reviewing stand. Those who found no room on the benches were made to sit in the middle of the road and watch. The ceremony began with one of the soldiers presenting arms and marching with vigorous strides to the gate and back. Orders were shouted in belligerent voices, the words virtually unintelligible. A second soldier repeated the same manoeuvre, stamping his boots and marching with an exaggerated goose step. He was a Sikh, his beard tinted orange with henna, while the first soldier had been a Hindu. Both men stood over six feet tall and were obviously chosen for their imposing stature and fierce demeanour. Across the border we could hear similar commands being shouted and the clatter of hobnailed boots. This posturing continued for at least ten minutes until the gate at the border was finally thrown open. On the other side we could see that an identical ceremony was being repeated by Pakistani Rangers, uniformed in black salwar kameez, with bandoliers and rifles. The two separate audiences rose to their feet and peered across at each other like the supporters of opposing football teams. All around me I could feel a bristling of patriotic sentiments as the two commanders came out to the gate and shook hands. At this point the spectators broke into applause and cheers. Two buglers played reveille and the flags were lowered in unison.

Once the Beating Retreat was over, spectators were allowed to approach within ten feet of the open gate and the painted white line that marks the border. There was a rush to get to the front and everyone pressed forward so that the soldiers had to shout and put out their arms to keep us back. Fired up by the nationalistic passions of the parade, the crowds on either side became aggressive. Shouts of 'Bharat Mata Ki Jai!' came from the one side and 'Allah ho Akbar!' from the other. For a moment it looked as if this jingoistic fervour was going to lead to a minor riot, but the BSF soldiers and the Pakistani Rangers stood between the two contingents, holding them back. Within a minute or two the hostile voices were stilled and as the muted shadows of twilight settled over Atari the spectators stood transfixed. For me this was the most remarkable and profound moment of the whole ceremony, when all of the tension and animosity, the bluster and bravado, suddenly melted into silence. For at least five minutes nobody moved and the spectators on either side simply stared at each other. Their faces were filled with bewilderment and curiosity, the kind of expressions that one sees in a crowd that leaves a cinema hall, blinking as their eyes adjust to reality.

Driving back to Amritsar, Mamaji and the two boys started laughing and joking in the back seat. As I listened to what they said I found myself laughing too, unable to wipe a foolish grin off my face. Even the driver, who had said no more than a couple of words all day, joined in the conversation. It was as if the proximity of the border and the intensity of emotions during the ceremony had animated each of us and we were overcome by an uncontrollable feeling of elation and catharsis. Both of the boys were giggling hysterically and their uncle couldn't stop talking. After a while the driver switched on the radio so that we had to shout to make ourselves heard over the sound of Hindi film music. Nobody said anything about the Pakistanis we had seen but there was an unspoken feeling in the car of having witnessed an event that signified more than just a cessation of hostilities. We had gone to the edge and back.

Approaching the outskirts of the city, we passed a banner announcing the Jubilee celebrations, along with a huge hoarding with a picture of Sita Ram Kesari, the Congress Party president. Mamaji began to make disparaging comments about Kesri's appearance, his dark skin, bulging eyes, and swollen lips. The boys were doubled up with laughter as their uncle explained that Kesri had once been a 'bandmaster'. By this time the traffic was growing thicker as we entered Amritsar and the driver was laughing so hard I thought he would lose control of the car. Mamaji wiped the tears from his eyes, as he told one political joke after the other.

Eventually we came to a stop near Arjun Mehra's workshop and showroom, located only a few hundred yards from the Golden Temple. The streets were so narrow that even the compact Maruti was unable to take us all the way and we went on foot through a labyrinth of gullies. On either side of us were lines of utensil shops, with brass and copper pots, aluminium bowls, and stainless-steel implements hanging from the ceilings and walls. At a crossing in the centre of the bazaar grew a twisted pipal tree, its branches constrained by the buildings on either side. In its roots I could see a small Hindu shrine and the stooped figure of a man lighting an oil lamp in front of a framed picture of Lakshmi, the goddess of wealth.

Arjun's showroom was on the third floor of a shabby looking building, up a dimly lit flight of stairs. Inside it was air-conditioned and comfortably furnished with chairs and sofas. As we entered, Arjun was in the process of weighing a set of wedding ornaments. He greeted us with a distracted smile and showed me a gold necklace inlaid with precious stones and pearls, worth more than Rs 50,000. One of the assistants in the showroom was sent to bring us Coca-Colas, which we drank as Arjun finished up his work. By this time we had all recovered from our fit of laughter and the boys looked tired and subdued. I was introduced to an older man named Munshi Ram, who had worked for the family for sixty years, having come across from Sialkot with Randhir Mehra in 1947. In one corner of the showroom stood a massive safe, built into the wall, and as they put the gold ornaments away, Arjun turned one key in the lock while Munshi Ram turned another. The safe could only be opened if the two of them were in the showroom together.

Later Arjun took me downstairs to his workshop where the ornaments were made—a stuffy, rectangular room in which fifteen men were seated on the floor at low wooden tables. The craftsmen were shaping the gold into tiny flowers, their petals and leaves inlaid with rubies and emeralds. Arjun explained that all the goldsmiths employed in his workshop came from Bengal and most of them had been working for his family since they were boys. Some of the men were tapping at the ornaments with small hammers and miniature chisels the size of toothpicks. Even under the glare of a fluorescent bulb, the yellow metal in their hands seemed to glow with a light of its own. On one side of the room was a single window, which was open but secured with a line of steel bars, like a prison cell. In the distance, over the rooftops of Guru bazaar, I could see the dome of the Golden Temple lit up against the night sky, like the bud of a gilded lotus.

2000

ABRAHAM VERGHESE

THE BANDIT KING AND THE MOVIE STAR

On 30 July 2000 the smuggler and poacher Veerappan kidnapped the elderly and popular Kannada actor Rajkumar and took him away to a forest hideout. The kidnapping roused passions in Karnataka and Tamil Nadu and generated much interest in the media. Then, suddenly—and mysteriously—in November, Rajkumar was set free.

It was after midnight on 6 August when my plane landed in Madras. On the cab ride into town the breeze coming through the window carried the scent of the ocean but also hints of coir rope, ganja, and jasmine. It was a complex fragrance, and it evoked an involuntary flood of memories, as if the olfactory cortex of my brain had roused the rest of the house. I saw clearly the faces of people I had not thought about in years.

One particular bend in the road, as we motored past St. Thomas Mount and the Officers Training College, brought to mind a one-eyed Anglo-Indian hooker named Blossom. It was my first time, and some upperclassmen at my college had taken me to a brothel. Blossom had been grinding chilli in the kitchen when she was pressed into duty. I still remember the scent of chilli wafting up from her hand as it lay motionless on the pillow. The rest of her was motionless too. 'Hurry up, child, we don't have all night,' she said.

ABRAHAM VERGHESE is a doctor based in the United States. He is the author of *My Own Country* and *The Tennis Partner*. 'The Bandit King and the Movie Star' first appeared in the *Atlantic Monthly*.

I left Madras twenty years ago. Two marriages and three children later I am a different man from the one who left. My return visits have been sporadic. But there is great delight in a homecoming. Only one thing spoils it: the city's new name—Chennai—grates on my ears. A delayed postcolonial regionalism has brought many such changes; the state to which the city belongs is no longer Madras state but Tamil Nadu— land of the Tamils.

I played the game of the returning native—looking for familiar landmarks, seeing if I could recognize them behind the hoardings and billboards and new apartment buildings that have so altered the face of the city. My cabby was a dark, moustachioed Tamil who sat scrunched up against the door, his shoulder half out the window, addressing the steering wheel and pedals in a sideways fashion. His toes, curled around the accelerator, looked like carved ebony. I asked him if there had been disturbances in Madras, as there had been recently in Bangalore, with the news that Veerappan had kidnapped Rajkumar. (I didn't have to say 'Rajkumar, the actor' or 'Veerappan, the smuggler'; the kidnapping had been front and centre in India for days.)

The cabby laughed at my question. 'Riots?' he said in Tamil. 'What for? What do we care about Rajkumar? He is nothing to us in Madras.' And then he added, with a strange authority and confidence that I was to encounter repeatedly, and always from persons far removed from the story, 'He will be released tomorrow. Definitely.' He was satisfied with his pronouncement. He looked at me and gave me a don't-mention-it wag of his head.

When we pulled under the glittering portico of the Taj Coromandel Hotel, it was crowded with socialites departing from a gala. The bejewelled women rustled by in their chiffon saris, calling good-bye to each other in voices like myna birds'. I smelled Shalimar, Chanel No. 5, Bijan. The men were stoic, more Old Spice than Drakkar Noir; they stood holding open the doors of the cars the valets had brought around. I was embarrassed by my rumpled clothing, the stubble on my face, and my eau de travel. But more than anything it was my bare upper lip that bothered me. All the years I lived in Madras I had worn a moustache. Now that I was back, I saw a moustache on every male face. Without one of my own I felt exposed.

Moustaches were on my mind because of Veerappan and his trademark facial growth. His moustache is called a *kattabomman*, which has historically represented passion and fierceness. Throughout India it is a staple of police inspectors, villains, ruffians, and zamindars (and, of course, actors playing inspectors, villains, ruffians, and zamindars in Indian movies). Not everyone can pull off a *kattabomman* (though, God knows, we all tried in college; but most of us wound up settling for the bottle brush, or the pyramid centered over the upper lip, or variations thereupon). One has to back up a *kattabomman*, ideally with a hollow-cheeked, sharp-nosed, and steely-eyed countenance as well as big shoulders and bulging biceps (though the wiry Veerappan has defied that rule). In college only my friend Eddie could pull this moustache off. It made him look fierce, even though Eddie was a sweetheart, a pussycat.

Veerappan's *kattabomman* is the prototype: it is shaped like the Arc de Triomphe, all but concealing his lips, its thick, oversized pillars dwarfing his face and hanging bushily off the edge of his chin. A secondary growth leads back to the angle of his jaw. The moustache dominates every image I have seen of Veerappan over the years. At times it seems as if the moustache—not the man—is responsible for killing more than 130 people and 2,000 elephants, poaching 88,000 pounds of ivory, and smuggling sandalwood worth millions. The fellow peering out from behind the *kattabomman* is a mere appendage, powerless but for those tusks. After The Kidnapping, Veerappan's wife—who was captured and released and who no longer lives in the jungle—had this to say about her husband: 'Only in appearance he looks frightening. But if you sit and talk to him, he is a very kind person.' A pussycat, in other words.

But this mouser achieved new heights of notoriety when he kidnapped Rajkumar, last 30 July. It is difficult for the rest of India (not to mention the rest of the world) to fathom the devotion and love that Rajkumar's fans in Karnataka (formerly the state of Mysore) have for him. With the advent of Star TV and the opening up of the economy to imports, all kinds of people and things have gained fame in India: Jennifer Lopez, Palm Pilots, *Baywatch*, Nokia cell phones, Monica Lewinsky. Then there is the homegrown fame of film stars in Bombay (or Mumbai, I should say). Twinkle, Tabu, Pooja, Dimple, Bobby, Sunny, Anil, and others adorn the covers of the glamour magazines and scandal rags that scream from vendors' carts. These actors live on a well-lit stage, and every beauty pageant they judge, every opening they attend, is carefully recorded. Marriage, divorce, falling in and out of love, all take place within the same incestuous circle—or so it seems to us observers. Periodically the actors' houses are raided by IT (income-tax) officers looking for black (undeclared) money; great wads of it often show up behind panelling, stuffed into mattresses, or buried underground. We begin to imagine that the stars speak not like the rest of us but in Bollywood lines. (*Woman from a lousy family tree, did I raise you to show me this day! Or You have mixed my honour in the mud. Get out of the house. From today you are not my son and neither am I your father. Assume that your father is dead!*)

But Rajkumar's fame is a league apart from the ephemeral Bollywood variety: it is made of broad cloth, enduring even as he reaches his seventies. Rajkumar grew up in poverty—a fact he has never tried to hide. Even if his onscreen persona invariably sports a wig and a debonair moustache, and even if lately his leading ladies have been young enough to be his granddaughters, offscreen he happily appears as himself: a pleasant, avuncular septuagenarian with a bald pate, twinkling eyes, a large nose, and a winning smile. He has been an ardent champion of Kannada (the language of Karnataka) and its culture. At one time the state government wanted to make the teaching of Kannada in schools optional rather than mandatory. Rajkumar objected, and it was as if God had spoken. Legions of fans rallied to the cause, and the government backed down in a hurry. He never ran for office, though he could easily have done so and won. Even in his 007 kinds of roles he refused to imbibe alcohol or smoke cigarettes onscreen, not wanting to be a bad role model for his fans. He was in good health, thanks to his modest and temperate lifestyle, and he still had the habit of rising at four every morning to practice yoga and chant *bhajans*. He was always early for his shoots. This humility—so much the exception in the movie business—is why Rajkumar (or 'Dr Rajkumar', as he is known for an honorary degree) is so revered by the common man in Karnataka. His repertoire has included roles as popular Hindu deities and saints. The colourful posters and calendars that decorate living rooms and shops in Karnataka often use Rajkumar's face to depict these figures (there being no gold standard, after all), thus sealing this divine transference. His millions of fans believe they have a personal relationship with him: he is brother, father, son, faithful husband, avenging angel; he is me and he is you and he is . . . God. 'You won't see this happening in Bombay,' a filmmaker told me a few days later, referring to such deification. 'It's as though self-esteem in the south isn't innate but exists largely as something we project on our heroes.'

The actors M. G. Ramachandran, of Tamil Nadu, and N. T. Rama Rao, of Andhra Pradesh, were similarly deified in their states. Both men used—some would say they were involuntarily catapulted by—their popularity to become chief ministers (the equivalent of governors in America) in the late 1970s and early 1980s, and they went on, in a Reaganesque manner, to hugely influence politics on the national scene. I remember that MGR, even when old and sickly, insisted on appearing in a white Cossack hat and gangsta shades, his neck and jowls hidden by a white shawl, and with the few square inches of flesh that showed covered in white pancake makeup. It was as if he sensed that only MGR the icon had any power; to reveal the mortal beneath would destroy everything. Rajkumar has never had such worries.

I wanted to get close to the forest where the abduction took place and where Veerappan and Rajkumar were hidden at that moment. I flew from Madras to Coimbatore, a town famous for its textile mills. In Coimbatore I hired a car and drove to Satyamangalam, a town in the foothills of the Western Ghats, a chain of mountains on the edge of the Deccan Plateau. Outside the police station I met the man who was to be my guide, and we headed to the forest.

Rajkumar's kidnapping took place on a Sunday. The actor and his wife were visiting his native village of Gajanur, about 130 miles from the city of Bangalore, their principal residence. Rajkumar's ancestral property in Gajanur borders the Satyamangalam forest, a dense jungle preserve covering 2,300 square miles and nestled between Tamil Nadu and Karnataka. Rajkumar loved to escape to this rural retreat, far from the urban bustle of Bangalore. He had just built a new house on the grounds but had not as yet moved into it, and the couple was spending the night in the old house. They sat on a straw mat, watching the local news on television. Rajkumar prepared a betel leaf for his after-dinner chew.

Suddenly men armed with Kalashnikov rifles burst in. Rajkumar recognized the leader as (or recognized the moustache of) Veerappan. The smuggler addressed the actor using the English word 'Sir' and ordered him to come with them. Rajkumar, who has played a calm, composed hero many times in his movies, stayed true to that role. He told his wife not to worry. His hands were bound behind his back with nylon rope. Veerappan handed a cassette tape containing his demands to

Rajkumar's wife, with instructions that she deliver it to the chief minister of Karnataka. The bandits, about a dozen of them, disappeared into the forest with their prize as quickly as they had come.

A few miles from Satyamangalam, just before we began the twisty mountain climb, we passed a Special Task Force camp. The STF has been in existence for a decade, its sole mission being to capture Veerappan (at which it has been spectacularly unsuccessful). STF men in khaki trousers slouched around, looking bored. Khaki shirts flapped on clotheslines behind them. My driver told me that the STF troops had been asked to 'stand down' in order not to jeopardize Rajkumar's life. Standing down seemed to come easy to this group, I thought as I studied them. Only their eyeballs moved as they watched my car go by.

The STF operation has swallowed many millions of rupees. Some editorialists describe the STF as an industry, and like many government industries it is also an inexhaustible source of graft. If the STF were actually to succeed in its mission, the well would dry up; therefore (according to this theory) there is no incentive to catch Veerappan. And besides, catching Veerappan would be a very dangerous undertaking.

Past the STF post the steep and narrow mountain road began its seemingly endless hairpin bends. My driver leaned on the horn as we came to the blind spot in each turn, but we never heard answering bleats from lorries coming down. This sinuous road connects Tamil Nadu with Karnataka. Because Veerappan is a Tamil and Rajkumar is from Karnataka, the kidnapping had heightened tensions between the two states. Commerce between them had almost come to a standstill. Large numbers of Tamils live and work in Karnataka, in the city of Bangalore in particular. In 1991 a dispute between the two states over sharing water from the Cauvery River had brought deadly violence against the Tamils in Karnataka. When word of Rajkumar's kidnapping spread in Bangalore, on 'Black

Monday', as it is now called, there were huge protests and many fears that Tamils were in danger again. One motorist was stabbed to death. Trains coming from Madras were stopped. Only a strong show of force by the police prevented a repeat of the bloodshed seen in the Cauvery riots.

We eventually arrived at the tiny village of Thimbam. Only two cars had passed us on the way. Both were hardy Ambassadors, with Gatsby-era contours, and both displayed press signs on their windshields. The mountain air was brisk, nothing like the dry heat of the plains below. Thimbam sits close to the boundary between Karnataka and Tamil Nadu and is also on the edge of the forest. The village was eerily quiet. I strolled down a path bordered by tall grass, keeping a keen eye out for cobras and conscious of the monkeys in the trees above who followed my progress. I soon came to a ledge that offered a sweeping view of a valley below. I lifted up my camera but lowered it again, because no lens could do justice to this vast valley and its dense forest, which deferred in the distance to mountains again, beyond which was a glimpse of more forest. Mudumalai forest, Bandipur forest, Satyamangalam forest—it is all one forest, and the names simply reflect its size and the direction from which one happens to approach it. In this huge preserve herds of elephants roam free along with all manner of other animals, of which wild boar are probably the most dangerous. Also somewhere in the forest, perhaps within hailing distance (Thimbam is a place where he has often surfaced), lurked Veerappan with his captive, Rajkumar.

Veerappan, who is now in his fifties, also grew up in poverty on the edge of the forest, and he has spent most of his life roaming within it. He moves from one spot to another, caching food in strategic locations. The terrain is difficult, and its few paths are well known to him; he has sown some of them with land mines. It is said that he has observers on hills and in treetops, and cannot easily be surprised. According to the Veerappan legend (a legend he helped to create), he was initiated into elephant poaching as a youth, and later branched out into the business of smuggling sandalwood, which is as expensive as it is uncommon. He began making the news twenty years ago as a smuggler of ivory. 'We target and shoot at the forehead,' he said in one interview, waxing eloquent about his first vocation. '[The elephant] slumps to death without even knowing that life is departing. Good death. To feed on its carcass birds come. Eight-point-four million living beings . . . Of all charity, feeding is the greatest.'

To become king of the jungle, Veerappan ruthlessly eliminated rival poachers, including a cousin of his. He was merciless with informers. Yet he helped villagers in places like Thimbam when they needed money for a wedding or funds to build a temple. In all likelihood the villagers here had worked for him in the past, hauling out headloads of ivory and sandalwood and receiving generous pay for their services. This generosity had won him a network of sympathizers who acted as his eyes and ears on the edges of his Sherwood Forest.

I had met briefly with a Veerappan sympathizer in Madras, a man who runs a lesser-known Tamil weekly magazine and who once served as an emissary for Veerappan. What he had to tell me was a rehash of what I had already heard and read. Nonetheless, I now had the eerie sense, as I stood looking over the forest, that because of that meeting Veerappan was aware of my presence.

How does one investigate a kidnapping when the main actors in the drama are hidden from sight? In Madras, Coimbatore, Satyamangalam, and now Thimbam, I had run into other Indian reporters—a congenial and helpful lot with whom I felt a strong kinship. (India's huge press corps, representing a plethora of papers and magazines, was something else new since my student days.) But we were all chewing on the same cud, the same slender set of 'facts'. The reporters offered speculation and rumours sotto voce. These, by virtue of frequent repetition, began to take on an air of unassailable truth. The outcome of this drama was predicted with emphatic punctuation: 'Definitely!' 'Undoubtedly!' 'He will never . . .!' 'The government must . . .!'

I knew one thing from my visit—the jungle, depicted in the press as an impenetrable overgrowth, was far from that. It was a dry deciduous forest, and walking into it was easy, with natural trails evident to the eye.

Things changed for Veerappan in the past decade, when India clamped down on the export of ivory. The bandit turned to the human trade, beginning a practice of kidnapping officials and even the occasional tourist or wildlife photographer. He demanded amnesty as well as money, and when the former was denied, he settled for the latter and released his victims. During the terms of the previous state governments in Tamil Nadu and Karnataka an intense effort was made to flush out Veerappan. The STF eight years ago was more engaged, and led by a fearless leader, Walter Davaram, who sported a bristling sergeant major's moustache every bit as fearsome as the *kattabomman* of his quarry. Many of Veerappan's associates were either captured or killed, and the gang was reduced from about a hundred to fewer than ten.

Somehow Veerappan survived. But his brother died in police custody (the police claim he committed suicide with a cyanide capsule), and that is said to have fuelled Veerappan's hatred for the police. He became a man hunter. He used land mines to ambush police patrols. He killed and even beheaded some of his pursuers. One story that has been widely repeated to illustrate his ruthlessness (and the Veerappan myth has become increasingly indistinguishable from fact) is that he smothered his infant daughter to prevent her cries from giving away his forest hideout when the authorities came close.

After the decimation of his forces Veerappan seemed to have gone into hibernation; newly elected state governments in both Tamil Nadu and Karnataka had all but forgotten about him. The Rajkumar kidnapping came after a two-year lull in Veerappan's activities, and it was, for both state governments, a rude awakening. Veerappan's newfound strength and the Kalashnikovs in the gang members' hands clearly stunned the authorities.

The ransom request was published in the national papers the very day I was in Thimbam. It, too, was atypical, in that the kidnapper did not ask for money. Instead he demanded that water from the Cauvery be released immediately to Tamil Nadu by the Karnataka government, and that compensation be paid to Tamil victims of the 1991 riots. He wanted the Karnataka government to declare Tamil the second language of the state, and he asked that a statue of the Tamil poet Thiruvalluvar be erected in Bangalore. Thiruvalluvar wrote his maxims and aphorisms around 2,000 years ago, and they are still used in everyday speech. There actually is a statue of Thiruvalluvar in Bangalore, but it is covered by gunny sacks. Bangalorians don't want it unveiled until and unless a statue of Sarvajna, a Kannada poet, is erected in Madras. Veerappan demanded the release of five militants belonging to Tamil liberation forces and of fifty-one members of his gang who had been captured in the wake of the killing of two police officers, Harikrishna and Shakeel Ahmed. All the evidence suggested that Veerappan had formed an alliance with disciplined Tamil militant groups who were sympathizers if not comrades of the Tamil revolutionaries waging war in Sri Lanka.

After two days I headed to Bangalore, where I found schools, colleges, liquor stores, and bars closed. As a mark of respect for Rajkumar, movie theatres, too, were shut, and all shooting on movie sets had come to a halt. Estimates put the losses to the film industry at the equivalent of $660,000 a day. In the aftermath of The Kidnapping the evening news showed film stars offering prayers alongside saffron-robed priests. Newspapers carried a picture of a starlet rolling on a temple floor, in a form of penance and sacrifice for Rajkumar's safety. For his fans, whose clubs are organized by street and neighborhood, Rajkumar's life was more important than their own; one fan demonstrated this by throwing himself in front of a bus.

Bangalore, once known for being a gentle 'garden city' with a mild climate, is now at the forefront of India's information-technology revolution, or 'Eye Tee', as I heard repeatedly. The city is home to Infosys, Wipro, and other world-class businesses. When I had visited the city five years earlier, pubs had been the new, new thing. Now it was cybercafés. Congestion, pollution, and rapid growth had predictably changed Bangalore, and Brigade Road, once the place to see and be seen in, was a street I barely recognized. As I drove through town, I saw scars of Black Monday everywhere, in the form of shattered windowpanes. The damage was most striking in the high-rises under construction in the Diamond District, an Indian version of Silicon Valley. Ammu Joseph, a journalist friend of mine who has lived in Bangalore for a decade, pointed out that the rioters who gathered in the streets the day after The Kidnapping targeted the city's affluent and the symbols of affluence, such as automobile showrooms. Writing in *The Hindu*, she said of Bangalore,

> *Enormous fortunes have been made here . . . but they have not trickled down in the form of more jobs, better wages . . . If some of the richest individuals in the country—even the world—live in Bangalore . . . so surely do some of the poorest.*

That night in Bangalore, I was with friends and relatives. The beer (obtained with great resourcefulness, since all liquor outlets were closed) flowed, and the food was fabulous. Like everyone else in southern India, we talked about Veerappan and Rajkumar. 'Why would anyone in America care about this?' I was asked, because in that room, at that moment, the story was really not of great importance. The riots of just a few days before were no joke, but the rest of it was a tamasha of sorts, an entertainment, although we were all nervous about how it would end. 'High drama,' I suggested. 'Life imitating art imitating life. Robin Hood kidnaps Elvis Presley.' But in a few minutes we had forgotten about Veerappan and Rajkumar. The forest I had walked in the previous day seemed a continent away.

There is another moustachioed character in this story, R.R. Gopal, the editor of a hard-hitting Tamil magazine called *Nakkheeran* (named after a mythical Tamil bard who offered a dare to Lord Siva). He, too, sports a *kattabomman* as his trademark. His magazine's style of investigative reporting has frequently embarrassed government figures and made *Nakkheeran* hugely popular. But in the Indian publishing world dangers abound for the aggressive journalist that are absent in the West: Gopal's printer, a man named Ganesan, died after being released from police custody. He had been arrested in retaliation for the publication of stories critical of the then chief minister of Tamil Nadu, Jayalalitha (herself a former film star). Jayalalitha's government harassed *Nakkheeran* but could never close it down; many believe it was the magazine's revelation of her corruption that brought down her regime. Just hours before The Kidnapping one of Gopal's reporters was murdered by 'unknown persons', according to newspaper reports.

Veerappan must have admired the pluck of the little magazine, because in past kidnappings he had sometimes requested that Gopal be the mediator, the man with the briefcase. Gopal had played the role of jungle emissary several times, the last mission taking place three years earlier. His video crew brought images of the bandit and his forest abode into the living rooms of a hungry TV audience. Gopal wrote a book in

Tamil on Veerappan. It is Gopal—perhaps by Veerappan's own design—who is responsible for the transformation of Veerappan from famous bandit to iconic figure, a superstar in Rajkumar's league. Yet Gopal's analysis of Veerappan has not always been flattering, and Veerappan is said to have been unhappy that Gopal profited at his expense. That may explain why, after the Rajkumar kidnapping, Veerappan asked for an emissary but pointedly did not ask for Gopal. Nevertheless, the governments of Tamil Nadu and Karnataka, both of which had been at odds with Gopal, pressed the journalist into his familiar role of mediator.

While I was still in Bangalore, Gopal went to Thimbam, where he was forced to cool his heels for two days before Veerappan's associates finally made contact with him and took him to the hideout. He emerged a few days later with the story. Photographs he brought back showed Rajkumar seemingly in good spirits and looking well. 'Whatever his desire, please fulfil it,' the actor said on tape, using the honorific 'Sir' to refer to his captor. 'He is looking after us with love and affection. He fully trusts us, and we have confidence in him.' Rajkumar, Gopal said, was enjoying nature and the outdoors and having long dialogues with his kidnappers. This was an unexpected twist, I thought. If, as Hindu tradition has it, there are four stages to a man's life (youth, family life, retirement, and renunciation), then Rajkumar had involuntarily entered the sanyasa phase: renouncing worldly duties and retreating to the forest to devote himself to meditation and spirituality.

Meanwhile, Veerappan, according to Gopal, was quoting Che Guevara and showing other signs of a transformation from robber to revolutionary. Perhaps he was also getting tips from the veteran actor on having a film made of his life. Veerappan was well aware of the precedent set by Phoolan Devi, a revolutionary who, after she surrendered and served time in jail, ran for and won a seat in Parliament. Her life story was made into the movie Bandit Queen by the director Shekhar Kapur, before he went on to make the Academy Award-winning *Elizabeth*. A diary of Veerappan's that was captured three years ago is said to have Shekhar Kapur's telephone number in it.

Gopal visited the forest several times over the next eight weeks. The governments of Tamil Nadu and Karnataka were ready to give in to Veerappan's demands, because they knew the public would not forgive them should anything happen to Rajkumar. The stumbling block now was the elderly father of Shakeel Ahmed, one of the policemen killed by Veerappan's gang. The father obtained a stay from the Supreme Court to block the release of the fifty-one prisoners connected with the ambush in which his son died. Meanwhile, the central government in Delhi and a sizable portion of the journalistic community and the public, at least outside Karnataka, were also against releasing these prisoners on the bandit's say-so.

In Bangalore rumors were flying. The most persistent one had to do with one of Rajkumar's sons, who is involved in the granite business; some granite quarries lie in Veerappan territory. According to this story, Rajkumar's son failed to pay money he owed to granite dealers, and this is why his father was kidnapped. As the days passed, the rumours became more inventive and surreal: Gopal, the journalist, according to one, is Veerappan! According to another, Rajkumar was fed up with his wife and son, and engineered this whole thing to get a little forest R&R. 'Definitely!'

It was the hundredth day of The Kidnapping. In the Indian movie business a hundred days is a significant milestone: when a film has a theatrical run that long, it is cause for celebration. But the story was no longer on the front pages of Indian papers. The crowds holding vigil outside Rajkumar's house had thinned considerably, and life in Bangalore was almost back to normal. The likelihood of a dramatic police or military operation à la Entebbe was remote, because the risk to Rajkumar would be unacceptable. Veerappan, too, was in an awkward situation: should he kill Rajkumar, he would unleash a backlash against ethnic Tamils. By all reports, Veerappan was tired of life on the run. He was bothered by asthma and chronic intestinal ailments. He wanted out of the forest.

N. Ram, the editor of *Frontline*, a respected fortnightly, arranged for me to get an interview with Gopal in his office at *Nakkheeran*, in Madras. It was a Friday evening, the 103rd day of The Kidnapping, and a surprise shower had left puddles on the streets and sidewalks which mirrored the gay lights strung over shop awnings. Colours seemed strangely brighter in the rain's aftermath: purple and orange saris in store windows, white jasmine strung through coconut-shined hair, yellow auto-rickshaws darting between lime-green Pallavan transport buses. I left my sandals on a porch and climbed the narrow stairs of a residential building to its second floor. I entered a largish room partitioned into cubicles and lit by fluorescent lights that didn't seem to reach the corners. The reporters and other employees were all men, all swarthy, and all sporting moustaches, but none wore a *kattabomman* like Gopal's. A shelf running around the room at head height displayed awards and trophies, most featuring a likeness of Gopal, or Gopal with Veerappan. There was a bust of Veerappan in a glass case: the inscription indicated that it was a gift to Gopal from a grateful kidnap victim. Larger trophies had the usual silver figurine replaced by cardboard-backed full-figure color cutouts of Veerappan and Gopal facing each other like stags about to lock antlers, their moustaches bristling. One could be forgiven for thinking that the office belonged to both men, so prominent was Veerappan's image. My escort whispered to me that some of these trophies were awards that Gopal gives to his best reporters, or his best distributors. His reporters are fiercely loyal to him; I sensed both a siege mentality and a strong esprit de corps at *Nakkheeran*.

An unsmiling Gopal came out and took me into his

air-conditioned office, which has a window overlooking the newsroom where his staff works. Under the glass top of his desk were displayed photographs, including the first ones of Veerappan published in *Nakkheeran*, relating to some of Gopal's most important investigative coups. Speaking in Tamil liberally sprinkled with English, Gopal told me that his first foray into Veerappan territory had resulted from his frustration at having to reuse an old police photograph of Veerappan every time there was news of the bandit: 'One time I changed the size, next time the tint. But I was fed up with having to use the same picture.' He offered a cash reward to the first of his reporters who brought him a photo of Veerappan. In 1993 one of them bravely walked into the forest and came back with the prize. This was at a time when several hundred Special Task Force people were supposedly looking for Veerappan. 'The first time I saw the negative, my hair was standing on end,' Gopal told me. 'I had to process the photo secretly. I had to pinch myself to see if it was real.' He was cautious about discussing Veerappan or Rajkumar, because in the absence of any real news the only sport in town was to magnify or distort the least utterance or gesture of Gopal. New members had joined the team negotiating for Rajkumar's release, apparently without consulting Gopal. Much had been made of this in the press, but Gopal said it did not bother him. 'I am the official government emissary. I have to see this through. My only goal is that Rajkumar should be released.' I sensed that he was tired of Veerappan—as Ringo Starr must be tired of constantly being asked what Paul is really like.

I had walked into Gopal's office prepared to dislike him—envious, I suppose, of his closeness to the story. Instead I found myself quite taken with him. If, as his critics have said, he has greatly enriched himself on the Veerappan story, there was little evidence of it. He walked me downstairs to my car; he would remain in the office for an hour or two more, he said, and then head to the printing plant for a final okay of the next issue of *Nakkheeran*. Asked for one last thought about Rajkumar, he would say only 'I am sure he will be released within the next few days.'

Indeed, a few days later, when it seemed that no one other than Gopal really expected it, Rajkumar was released. On 16 November the thespian appeared in Bangalore, helicoptered in from the forest. The pilot of the helicopter made two landings in the city, as if to unsure exactly where to take him. Finally Rajkumar was delivered to the Vidhana Saudha, the seat of government, where an unusual press conference was staged in the assembly building. Rajkumar, dressed in a simple white shirt and dhoti, appeared dazed and overwhelmed by the outpouring of joy from thousands of fans outside. But then, what should have been the clear denouement of this prolonged abduction instead became a source of further confusion. Referring to the negotiating team that had last visited the forest, Rajkumar gave credit for his release to one of its members, a woman who called herself Dr Banu. Rajkumar said that she had coached him to act ill and then persuaded Veerappan to let him go. At the press conference, while she periodically whispered into his ear, Rajkumar described her as a goddess: 'It was as if I saw Devi Shakti in her.'

But the next day Banu turned out not to be a doctor at all. The rescuer of Rajkumar was, in fact, in the granite business. The *Times of India* uncovered court records showing that she had been accused in 1996 of cheating an Italian granite businessman to the tune of about $100,000. Her links, if any, to Rajkumar's son or to Veerappan are unclear. The goddess, without explanation, cancelled a press conference she was to hold. Rajkumar, contradicting what he had said in front of millions of television viewers all over India, released a statement downplaying her role and giving credit to government emissaries. There were strong rumours of a big payout to

Veerappan and his militant Tamil partners, and strong rumours that the whole kidnapping had come out of a granite deal gone sour. Among people I talked to in Bangalore there was growing resentment: if in fact The Kidnapping had little to do with Tamil nationalism, but instead arose from a private matter involving Rajkumar's son and some granite dealers, then the millions of dollars it had cost the state of Karnataka should be reimbursed. There was brave talk of night-vision goggles, heat sensors, and going into the jungle to capture Veerappan. There was equally brave talk of taking politicians and STF members to task for the atrocities committed against villagers and other detainees in the name of catching Veerappan. Rajkumar declined to be interviewed.

When I finally left Bangalore, I drove past the statue of Thiruvalluvar, which sits, still wrapped in gunny sacks, on a pedestal in the centre of a traffic circle. I left with a sense that the story was even murkier than when I began. But this is the nature of things in India: the harder one scratches, the more complexity is revealed. I thought back to Ganesha Chaturthi, the festival celebrating Ganesha, the elephant-headed god (the most popular of Hindu deities, the god of wisdom and prudence), where clay images of Ganesha are always immersed in lakes and rivers and other bodies of water. In recent years the festival had become more and more elaborate, and a major element of entertainment had been thrown in: film screenings and dance performances were now common. Of late, too, intricate tableaux had been constructed around the statue of Ganesha. In 1999 the tableaux featured Indian soldiers, the heroes of the Kargil war with Pakistan over Kashmir. But last September in Bangalore one tableau had Ganesha leading Rajkumar out of the wilderness. And there, peeping through the trees like a Cheshire cat who can never leave his forest, was Veerappan.

2001

VIJAY NAMBISAN

MEMORIES OF BIHAR

*For sixteen months, in 1996-97, Vijay Nambisan and
his wife Kavery, a surgeon, lived in a small town east of
Patna, where Kavery worked in a hospital run by nuns.*
                                                    —ed.

Our voyage back [from Mailpur] was much swifter and
more comfortable than the journey out. The wind was in our
favour, and the skipper and his mate jury-rigged a kind of mast
and attached to it something like a ragged bed-sheet, or perhaps
his spare dhoti. This worked remarkably well, and no punting
had to be done.

More than two-thirds of the way back, just before we drew
into the swollen main channel again, I saw something round and
white, with black strands attached, lying in some reeds at the
foot of higher around. Akhilesh had seen it too, and he said with
an uneasy laugh, '*Kisi ka sar kaat diya*'—someone's head has
been cut off. It was indeed a skull, and a woman's presumably,
from the long hair; it had been cut off, most likely with a sword,
and though the cut seemed clean the lower jaw appeared to be
missing.

We passed perhaps five metres from it, and all our eyes were
fixed on the ghastly object. No one said anything. What was

VIJAY NAMBISAN has worked as a journalist in Delhi, Mumbai, Chennai,
Bihar and Kerala. A selection of his poems appeared in *Gemini*, a two-poet
volume published in 1992. 'Memories of Bihar' is an extract from *Bihar is in the
Eye of the Beholder*, an impressionistic account of the sixteen months he spent
in Bihar in the mid-1990s.

there to say? Swords are common enough even in this age of Kalashnikovs; and in Bihar you don't have to go particularly far out of your way to see an intimation of mortality. There wasn't any point in going to the police, of course; they had enough fresh corpses to ignore or inter.

> PATNA, June 27. At least 88 human skulls were seized at Patna railway station today, according to police.
> The Government railway police officials told PTI that the skulls were found in a polythene bag lying unclaimed in the room of ticket collectors. They said so far no arrests have been made. An investigation had been ordered . . .
>
> —A 1999 newspaper report

The staid dictionary I subscribe to doesn't admit it, but I'm pretty sure 'skull' was once used as a colloquialism, in either the US or Britain, for a ticket to a show or game. Perhaps some connection with scalper, too . . . How fitting, how *congruous,* to find eighty-eight skulls in the ticket collector's room.

I've seen many weird things at Patna Junction, but never a skull in the bare sense of the word. This grisly news item reminded me at once of the skull in the fields I'd seen almost two years earlier. Eighty-eight skulls all in one bag could have almost any explanation in Bihar; from being the fetishes of some grotesque cult to being the relics of passengers whose train had suffered an unusual delay.

Of course the truth, which a newsmagazine later made clear, was more prosaic. This bag was only a token of the racket which supplies medical colleges with portions of the human anatomy. It was illegal, naturally, and no one claimed the skulls.

But I wondered, that day, sailing back from Mailpur, if we had seen not one skull in the field but eighty-eight, what would we have done? I suppose we should have reported it: even in

Bihar, eighty-eight skulls in one spot takes some explaining. But say five or six?

I'm not sure. I guess we'd have sailed on by.

I just hope those eighty-eight human beings were dead *before* their skulls were detached.

Violence was something we could expect every time we stepped out of the Hospital Campus. I don't say it ever happened; but it could be expected. It wasn't unlikely. One evening Kavery and I were walking outside the quarters when we heard the rapid chatter of automatic gunfire from the town. We stood outside, waiting for Kavery to be called to the operating theatre; but in a few minutes two of the boys who lived upstairs came screeching back through the gates on a scooter. William Williamson, whose scooter it was, was a Tamil from Jamshedpur who had just recently joined the Hospital as X-ray technician. He was unused to the pace of life in M—— and was ashen and stuttering:

'I'd just gone to the market to buy eggs . . . I'd given a ten-rupee note to the shopkeeper—when someone opened up at the top of the street. He was firing down it in our direction. The shopkeeper downed his shutters at once, we just jumped on the scooter and fled.'

Ranjit, the laconic and handsome local on the pillion who worked in accounts, was clutching a bag of groceries and was more casual about the whole thing. 'It was just some guy skylarking,' he said. After half an hour I heard them drive off again to get the eggs. The shutters would have come up again in five minutes if it had been just someone skylarking, and Ranjit was right.

We had heard stories about the violence in M——, and in Bihar generally, before coming, but we had had no idea how common it was. We had reckoned on occasional murders and dacoities, not things that went bang in the night every other night.

Everyone, even in the south, has heard stories of the violence in Bihar. A classmate of mine in college, Krishna—this was fifteen years ago or more—got his first job after graduation with an engineering company which was putting up conveyor belts at some power plant in the Dhanbad area. He had an old Bullet then, which he had spent much time and money on maintaining and was keen to take with him. I remember he used to go out to the Marina with it and practice making U-turns in the sand in top gear; because, he said, he'd heard the *dakus* in South Bihar specialized in blocking a lonely road at night with a felled tree, and the only thing you could do if you came up against something like that was to turn right round and make tracks in several opposite directions.

In our time, the roads were so bad it wouldn't have been any trouble making a U-turn. You never would be in top gear, even if you were foolish enough to drive alone on a lonely road at night.

Krishna didn't take his Bullet with him, but he came back with a few stories. He told us of how the tribal people were being corrupted, how they were persuaded to sign away their rights to the land for a few cases of country liquor. I'd only read about that before, with the American Indians and the Polynesians.

Some days after we'd first reached M—— in '96, a shopkeeper in the market was shot dead in his sweet shop, in broad daylight, for a few kilograms of *mithai*. Five men had come to the shop and asked for the sweets, then refused to pay. The shopkeeper naturally, but stupidly, refused too, at which angered by his lack of bonhomie—it was the festive season—they shot him point blank.

I went into M—— many times, to buy this or that, to catch a train to Patna or a bus to Begusarai, usually returning after dark. I never had any trouble, but it wasn't really advisable for a foreigner to do it. The gods who look after fools and madmen and drunkards guarded me. But there were many times, especially on the trains, that I felt violence only a hair's-breadth away.

More than once there was a dacoity on the railway line the day after one of my trips. In one of these, a doctor from the Hospital was among those robbed. Of course nobody on Bihar trains carries much money: he lost a couple of hundred bucks, and his watch chain being unlinked it had ridden up his loosely rolled sleeve so the dacoits didn't see it. After that I carried most of my money in my shoes, and wore a cheap watch; but I kept something, 200 rupees or so, in my wallet so that the dacoits wouldn't shoot me out of frustration . . .

Train dacoities and fights are small-time stuff. The real violence was in M——, almost palpable at times even in the cloister we were residents of. There were two gangs of 'criminals' in the town, and when trouble flared up between them a hush fell over the Hospital campus too. We became used to hearing the rat-tatatata of automatic arms, often in the middle of the night, sometimes soon after dusk, once or twice around dawn.

After the first few such incidents we became resigned to the fact that Kavery would almost inevitably be called to the operating theatre. 'Oh shit,' I would mutter as I got from under the *razai* and out of the mosquito net and stumbled towards the intercom while Kavery got out of the other side of the bed and struggled into her clothes, saying, 'I hope they're dead.'

This is not really as nasty as it sounds, for on almost every occasion those killed and injured were 'criminals'. On one horrific morning it was different. We heard the gunfire very early, long before a winter sunrise. One of the gangs had ambushed the other. Among those killed was an eleven-year-old girl who had been brushing her teeth on an upstairs terrace and had leaned over the parapet to see what was happening. But usually the gangsters were considerate enough to only eliminate each other. There were plenty of willing, and able, replacements.

Other people shared Kavery's sentiments, and some of them had been put to more trouble by the gangsters' activities than merely being routed out of bed at two in the morning. In late 1996 the lieutenant of one of the gang leaders, a much-wanted man named Ashok Singh, was brought by the cops to the Hospital with two bleeding stumps where his hands had been. He had been carrying a couple of country bombs to do a neighbour a good turn, but they'd gone off early as often happens.

Ashok Singh was also, it transpired, a Calmpose addict, but Kavery didn't know that as she looked down at him and saw the glazed, desperate look in his eyes. The police *daroga* outside the theatre told her casually, '*Marne deejiye usko*.' Let him die. She retorted, 'That's your job, mine is to save him,' and went in. Later—after an operation which consisted of tying the blood vessels and nerves, trimming the forearm bones and closing the stumps—as she went on her rounds she found his mother and brother with the still unconscious Ashok Singh. They were both well-dressed and respectable. The mother was weeping but not in the turbulent rustic way. 'Doctor saab,' the brother burst out in the policeman's own words, 'let him die.'

Ashok Singh was removed to Patna Jail. For all I know he's there still. If he ever gets out—he had a few murders to his name—he's unlikely, without hands, to find an opening in his trade again.

Thinking about it, why should Ashok Singh have been carrying country bombs? The gangs are equipped with the very latest weapons, and they're quite cheap. They tote AK-47s and even –57s, while the police go around with the equivalent of Lee Enfields (the only relatively well-equipped police force is the Patna Armed Police, and even they don't have Kalashnikovs). Everyone in M—— knows where the arms dropped in Purulia some years earlier went.

But country bombs are also popular, and there is an unfailing demand for them. One morning in late 1997 a boy of about fourteen was brought to the Hospital with a gangrenous hand. It was obvious that the original injury was the result of an explosion. It had not been treated for a while, and the wound had become septic and was now actually crawling with maggots. (This is not uncommon in rural areas, where hospitals are resorted to only when it is too late.)

Questioned, the boy said a firecracker had burst in his hand. But Divali was still a month off, and the doctors dragged his story out of him a word at a time. He said he had been working in a bomb factory.

Much has been written about child labour in the fireworks factories of Sivakasi; should we be surprised to learn that children are cheaper to use and more dispensable in the manufacture of illegal arms as well?

The boy's story was backed by such strong circumstantial detail that it was impossible to disbelieve. He said homeless boys like himself were picked up in the cities and brought to Bihar. He himself was from Old Delhi—a curious instance of reversing the flow from the villages to the town which everybody deprecates.

The boys were set to work in groups of two or three beside the Ganga, each group a couple of hundred metres from the next in case of accident. And there were many accidents, quality control not being terribly important to the manufacturers. When something went off bang and the workers were injured, the Ganga was a handy means of disposal. This boy had somehow escaped and got to town whence some Samaritan had brought him to the Hospital. Of course, his hand was a write-off, and he was told most of his arm would have to be amputated. He protested, but the doctors told him there was no alternative. Next morning he was missing. He had probably slipped away in the middle of the night to catch a train to Delhi.

Arms manufacture is a cottage industry in Bihar, and

probably—like the fake degree racket—brings in crores of rupees. It's a lucrative business, since there is no tax, and no bribes to be paid to government inspectors. Not two kilometres from the Hospital campus there were shacks by the Ganga where a single-shot pistol could be bought for Rs . . . But why should I give that away, or the method of manufacture? I might want to go into business myself one day, with the help of friends who're qualified engineers. Or I might want to eliminate someone, and the way things are going in this country that will be sooner than I would want to think.

By single-shot, above, I mean the pistol can only fire once, after that it's unusable. But one shot is enough to settle a feud, that is if the thing doesn't blow up in your hand . . . Either way the feud is settled. Sophisticated weapons are also cheap: You can buy an AK-47 in M——, if you have the right credentials, for just about what a handgun costs elsewhere in India if acquired through legal channels.

But simpler weapons are still used. I have seen reports of tribespeople using bows and arrows to kill gangsters who had threatened them. The senas of the landlords and the Left both have the very latest in automatic hand-held weapons, but their victims are often reported as having been hacked to death . . . or sometimes burned alive. I have never asked anyone in a position to state the reason with authority why they should use such antiquated implements, but I would imagine it is simply to make a point and frighten the victim's friends. God knows there is nothing soothing about bodies riddled with bullets, but what can be done by an imaginative person with a sharp edge, or fire, is much more horrifying, as we saw in the Graham Staines 'incident'.

But in M—— we quickly grew accustomed to all this. At least I never had to see the victims of the gang wars, and those who work in a hospital are very soon inured to human suffering. If they don't learn to shake off what they have seen when they go off duty—that is if they haven't already been conditioned by medical college—they quickly find other jobs.

Kishan—our medical-rep friend—though he once had his troubles from one of the 'criminals', was not the man to go in awe of anyone, and he was friends with some of the gangsters. I suppose if your town was M——, you had grown up and attended school with some of the guys, or you did business with them in one way or another. They might have bought aspirin from him, or arsenic. The day after the Divali of 1997, Kishan came to the Hospital on work and dropped by at our flat for a smoke. He was quite hung over, which is usual for the day after Divali. They'd had a wild time the previous night, he said. Early in the evening they'd run out of fireworks, so they set some bombs in a row and touched those off. It had been a jolly Divali.

How many people do you know who can procure country bombs when the fireworks run out on Divali night? Bihar certainly broadens the mind.

2000

DAWOOD ALI MCCALUM

GWALIOR TODAY

Ten past one. No let up in the rain since we left Delhi five hours earlier. The Punjab Mail pulls into Gwalior Station no more than a few minutes late. I am amazed at how nervous I feel. Like it's my first day at a new school. Why? We've been talking about this visit for the past three years. Years during which the book on my lap, carefully wrapped now to protect it from the rain, has been my constant companion. I can quote from memory it's summation of my destination:

> *The capital of the premier state of Central India is composed of three towns: Lashkar, lying to the south of the Fort and on the site of the Scindia camp; Old Gwalior, lying below the north end of the Fort hill and dating from ancient times; and Morar, east of the Fort, which was for a time the British Cantonment.*
> *With its up-to-date facilities such as water supply, drainage, electricity, medical services and town planning, Gwalior today compares favourably with any other city in the country.*

Dog-eared and hard-backed, bound in faded red and lettered in tarnished gold, *Gwalior Today* was long ago lent and

DAWOOD ALI MCCALLUM is a director of a charitable trust which works with governments throughout the Commonwealth. An avid traveller with a passion for India, his working life is currently divided between the UK and East and West Africa. He is the author of *The Lords of Alijah*, an epic novel set in nineteenth-century Gwalior.

never returned. Published by the Government of Gwalior in 1940, it is to be our guide now, almost four decades later.

For today it, at least, has come home.

'Hello, scallywag,' booms Dada as he offers me a corner of the tarpaulin he shelters under. I step down from the train and am immediately in his thrall.

Dada is who I want to be in my next life, namely everything I affect to despise in this. Lithe, tall, erect. Lots of hair. Good looks. He tilts his head back slightly as he talks, a smile and a cigarette never far from his full lips. Irresponsible, irrepressible and irreverent; he has the beguiling arrogance befitting to one so unfairly favoured by nature and fortune.

'Packed lunch and beer in the car, OK?' he says, as he waves aside ticket collectors and porters. His accent and colloquialisms are those of Gwalior State and expensive public schools. He sounds like a First World War officer airily announcing that we are about to go over the top. Not for the first time, I fall in: silently acquiesce. It's a class thing, I have no doubt.

'You've brought it with you?'

I hold up the book, shrouded in a plastic bag.

'Good man!'

Dada's Ambassador is two-tone green and, not to put too fine a point on it, has seen better days. More than a few, in fact. The single, wheezing wiper tocks like a metronome, back and forth across the cracked windscreen, momentarily revealing a demi-circle snapshot of the road ahead which the thick rain promptly distorts and obliterates once more. We seem to be progressing in stroboscopic flashes.

We had agreed to make this trip, to search out and record the surviving remnants of Gwalior State, some months earlier. Dada had been regaling me with tales of his childhood over late drinks and early lunches for ages. Not just the anecdotes of Princely India—tiger shoots, durbars, nautches and parades—although a number of them had been cracking stories—but accounts of power, politics, intrigue and, perhaps more prosaic, but to me equally fascinating, the daily workings, the minutiae of administering a vast, populous state. How much remained, we wondered, thirty years on from Independence, Partition and Integration.

In the coming days, we were due to visit the Palace, the Fort and the Central Jail. Speak with the Rajmata and the erstwhile Maharaja. Interview lords, ministers, artisans, craftsmen and convicted dacoits. Try to get beneath the surface of the here and now.

But first, like any new boy, I'm to have an afternoon's orientation with one of the Prefects.

'Jayaji Chowk,' says Dada, tossing an empty beer bottle on to the back seat. 'Go on, look it up. I can see you're dying to. '

I unwrap the book, and turn its foxed, yellowed, familiar pages with care, for they are brittle as papad.

'*Jayaji Chowk*,' I read, '*can be regarded as the hub of Gwalior. The statue of Maharaja Jayaji Rao which forms the centre is surrounded by a public garden, filled with flowers and trees. The wide road running round this garden is lined with fine buildings including the Town Hall and Theatre, the State General Post Office and offices of* Jayaji Pratap, *the State newspaper, the Victoria Memorial Market, the Offices of the Municipality, the Gorkhi or Old Palace, the Alijah Durbar Press and the Imperial Bank building. The grouping of such institutions around this square makes it the busiest part of the city and gives an imposing picture of Gwalior's prosperity.*'

Well . . . At the moment, with the lunch-time traffic coagulating around us, it seems more a metaphor for contemporary India: hard pressed, heterogeneous, impatient— and wet. Ox carts and auto-rickshaws and cyclists, government cars with darkened windows, and gaudily decorated, overloaded lorries all crowd in on one another. Horns blare, engines roar and bells ring. A helmeted father on a scooter cuts in before us, his adolescent daughter perched, elegantly side-saddle, on the pillion behind him, a younger child standing between his pyjama-ed knees. All three are soaked.

'The secret of surviving the monsoon,' Dada explains as he reaches for another beer, 'is Liquid Equilibrium: to be as wet on the inside as you are on the out.' We grind to a halt, and I open up our lunch—parathas, aloo-ki-bhaji and dry chutney—and we picnic amid the cacophony. Next to us is a tempo, a three-wheeled bus, which roars and snorts and belches out blue smoke, thrusting its upturned snout forward. Its driver winces and curses as the metalled axle hub of a two-wheeled, horse-drawn tanga scrapes against his paint work. The tanga-wala, with eloquent contempt, shoots a red jet of sputum onto the road before him, flicks his whip at the callused rump of his bedraggled horse, and swerves neatly aside.

We splash forward, in fits and starts, until a herd of water buffaloes completely paralyses the street. The protests of men and machines reach a crescendo. The bewildered beasts turn this way and that, spot an escape route and set off toward it at a brisk trot, out of the traffic and, judging from the strangled cry of their herdsmen, in completely the wrong direction. We follow their lead, off round behind the Gorkhi, to our first objective.

We pull up beside an entrance, perhaps ten feet wide and fifteen high. The heavy gates are locked against the outside world. Our pounding and shouts eventually bring forth the chowkidar, in dirty, torn vest and stained dhoti, rubbing sleep from his eyes. Recognizing Dada, he joins his hands, namastes deep and leads us, at a crouching trot, through an abandoned garden, gloriously green, overgrown with creepers and fruit trees long run wild, among which a pair of mongoose scamper, scrap and play, their sleek bodies liquid as quicksilver. The street sounds fade as we enter the abandoned *bara* through a doorway around which coloured chalk elephants march and village girls dance.

'Done for the daughter's wedding,' says Dada. 'The place was opened up to accommodate the *baraat*.'

'Recently?'

He shakes his head. 'Years ago.'

From the ceiling of the cavernous entrance hall, a breathtaking enamelled glass chandelier hangs, thickly coated with dust and cobwebs.

'Art-deco,' says Dada, 'was big in Gwalior.'

On either side of us, broad stairways sweep up in opposite directions. Half way up they swing back on themselves to continue their ascent towards each other. It looks like the lobby of a grand hotel, or a long abandoned stage setting for a Busby Berkeley musical. We climb the stone stairs, a wrought iron banister writhing and twining its way up at our side. On the first floor, we wander through room after room. All empty, each identical. We push open pair after pair of narrow, half-glazed doors. Opaque, chamfered glass bearing the family name and the coat of arms. Every so many rooms is a stripped bathroom or toilet, superbly tiled. In each there are the stumps of brass pipes, the remnants of smashed porcelain fittings. The silent rooms are carpeted with pigeon droppings giving off an acid pungency as we tread on them. Where a pipe or wire traverses the room, its route is traced on the floor in a neat ridge of extra deep droppings. Occasionally, a spread of dry feathers and darkened stain marks the violent demise of a bird that let the desolation of the place put it off its guard.

A corridor takes us alongside the great Durbar Hall. At some time, the palace had been requisitioned by the government. Those who had occupied the building then had marked out a badminton court in white paint on its massive carpet. Nails had been roughly hammered into plaster—neo-classical pillars to support the net. Rotting fabric, broken glass, pigeon shit.

'Why have we come here?' I ask.

'To see if you can imagine what once was.'

But I can't. It's just a big, sad, empty place. This isn't how I had thought it would be.

We drive around Old Gwalior, in a deluge. The rain drums on the roof of the car and seeps through leaking door seals. Our windows steam up. In the doorway of a tiny shop, two women, a child and a cow stare glumly at the muddy water coursing through the steep, narrow street. At the sound of our approach, all four heads turn in unison and follow our progress until we are out of sight. A hundred yards further on, where two gullies converge, rain from roofs and gutters higher up collects, combines and gushes on, its energy renewed. A tiny child squats at the confluence of the rushing, bubbling torrent washing a battered saucepan, her long hair plastered to her naked back, utterly absorbed in her task. The road suddenly broadens out. Yoke buffalo and their drivers huddle under a sagging tarpaulin draped across the shafts of their heavy carts.

'Nomadic tribes from Rajastan, blacksmiths by tradition. They go from place to place in these caravans with their bellows and whatever and they make things. Axe blades, hammer heads, whatever.'

In the next road we fall in behind a tractor and trailer, both spilling with jubilant young men. Their expensively cut white shirts are splashed orange, red and yellow. The rain, which has pasted their ruined clothes onto their bodies, dilutes the dyes and spreads them further. Their hair, cut long, is stained with the same patches of colour. They shout and wave their arms, jumping on and off the moving vehicles. One wears a garland of flowers.

'Students celebrating the victory of their candidate in a college election.'

Their progress is watched with weary eyes, for their exuberance has an undertone of latent aggression.

'Look!' cries Dada, 'On your left, Mohammed Ghaus.'

He points to a Mughal mausoleum, its cupolas and arches reminiscent of Fatepur Sikri. 'Look at the sandstone screens. Jali work. Stone made delicate as lace. Take a picture.'

I grope for my camera, and wind the window down.

'Too late. Look there, Tansen's tomb. Good shot that.'

I miss that too.

Dada sighs. 'All around here are all sorts of fantastic things, but you must keep your eyes peeled. And you're going to have to be a bit more handy with that camera . . . There!' He brakes hard, and I lurch forward. 'Right there; do you know what those are?' he asks, pointing to what look like concertina-ed frameworks of coathanger wire suspended from hooks on a wall.

I shake my head.

'Tazzia frames! The Maharaja reintroduced the tazzias a few years ago. Muharram used to be one of the most important festivals in the State calendar. Noble families, public institutions, community groups would all compete to see who could build the most magnificent tazzia. Not the largest, obviously, none could be bigger than the Maharaja's, but the most lavishly decorated, or most colourful. They are supposed to represent the mausoleum of the Imam Hussain. All our houses have an Imam *bara* in which our tazzia would be displayed for the first ten days of Muharram. Then, on Ashora day, the tazzias were paraded and then buried in huge pits. Everyone wore green, Muslims, Hindus, everyone. It was splendid! It's been going on here for hundreds of years.'

'Part of the glory that was Gwalior, huh?'

'Yup. And I'll tell you another part: one Muharram, back in the '20's or '30's, a party was parading their tazzia along the road when they found they couldn't get it under a tree because it was a metre or so too tall. So they were just about to shin up and saw off the offending bough when the local pandit appeared on the scene. "Oh no, you don't," he says, "that tree is sacred." Stand off! A crowd gathered. Feelings were running high. Confrontation was in the air! Now, what would happen anywhere else? Communal riots? Lathi charges? Death and destruction? Probably. What happened here? The Home Minister picked up the phone: "Public Works Department? Send a road crew round to so-and-so. I want the road lowered by four feet. Jump to it!" Look up the park in *Gwalior Today*.'

'*King George Park*,' I read. '*Laid out by the late Maharaja in a portion of his Palace grounds which he set aside for the use of the public. There are good roads, green lawns and quiet retreats . . .*'

'Read on,' says Dada impatiently.

'*A special feature of the park is that in it are a Hindu Temple, a Mohamedan mosque, a Sikh gurudwara and a Theosophical lodge—all built and maintained chiefly at the State's expense. A fine example of the broadmindedness with which the late ruler viewed the faith of his subjects.*'

'Need I say more?' Dada asks, smugly.

'Your family and the Scindias were pretty close, huh?'

Dada lights another cigarette, his knee raised up under the steering wheel to keep us going in a more or less straight line.

He exhales. 'Sure. We were one of the big jagirdars in the State. From the outset, although Gwalior was a Maratha durbar, with a Hindu Maharaja, it's senior nobles came from a wide range of backgrounds. The band of brothers included Sisodia and Chauhan Rajputs, Muslims, Gujarati Brahmins and Italian Catholics. All fiercely loyal to each other, the Scindia and the State. We call each other by family titles—Motidada, Boasahib, Bhaiya, Chhoti-jiji . . . We even required all newly appointed British Residents to present their credentials not only to the ruler, but to each of the heads of our ten families. You can imagine how much they must have enjoyed that! The representative of the Viceroy and the Queen Empress having to bow and fawn before this mixed bag of scallywags!'

I check out *Gwalior Today* on the subject:

'*Gwalior state can truly be said to have a prosperous and contented aristocracy which has been impressed with the necessity of interesting itself in State administration and is capable of taking a direct and personal interest in the administration and betterment of its estates.'*

Dada laughs when I read this to him, but he won't tell me why.

We turn into a muddy courtyard. The rain has stopped at last, and there is a strange stillness in the air. To our left is a line of trees, alive with birds. To our right, a small chapel with an arched portico. Painted terracotta and cream, it is very Tuscan, but for the bulbous onion-dome surmounted by a cross half hidden behind its bell tower. From within come the thin, high voices of children, singing in Hindi to a very European rhythm. We stand and listen, until the doors swing open, and two nuns lead out a crocodile of infants, dressed identically in blue and white, in pairs, holding hands. Shortly after, a priest emerges, carrying a huge black umbrella. He squints up uncertainly at the sky. He is very old, and very thin. His lined face seems abnormally dark against the stark white of his beard. He wears an orange cassock, sandals and a heavy silver cross that seems to weigh him down.

'Good afternoon, Father,' says Dada, leaning back and speaking out of the corner of his mouth in a vain attempt to hide the stale alcohol on his breath. 'I want to show my visitor here the chapel.'

The old Priest smiles wearily. 'You are welcome. Go in.' He points to a youth about to close up the doors. 'He will show you round. I must rest now.'

Inside, the chapel is spartan, dark and dominated by memorials all of which bear the same name: Filose.

'Sacred to the memory of Espirance Filose, Wife of Maj Julian Filose
the dearly loved mother
of Julian, Simeon, Anthony, Peter, Florence and Michael Filose.

She was born in the year 1801 on 7 September and died
in Gwalior
on 23 December 1874.
The latter three surviving sons who lived to mourn her loss
beg of you dear Christians to pray for the eternal repose of her soul.'

'In loving memory of Lt Col Sirdar Sir Michael Filose, KSS KCIE
Born at Lashkar 18 April 1836
Died at Lashkar 5 February 1925
Youngest son of Maj Julian and grandson of Col Jean Baptiste Filose
Served under three Maharajahs
Commissioned Captain at the age of two and a half years by H H
Jankoji Rao Scindia
Designed and constructed the Jai Villas Palace
And was Sir Suba of Malwa in H H Jayaji Rao Scindia's reign
Knighted by his Holiness Pope Pious IX in 1874 during the reign of
H H Madhav Rao Scindia
He was Chief Secretary of State
And was knighted by his Majesty the King Emperor at Delhi in
1913.'

'Sirdars of Gwalior State for two centuries,' whispers Dada, 'riding side by side with my forefathers, and the Maharajas. The British kicked out all the other so-called European military adventurers after the Battle of Assaye in 1803. All except these scallywags.'

'What happened to them?'

Dada looks round, his glance taking in the plaques on the walls and floors, and his mouth hangs open. 'They died,' he says, as though he can't quite believe anyone could be so dumb. 'Obviously.' He checks at his watch. 'Time for one more visit,' he says. 'The Scindia's will have arisen from their siesta and be prepared to receive visitors.'

'I thought the Big man was in Delhi.'

'Oh he is,' Dada assures me. 'We're off to present our

nuzzer to his great-grandfather.'

'*Chattris or cenotaphs, which commemorate departed members of the royal family number ten. Those of the Maharajas Daulat Rao, Jankoji Rao and Jayaji Rao being the most important . . .*'

We enter the vast and gorgeously carved *chhatri* of Jayaji Rao. At the entrance, we slip off our shoes, and Dada performs *mujra*, the traditional greeting of the Maratha nobles of Gwalior. A slight bow, right hand flapping in front of the chest. Through a marble hall, past a Nandi bull and Shiv-lingam, and into the presence.

Jayaji Rao is carved from black marble. He wears a purple angharkah and red pugree. He sits, one leg folded beneath him, one knee raised, as though on the *gaddi* of old. He glares at us with silvered eyes.

Each morning, as in every other *chhatri*, the statue is washed, dressed in State regalia, bejewelled and garlanded. At lunch time, roti, rice, daal and dahi are placed before it on a silver thali. After lunch, the hands and feet of the statue are massaged, and the fine clothes replaced by pyjamas. A tiny bed, complete with miniature linen and mosquito net, is placed beside the statue and the *chhatri* closes for a few hours. Then, in the late afternoon, the statue is re-dressed, and prepared for the evening. Priests read from holy writ. Musicians play to entertain the literally death-defying king.

Behind Jayaji Rao hangs a cloth of gold. There is a heavy silence in the perfumed air. A gecko clings to the marble above the statue, its motionless body so pale it seems translucent. As I stare, I swear I catch Jayaji Rao's chest rise gently, and fall. I feel a profound sense of disquiet, and am glad when Dada again performs *mujra* and begins to back toward the door.

As the bloated monsoon clouds purple and darken like a bruise, we head at last for Dada's own crumbling *bara*. The Magrib *azaan* tannoys through the darkening streets. The twilight is heavy with smoke from damp wood. There is something disconcerting me still about the state of suspended animation in the *chhatri*: The sense of displaced time and space. I am suddenly convinced that there is something in this place, not necessarily wholly good, but undeniably important, that sits under sentence of death. Or perhaps it has already died, but hasn't yet understood, or, like the long dead Maharaja in the *chhatri*, refuses to accept, the nature and import of it's own passing. The clouds begin the break up.

Immediately outside the gates of Dada's *bara* a *gaushala* nightly forms. Women squat, heads covered, beside huge piles of limp fodder and guttering oil lamps, and just about all the cows in the three towns converge upon this spot. Sinners, supplicants and, yes, even scallywags hand over a few coins for a crack at redemption and a handful of grass. They cast their offerings before the cattle, who watch them fall to the ground with priestly indifference. It takes much rump slapping and tail pulling, and many an offended stare from bovine eyes, before we manage to clear a path through.

The car is parked in what looks like a vast, ornately decorated kennel for a giant elephant, but which I identify, with a glow of satisfaction, as an Imam *bara*. The gates crash closed. In the courtyard, bats circle, jink and dive. I can smell chapatis roasting on charcoal. We glance up, and see a single star. I head towards the door, *Gwalior Today* tucked safely beneath my arm, until Dada places a hand gently on my chest, halting me. 'Don't go in,' he says, 'not yet. Not until you've seen the second star.'

So we stand together, in silence. Until the second star appears.

2001

ALLEN GINSBERG

BURNING GHATS

TO GARY IN LETTER:
Humans eyes & lips blackened & crackling in flame, hair
smelling with human fat dripping from neck as skin turns bright
red & burns—
  Under the great Howrah bridge, an eternity style bridge
with all Calcutta passing over it in bullock cart auto tram bus
bicycle or dragging leprous foot—
  A sustained wild roar that rises and falls like music,
crescendos of Trolleycars and trucks reechoing under the vast
steel roof that collects the vast Noise into one vast oceanic
crash—Om—
  Saddhus sit there with Will's Gold Flake yellow & Red
Neon shining from across the waters below bridge—just like
home, Westminister, Brooklyn—
  a cover photo of beautiful small-faced cripple beggar girl
sleeping under her black umbrella—
  Boys poking the corpses with bamboo poles, a lawyer's
shoulders and head seared and puffed up over the flames,
pushed by attendants so it falls into the central red coals—
  Ten feet away group of saddhus & devotees around
improvised mandir with flowers & incense and prasad on a
cloth, shouting loud Boom Boom Mahadeva! lifting faces to sky

---

ALLEN GINSBERG was the most prominent and successful writer of the Beat
generation. His best-known work is the long poem *Howl*. 'Burning Ghats' is
extracted from *Indian Journals*, a selection from the notebooks and diaries
Ginsberg kept during his stay in India in 1962-3.

eyes closed hands clasped to mouth as if in prayer, except in their hands little red clay pipesful of Ganja—passing around the pipe with great mantras—

Saddhu dancing to blind beggar's drum on the pathway, thin armed snakey hip sex gestures & slow shuffles—

Eating prasad with exquisite deliberate gesture both hands to mouth wolfing it down & going to the next circle of teaheads to try their pot & prasad.

The corpse smoke rolling over their heads, bodies burning—one of the worst areas of the Bardothodol & demons with long Bamboo poles pushing that meat into the flames.

Lying in bed, one hard electric light foregathering little green flying insect sparks 3 feet around its reflection on whitewashed   wall   in   roof   cell   of   Mohamedan hotel—Calcutta—

Corpses heaped with flowers in a litter carried thru streets disappear right in front of you like burning a big meat doll or pillow or Sofa—

Dolls of meat—with feet & hair

DEC 13, '62—

Out with Peter Thurs. nite to Manikarnika ghat. Sat on stone ledges above the ash sand shelf filled with woodpile fires aburning, cows putting their big nose heads near under the foot of the pile bed—flame lighting his forehead, eye most closed, chewing some yellow stalks of straw kindling—boy chased three cows out of the rectangle garden of fire—they were eating up a corpse litter prematurely—or horsing around in the way—the nearby corpse masked in white shroud lay back in the flames & turned black, knees hanging down, the veil burning away and one ear sticking too far out, later became a thin black mummy in flames—the furthest we saw lit up, later the bamboo attendants thwacked it in the middle and turned it face down in the flames, skull hanging over the side in the fire—the middle corpse had

burnt thru the belly which fell out, intestines sprang up (that is)
like a jack in the box charcoal glumpf—then its right leg and
foot came up in silhouette as the pole boy shifted it to the top
first, then the other leg and foot spreading big toes was poled up
and over bouncing like a soft log—and his hand (or hers it
seemed to have a charred bracelet round the forearm) slowly
lifted from the chest as the bulk burned—fires playing orange
around from black cranium along the sides, over the lifted
hand—and the two feet flung back over detached and burning
over the middle of the bed—like burning fear away—I thought,
burning the dross inside me—Dogs curled asleep on the shady
steps as the moon rose over the western sky with Orion near,
and the flat plate of Ganges stretching up to the faraway river
shore beach—fires reflected in the waters as we went away,
white mist reddened flaring out over the water, blocked by the
huge castle embankment steps & high Dharmashala of brick
where the dying came to spend last days breathing smoke.

18 DEC '62—
Sitting on rock at Harischandra Ghat—down below a sand
slope at the water's edge blackened with ashes, a high pile of
firewood ablaze and a man's head bent back blackened nose and
mouth unburnt, black fuzzy hair, the rest of the chest belly
outlined along down thighs at top of the pyre, feet sticking out
the other end—now turned toes down—cry of geese and rabble
of white longnecked good goose swan boids pecking in the
water's edge a few feet from fire.
   Nearby scows filled with sand from the other side of the
river, laborers carrying baskets of grey sand up the brick
stairway from the river— 'Oh—the head's going to fall off—'
The pile darkening, white ash floating up—a few watchers
squatted on bricks facing the pyre—Pole man comes and tucks a
foot into fire—then circles around and pushes length of pole
against the black head (lain back with open black throat and

adam's apple silhouetted against the small flames against the green river) till the body's balanced on the centre of the collapsing charred logs. Donkeys led along the sand path, children running with kites, a black baby with no pants & pigtails, balancing a stick of bamboo—A saddhu in orange robes sitting up on a stone porch on the embankment under turrets of an old small castle—rather Venetian the scene—Rectangular-sailed boats going downstream—the air above the pyre curling in the heat, like a transparent water veil between my eyes and the greenfields and tree along the horizon on the other side of the Ganges—and the embankments, red temple spires, toy mosques, trees and squat white shrines walling in the bend of the river upstream to the long red train bridge at Raj Ghat an inch high.

P. SAINATH

REPORTS FROM ORISSA

A DISSARI COMES CALLING

Malkangiri (Orissa): We had waited nearly three hours for the chickens to be slaughtered. They hung upside down from the hand of the medicine man's assistant. And, in the philosophical manner of their kind, still pecked around for any available food. Meanwhile the two dissaris—hereditary practitioners of traditional systems of medicine in this region—went on with their ancient rituals. There was one major departure, though. At the end of their session, the main dissari, Gobardhan Poojari, could be giving the patient something quite modern. Like chloroquine or Flagyl, depending on his diagnosis.

Gobardhan's real name is Hanthal, but he wears the 'Poojari' label quite proudly. When he said we could join him on his rounds in the remote Bonda hills, we were happy. We knew that we were to be witness to something unusual. Just how unusual, we did not quite realize.

Gobardhan's techniques combine indigenous and allopathic medicine. His work here is part of a strategy aimed at ancient tribes in Malkangiri. The idea is to persuade them to blend life-saving modern drugs into their traditional health

PALAGUMMI SAINATH is a Bombay-based freelance journalist. His work on rural poverty has won him several awards, including the Lorenzo Natali Prize, the European Commission's prestigious award for journalism. 'Reports from Orissa' comprises two extracts from his book *Everybody Loves a Good Drought: Stories from India's Poorest Districts*, which is based on a series of reports he filed for the *Times of India* on the living conditions of the poor in rural India.

systems. Dissaris often serve as village priests, too, and enjoy high respect here, says Surendra Khemendu of the NGO Anwesha. Thus, 'they greatly influence health beliefs and practices where modern medicine has not yet made big inroads'. Dissaris render health services at their own homes and at those of their patients.

Khemendu himself is studying plant-based medicines. He says: 'The traditional dissaris tend to combine the use of herbs and roots with medico-religious practices. They are a mine of knowledge that has real cures for some ailments.' But there are diseases against which tribes like the Bondas have no protection. So the need to reach effective cures through an acceptable medium arises. That medium is the dissari.

Malkangiri's energetic Collector, G.K. Dhal, is all for the experiment. His officials are training some dissaris. They are being taught to handle drugs for malaria and diarrhoea, both major killers here. 'The dissaris continue their traditional rituals,' says Dhal. 'But we encourage them to deliver life-saving drugs at the end of those.'

And so we are in the Bonda hills with Gobardhan. He is a Dom harijan, but is known here as the 'Bonda Doctor' on account of his patients. His first aid box has 'Only For Bondas' boldly inscribed on it in English. That is a language neither he nor any member of his clientele follows in the slightest degree. But he is proud of the box. At the river's edge sits the young patient, rather forlorn. A second dissari stands ankle deep in flowing water, chanting mantras, an assistant holds the unfortunate chickens as Gobardhan prepares for the sacrifice. The bright sun isn't doing anyone much good, especially the patient.

There can be little doubt about the value of the experiment. It does make the hours of trekking through the Bonda hills worthwhile. Yet, it can run into problems—if the trainers have not been thorough, or if some rituals backfire. Gobardhan is an intelligent man and on the whole, a useful doctor. But his ritual involves guzzling large amounts of mahua wine. (The ancients wisely made this part of the ritual rather than part of the payment, tying business with pleasure at no cost to the dissari.) Four hours into the show, Gobardhan is consuming more evil spirits than he is battling.

Meanwhile the second dissari reads his verses from a palmyra leaf. *'Aam rishi, jaam rishi, naam rishi, kaam rishi . . .'* he intones, breaking off only to inform Gobardhan that he too is entitled to the mahua wine. Gobardhan mixes in a few secular oaths along with his religious ones to tell the second dissari what he thinks of him. But he grudgingly parts with some. The latter then resumes: *'Yam dhoot, brahm dhoot, karm dhoot . . .'* We are later to learn that the palmyra leaves are a formality—he isn't literate. He just knows every word by heart. The patient shifts uneasily as Gobardhan blunders about with a knife, preparing for the sacrifice. Rather him than us, think Khemendu and I.

Gobardhan then holds the menacing blade between the toes of his left foot. As dissari two reads the verses, he beheads one bird by drawing its neck across the blade and throws it into the river. Moments later, the second follows. The third has its wings sliced off and is then allowed to peck at seed—whereupon it stops screaming and proceeds to eat as if nothing has happened. But soon, Gobardhan, having had yet another swig, finds he has left the job unfinished. The bird joins its companions in the river. The second dissari thoughtfully picks up all three birds from the water a little further downstream. Plans are made for dinner, Gobardhan gives no medicine to the patient and the session ends. As we move off, we learn that the patient was Gobardhan's own son.

Next comes a house call. A tough, if aging, Bonda warrior says his son is down with dysentery. As Gobardhan staggers around waving a strip of tablets, the old man lets flow rich oaths: 'You drunken pig. Stick to your pooja and I'll trust you. Don't mess with things you can't handle.' He seems to sense that

Khemendu and I are from another world. The one where people are presumed to be able to 'handle' such things. He gives us the tablets to check if Gobardhan is treating his son properly.

Gobardhan has got it right this time. But the old warrior has a point. Words like 'chloroquine' and 'paracetamol' are not easy to handle even for English speakers. For a tipsy dissari, mixing mantras with mahua, they can be tricky and harmful if interchanged. Clearly, the trainers in this project have to be very careful. Between what they think they are imparting, and what Gobardhan absorbs, is a complex chemistry.

In the interior, we find the traditional dissaris to be an intelligent lot. Hadi Mandra of Dantipada village has never seen the world outside of the Bonda hills. Yet, whether for snake bite or fractures or fever, he has an answer. Hadi shows us many local remedies. These include the root of the mango tree, handa, tulsi, amla, chandau, neem, papaya, donger, biguna and many other herbs and roots. He also works as a vet when needed. His fee is modest: some rice or chicken, mahua or solabh liquor.

He plans to train his grandson Mangla soon, in what to collect from the forest, what to use, how to use it and when. He has heard of dissaris like Gobardhan but won't accept them. Not until he has seen them prove their worth. 'Who has trained them and how well?' he wants to know. A legitimate question, decide Khemendu and I, recalling the day spent with Gobardhan. For some ailments, the services of Hadi's fraternity are invaluable in an area where doctors and hospitals are few or ill-equipped. One doctor brought here by a foreign-funded NGO ran away after seven days, terrified by the Bondas. He resurfaced months later as a 'water management' adviser to another foreign-funded NGO.

Attitudes here are complex. On the one hand are those who over-romanticize tribal health systems. These are mostly people who do not subject their own kin to it. On the other hand are those who dismiss indigenous medicine as absurd. Their mantra is the unthinking peddling of some forms of allopathic treatment. Both stands lack balance.

The romanticists can't say why adivasi children should not get the same medical facilities that children elsewhere do. Nor why, if tribal medical systems are so complete, must adivasis suffer such high rates of death from disease and the worst infant mortality levels. The pushy allopathic camp cares little about preserving traditional knowledge of real value.

Perhaps commerce intrudes. 'Traditional medicine'—as redefined by urban elite—is now a huge industry. The global herbal remedy market alone was worth close to Rs 20,000 crores in 1993. Oddly, the reverse is unfolding in much of rural India. There, no villager seems to feel cured unless put on drip, or given an injection. This craze for allopathy has given rise to massive quackery. In the context of these extremes, the 'Bonda doctor' idea has great potential. But, working under grave limitations, the risks it runs are many.

AND SILENT TREES SPEAK
Cut-Off Area, Malkangiri (Orissa): Acre upon acre of dead forest. Trees without a single leaf that still seem to speak—sticking out above the silent waters, decades after they were submerged. A reminder of the ninety-one villages swept away by the Balimela reservoir and other Machkund river projects. The ferry, noisy till this point, falls silent. It moves slowly because it has to. Built to transport sixty-six people, it is carrying close to 370.

The passengers' minds seem to speak: here people lived. Here, once, children played. For some on the ferry, that was a personal experience before their villages made way for a progress they never shared. And as the launch traverses the dead forest, we approach one of the loneliest parts of the Indian mainland: the 152 villages isolated by the Balimela and accompanying projects. A land so remote that even the official name for it is 'The Cut-Off Area'.

Perhaps no other river of comparable size produces so much hydel power as the humble Machkund. It churns up 720 MW annually—shared by Orissa and Andhra Pradesh—through different projects. The 152 villages, completely isolated, afford two states huge amounts of electricity by their sacrifice. Yet, it is virtually impossible to find a single household with electricity in any of these villages. Even the semi-pucca structure in Dharlabeda village where we spend the night has never seen a single bulb. Never mind that it is the panchayat office.

For those who live here are among the poorest of Indians. A woman in some of the cut-off villages can earn as little as Rs 4 for hours of weeding work in the fields. Isolation goes with deprivation here, ensuring that people have no voice. So the services extended to them are minimal. If you leave for the Cut-Off Area for the smallest of chores from Chitrakonda, you can only return on the third day, really speaking. The single launch operating today is old, overloaded, dilapidated and dangerous. It sets out late in the morning and will take many hours to cover its sixty-two-kilometre route, stopping at several points between Janbai and Jantri. We board at Chitrakonda and head for Palaspadar.

Along the way, people from the cut-off villages approach the launch in small boats. The launch becomes a moving market place—and their only contact with the outside world. Boarding it are Gadabas, Parojas (both ancient tribes) and even Bengali refugees from erstwhile East Pakistan settled in this region after the 1965 war. They buy things they need from the launch staff and sell fish and other produce to them.

A Bengali couple, having rowed a good distance to reach the craft, are now bargaining with passengers and staff. After a while, the man returns to his boat and rows off, leaving his wife behind to conclude the transactions. That will take time. So she will get off a few stops further down the Cut-Off Area—and walk back many kilometres to her home through the woods along the river bank in the gathering darkness.

People pay bribes to get jobs on this ferry. You can hawk wares at outrageous prices to a captive clientele in this seller's market. And the launch staff are a smart bunch of entrepreneurs. Bidis are probably cheaper in Bombay, but those living in the Cut-Off Area have no choice. Sometimes, the exchange is on a barter basis on this launch in Malkangiri.

Down the Machkund valley, you might run into the Didayis, a small tribe of less than 5,000 people not found anywhere else. The river itself goes on to take the name Sileru further down. It also becomes the boundary at some points between Orissa and Andhra Pradesh. Things looked quite different before the Machkund hydro-electric project—one of the earliest. The old gazetteers wrote of what they believed was one of the greatest sights in all India. The Machkund flinging itself over 300-foot walls of rock into a boiling pool hidden by dense clouds of spray that painted a permanent rainbow where they met sunlight. The Balimela power project, which began in 1962-63, ended that.

Landing at Palaspadar, we walk ten kilometres to reach Dharlabeda, passing through lonely, beautiful woods. The thick, whispering forests give you a sense of what even the submerged area must have once looked like. In Dharlabeda, the Village Level Worker (VLW) from Chitrakonda is distributing free sacks of groundnut. He takes everyone's signature in advance, but leaves blank the column stating the quantity given to each family. The VLW's judgement is arbitrary and he does not use a weighing balance though one is available here.

All the sacks of groundnut have this painted on them: *Do Not Accept Unless Sack Is Closed and Sealed.* All the sacks arrived open, with no trace of a seal. 'The groundnut,' says village head Saduram, one of the area's few educated individuals, 'is given out to encourage people to grow it. But mostly it gets eaten, people here are too poor.' People like Arjun Pangi, for instance, a Paroja tribal in whose hut we spend part of the evening. Pangi and family are so poor that 'even the moneylender will not lend us anything. He feels we can never repay him even partially,' says Pangi.

The moneylender's reading seems right. There is not a single possession of any value in the hut.

The coolie work he does—when there is work to do—fetches Pangi perhaps two kilograms of rice for a day's labour. Pangi and his family also go out and collect roots, berries, leaves and bamboo shoots. These make up the bulk of their diet on some days. 'Our time has gone,' says his friend Anandram Khilo. 'But perhaps one day our children, if they get an education, will lead a better life than this.'

Throughout the Cut-Off Area are villages with schools but children too poor to go to them. Also people who get steady work for no more than four months in the year. There is also a thirst for land among the worst off. 'If I had just two to three acres,' says Pangi, 'life would be fine.' But what about the officials who are supposed to come here and make such things possible?

Saduram laughs: 'The Collector has come here more than once. He means well. But many other officials just sit in Chitrakonda and send in their reports. Or they come up to the landing areas and send runners to call people from different villages to go there and meet them. When an official summons you, there is no choice. Once a party of journalists came and sat with the officials on the river bank. Some villagers had to walk over twenty kilometres taking food for them. After that they went back and wrote, I think, about how we live here—without ever being to our villages.'

'Do the people who live here have any reason to feel they are Indians?' asks Kawasi Kamraj, an emerging tribal leader. Kawasi being with us made our stay in the Cut-Off Area possible. 'In what way do they share in the national life? Governments may change, their lives don't. These people are invisible, though there are some 30,000 of them. They are untouched by any of the gains of the projects they sacrificed for.'

There are some signs of development, though. The village sarpanchs are building new, pucca houses for themselves.

In official reckoning, 1,200 families, mostly adivasi, were evicted to make way for the Balimela project in 1962-63. This figure appears flawed. For one thing, it does not seem to have recorded correctly the number really evicted. Next, the figure ignores many thousands outside the designated submergence zone who were devastated when their life support systems were literally drowned. It also disregards those in the Cut-Off Area who suffered all the adverse effects of displacement without being 'evicted'.

Even those evicted were hardly compensated. The old official record shows that the state spent Rs 35 lakhs on 'resettlement'. That's Rs 500 per individual if we accept the figure of 1,200 families. The amount spent on the 'staff vehicle', on 'salary to be paid to revenue department' and on 'shifting charges', was Rs 8.2 lakhs. That is well over double the amount spent on 'building(s)' and on 'land for building(s)' for the thousands evicted.

As we sit in the semi-darkness of Pangi's hut, offered food by people who go hungry half the year, Angra Hanthal tells us: 'Many who lost land in the submerged area were never looked after. In the early years, they told us our names would come in the record a little later on. In our innocence, we believed these things. Some of us, after coming here, occupied some land, half an acre to an acre, maybe. We even got pattas, but the land quality is poor. Only the forest is the great provider here.'

'After coming here,' says his wife, 'there were so many things the children needed we couldn't provide them. We had no money and even if we had money, we had no place to buy them—medicines, clothes, foodstuffs, so many things. You see them grown up now, but coming here hurt us. It hurt our children worse.'

On the return journey, the same silence falls. The trees, their branches like so many shrivelled fingers, seem to point at us accusingly. Thousands of acres of forest with prime teak and other rich produce were destroyed here forever. Their total worth was several times the Rs 57 crores spent on the Balimela power project. The combined investment in all development projects in Orissa since independence is eclipsed by the commercial value of renewable timber and forest produce lost in making way for them. The gung-ho attitude of the early decades is captured in the ugly concrete slab at the Chitrakonda pier. This announces, almost proudly, that the number of villages submerged by the project was ninety-one. All around, the hills show signs of electric installations. But in the Cut-Off Area, there is only darkness.

1996

BILL AITKEN

THE PROMISED LAND

Piecing together my fragmented notes I deduce that in February 1988 I caught the Malwa Express to Vidisha in Madhya Pradesh to kill two birds with one stone, or rather, to celebrate two passions in tandem—the goddess Narmada and steam traction. My original plan entailed proceeding down the Narmada valley and ending up in Dabhoi, near Baroda in Gujarat. This is the promised land for narrow gauge railway enthusiasts. In the event, I ended up in Mumbai, giving a slide show to the Himalayan Club on a third passion—the mountain goddess Nanda Devi. This detour meant I had to lug around on my back a hundred slides and psychologically, it meant I would take fewer risks with my itinerary, lest I damage these hard-won transparencies. If it seems laughable that the world's worst photographer should be so protective of his slides, my defence is that they are symbolic of the sweat I had put into my search. In a sense it was a relief my slides were so lousy. Had they been of *National Geographic* quality, I would have had kittens ensuring their safety.

My travels around Vidisha proved to be another wonderful rural experience of the kind only Madhya Pradesh can provide. I was galloped around the archaeological sites in a horse-drawn tonga and then made my way to Sanchi, clinging to a rope while

BILL AITKEN has lived in Himalayan ashrams, undertaken many excursions across India on his motorbike and by steam railway, and written on travel for newspapers and magazines for several years. His books include *Seven Sacred Rivers*, *The Nanda Devi Affair* and *Riding the Ranges*. 'The Promised Land' is an extract from *Branch Line to Eternity*, his tribute to the lost era of steam.

standing on the tailboard of a roaring jeep jammed full of villagers going to the market.

At Sanchi I met an English gricer (train spotter) who collected platform tickets. Thanks to his enthusiasm, I had another dimension of railway history opened for me. Incidentally, though main line trains do not normally stop at Sanchi, there is some small print in the timetable that reads: 'On application to Station Master (this) train will stop at Sanchi to pick up or set down air-conditioned or first class passengers and their servants and second class passengers when travelling in parties of not less than 10.' Any romantic who labours under the impression that socialist egalitarianism is the life blood of the railways will realize from this rubric that revenue raising takes precedence over fraternity; and the terms are strictly cash.

Moving on to Bhopal, I made the error of going to the bus station to seek information. I wanted to visit Patalkot, a Stone Age village near one of the subsidiary sources of the Narmada. My eyes lit up when I was told I should go via Chhindwara, for this lay on the Satpura narrow gauge system. Though I knew the chances of finding steam to be slim, the prospect of investigating the line was exciting. Had I gone to the railway station in Bhopal, I would have found out a more direct route to Patalkot via Parasia by the broad gauge. Parasia is a coal mining township west of Nainpur Junction.

The bus journey to Chhindwara was through delightful broad-leaved jungle but, as I had expected, the old railway station yielded only diesel. Had there been steam, I would have felt compelled to ferret out the tiny branches the Satpura locos once serviced.

Instead, I caught the morning 2 PC passenger that ran for 28 km to the coal depot. (From Khirsado Junction, another branch extends for 9 km to Barkui.) The station at Parasia was low slung and basic, but the platforms were big, to host both narrow gauge and broad gauge coal traffic. One oddity is that the broad gauge comes under Central jurisdiction, while the narrow gauge belongs to the South Eastern zone.

So backward was Parasia that the old-fashioned bioscope on the platform was sought out by children as a rich source of entertainment. As the colliery township was under a pall of black smoke and its accommodation seemed primitive, I decided to catch a bus to Tamia, which is near the site of the Stone Age village.

It was a brilliantly scenic trip, made more memorable by the friendly bus crew who treated the passengers to slapstick comedy along the route. Once again, Madhya Pradesh had come up trumps as the most tourist-friendly state. I spent the night in a bungalow set on the edge of a dramatic escarpment and the next morning, I explored the cliffs that fell away under it. They turned out to be the perfect practice wall for a budding rock climber. Tamia also boasted a tribal university affiliated to the Jawaharlal Nehru University in Delhi.

After my early morning explorations, I hired a bike to ride along the great rift and was puzzled as to how such a good stretch of road came to exist in these backwoods. It seemed the Stone Age village had become a tourist spot and learning that, all desire to visit it evaporated.

From Tamia I took a bus to Pachmarhi, the small hill station that is perched near the highest point in the Satpuras and overlooks a marvellous swathe of jungle country to the south. To the north lies Itarsi, where the great crossing of railway lines occurs—here Delhi-Chennai trains meet Calcutta-Mumbai traffic. Of all the hill stations I have visited, Pachmarhi comes closest to the British ideal of a sylvan retreat. Nature is still supreme in Pachmarhi and the Madhya Pradesh tourism arrangements are tasteful and subdued. What a contrast to my home town of Mussoorie, once called Queen of the Hills, but now rendered a common slut by the vulgar mismanagement of its affairs since Independence; the station's natural beauty bartered away for cheap and nasty tourism development.

It was cold enough in February to give me chapped lips and

I was loathe to leave the leafy walks and magic waterfalls of Pachmarhi. The nearest railway station of Pipariya offered no through train to my next stop, Hoshangabad, so I took a bus to this scenic town on the Narmada. Long before I set eyes on India, I had been in touch, as an undergraduate, with Banwarilal Choudhri, a Gandhian worker whose village lay next to the rural Quaker centre of Rasulia near Hoshangabad. I recall the early days when my idealism for the Bhoodan movement was fierce enough to blind me to the difficulties of rural reforms. I realize now that Banwarilal's greatness lay not in his ideology, but in his natural human qualities.

In Hoshangabad I hired a bike to ride to the banks of the blue river and marvelled at the difference in reception a tourist may find in different parts of India. Unquestionably, the most warm welcome awaits him in Madhya Pradesh. Everywhere I went in Hoshangabad, I was hailed and invited in for a cup of sweet and refreshing desi chai. What a contrast to the ghats at Nasik in neighbouring Maharashtra, where xenophobia runs quite high, or Ankleswar over the border in Gujarat, where I received the rudest reception in the whole of my travels, second only to being thrown out of Ayatollah Khomeini's mosque in Qum, Iran. Was it a coincidence that both these incidents occurred in dry states?

I was headed now for the lower reaches of the Narmada, where the controversial dam is the cause of extreme emotions, both for and against. This gigantic project appears to have been designed on the back of an envelope that no one has ever seen. To cover up the embarrassment of spending huge amounts of international aid, the Gujarat government had recently declared the project to be under the Official Secrets Act. So, I was not allowed access to this ultimate white elephant, supposedly built to supply water to the ordinary citizen, but which for forty years has not provided a drop.

My next port of call was Omkareshwar, another pilgrim place on the Narmada, access to which is by boat. I caught a train from Hoshangabad to Khandwa and had to stand for the 200 km broad gauge run. Omkareshwar was on the metre gauge line out of Khandwa and needless to say, there was no question of standing on the smaller line. The 55 km journey by evening fast-passenger was as relaxed and productive of literary output as the broad gauge had been disagreeable and unconducive to note-taking.

Omkareshwar is a jewel and the most exciting way to experience it is to be rowed around the island, though now the outboard engine has arrived to shatter the quietude. This must be one of the most inspiring sections of the river. Moving downstream to the formal ghats at Maheshwar, I found the architecture of Rani Ahalyabai's palace to be every bit as harmonious as the natural cliff scenery around Omkareshwar had been.

From Maheshwar I took a bus to Mandu, located on a wooded knoll distantly overlooking the Narmada. I had first visited Mandu four years ago, and its fabulous mix of natural beauty and exquisite, early Islamic architecture had left an indelible impression. But on my return, I found that a fanatical, high-caste mindset to revise historical reality had set in. Mandu had been converted to a Hindu identity, which would have been laughable had it not been so bogus. Instead of concentrating on quality infrastructure, the authorities seemed to have escaped into fantasy land. Nothing exemplified this better than the flashy, tiled bathrooms of the tourist bungalow which had chrome fittings worthy of a palace, but without any water in them.

The next morning I caught a bus to Dhar and was quite impressed by the antiquities. It was easy to see in Dhar why local resentment at medieval Muslim excesses had led to the bizarre transformation of Mandu into Mandhavi.

As I drew nearer to the border of Gujarat, the free and easy flavour of Madhya Pradesh waned and surly attitudes increased. I took another bus that passed through the village of Bagh, famous for its caves and textile dyeing, but decided not to get off because of its poor transport connections.

After a dusty day I came to Chhota Udaipur with its narrow gauge terminal, part of the Dabhoi system. However, road transport had so taken over passenger traffic, that this section was on its last legs. The station was locked and looked abandoned. Only one train a day arrived from Pratapnagar (100 km away) at noon and returned at 2 p.m. My dream of riding a ZB to Baroda in the morning evaporated as comprehensively as my prospects of seeing the Sardar Sarovar Dam. Instead, I walked around the pleasant little town, marked the diamond polishers at work in several shacks (under contract from the seths of Surat) and was rudely shooed away when I tried to take a photograph of the royal residence through the gates. As I meandered around the town, I mused on the fickleness of transport fashions. According to R. R. Bhandari, former curator of the Delhi Rail Museum, the Gaekwad's Baroda State Railway (GBSR), by the 1940s, was 'huge and profitable'. The section between Bodeli and Chhota Udaipur yielded incredible returns for a narrow gauge line. Yet, less than fifty years later, this same section had closed due to lack of traffic.

Dabhoi, where I made my way the next day, has some remarkably aesthetic Islamic architecture on show, but the chances are the international visitor will be a steam buff who makes a beeline for the world's busiest narrow gauge junction. I was fortunate in catching the last of the steam fleet, although several services had been curtailed for various reasons that ranged from drought to flood. The Chhota Udaipur service ran till 1994, but in the 1995 Bradshaw, a note reads: 'Running suspended due to breaches'. Curiously, every year thereafter, the name Chhota Udaipur appears in the timetable index, but the line only hosted trains as far as Bodeli, some 37 km short of the beleaguered terminal.

A small, unprepossessing station, Dabhoi announces its significance from a platform board advertising connections to

Chandod, Timba, Tankhala, Chhota Udaipur, Pratapnagar, Miyagam and Malsar. Extraordinarily, all these refer to narrow gauge options. Passenger traffic was quite brisk and I spotted two trains headed by ZBs waiting to steam out.

I also spotted half a dozen engines in the shed. They were mainly ZBs, but the odd WT and P class was also in the line-up. The Western zone, known for its smart turnout, keeps all these engines well groomed in a black and maroon livery with yellow dividers.

Dabhoi was indeed the promised land for the collector of narrow gauge steam records. In its heyday, it hosted forty locomotives and the five lines radiating from it totalled 359 km. In his monograph, *Western Railway Narrow Gauge System* (published in 1998), R. R. Bhandari provides an excellent, illustrated survey of Gujarat's long-lived narrow gauge lines. Perhaps because Baroda was a curiously scattered princely state with highly urbanized citizens, its rulers had to be men of foresight. With the coming of the Bombay-Baroda and Central Indian Railway's broad gauge from Surat to Baroda in 1855, Khanderao Gaekwad, on his own inspiration, decided to link it up to his state's interior by means of a 2'6" gauge. This was the earliest narrow gauge line built in India (actually a tram way) and it ran from Dabhoi to Miyagam. However, it was too lightly laid for the three steam locos Khanderao had been persuaded to buy from a Neilson salesman. Opened to bullock-hauled traffic in 1862, the line was relaid to allow the Neilson engines to run in 1873. Known as the Dabhoi Tramway and Gaekwad's Dabhoi Railway in the early years, the short trains had two passenger boxes and two floats for bales of impressed cotton. Grain and bamboo were also transported and continue to be to this day. The Dabhoi line was also important for the psychology of the Independence movement, being the first wholly Indian venture floated without imperial aid.

The 33 km from Dabhoi Junction to Miyagam Karian Junction still sees five trains a day, though diesel has now replaced the steam fleet. An occasional steam service is run to recall the flavour of this historical section. When I visited the line in 1988, the timetable included thirteen narrow gauge services for the whole of Gujarat, down from seventeen that appear in the 1976 timetable. By 2000, the lines had reduced to a single digit and presumably will continue to fall, since the bus is quicker.

The locos employed for these level tracts (Dabhoi is 43 m above sea-level) have always been light and trim. The three Neilsons were 0-4-0 saddle tanks, which later merited a change to tenders. Kitson and Bagnall engines were also used and after the opening of Calthrop's Barsi Light in 1879, large 0-8-4 tank locos were tried on certain sections. With the advent of IRS (Indian Railways Standard) locomotives, the sleek and comely ZB became the largest single class. This elegant 2-6-2 with six-wheeled tender came into service in 1928 and a large batch was ordered for the Dabhoi line in 1951. Bagnall built the first four, numbers 1, 56, 57 and 58 in the early thirties and numbers 59 to 68 were built in 1953. Thereafter, numbers 69 to 76 were made by Corpet Louvet (1953) and numbers 77 to 91 and 117 to 122, by Kraus Maffei between 1953 and 1960. These details are important because being so well cared for, several ZBs have found their way to preservation status. Number 66 has been preserved at Pratapnagar and number 72 at Godhra (now earmarked for an engineering college). Realizing their collector's value, the railways had the good sense to auction some of the condemned ZBs and at least one has gone to a private citizen. ZB 68 can be seen at the Delhi farmhouse of Arun Mohan, a senior advocate of the Supreme Court.

The older locos on view at Dabhoi indicated the earlier standard preferred by the GBSR. This was the W class, with later variants. A finely preserved example (W 574) stands before the impressive stone edifice of the Ajmer divisional headquarters. Together, these quality works in stone and metal make for a memorable portrait of the enduring character that the Western zone is famous for. W 574 goes back to the original lot of engines supplied by Bagnall in 1913. W-1 596, spotted in the yard at Dabhoi, dates back to 1949.

The extent and variety of the Gujarat narrow gauge lines deserve a book rather than a chapter. It was bad luck that time was against me when visiting the five spokes out of Dabhoi, to record some of their brave history. But to illustrate the dog-in-the-manger attitude of officialdom, when I enquired about the one-off surviving K class shunter (built specially for the Piplod-Baria line), the Pratapnagar workshop foreman froze as though he had been asked to reveal a secret nuclear device. I shrugged off this paranoia, knowing that at least K 563 was in good hands. Sooner or later she would resurface and I recently heard that this 2-6-4 Kerr Stuart side tank has been bought by the National Rail Museum.

The other two classes I saw at Dabhoi were of equal vintage status. The two Bagnall P class locos, 605 and 606, dating from 1929 and 1949, were machines too lean for the characteristically chubby look of the W and ZB standard locos of the GBSR, and one has to look elsewhere for their origin. They had been ordered for the Cutch State Railway and became redundant when that system went metric. The other ancient class I saw was Bagnall WT 596, of 1926 vintage (Delhi's Rail Museum has No 594). I saw this class again in the course of one of my metre gauge marathons, marooned high and dry in a little enclosure at Morbi. Not only had the surrounding lines been changed to metric, but the sole surviving narrow gauge branch had been washed away. W 585 stood forlornly, with a weather vane on its steam dome, while an even more bedraggled WT lurked on an overgrown siding. How are the mighty fallen! A hundred years ago, Morbi was the centre of narrow gauge engineering excellence that extended to the building of locomotives.

An opportunity to sample the Dabhoi line arose with the convenient departure of the afternoon train for Chandod, three

stations away and (unknown to me) on the banks of the
Narmada. It was a delicious 45-minute journey to cover the
seventeen kilometres to the wide, flowing river and the gait of
the engine earned her the name *Blue Danube*. The passenger
complement wasn't crowded for a 4 p.m. start—presumably,
pilgrims went by the morning train. Because of the age of the
line, everything went like clockwork, but best of all was the
smooth progress of the ZB. Everything about *Blue Danube* was
delightful, from looks to performance. During the last years of
steam running, the ZB was second to the ZE in terms of strength
and numbers. But in appearance, the ZB, in my opinion, easily
comes first. Also in smoothness of motion. She seemed to be a
thoroughbred whereas the ZE, with its extra set of driving
wheels, was a pedigree Clydesdale.

There was a train back from Chandod, but a passenger
bound for Rajpipla came up with the exciting alternative of
taking the ferry across the river and catching a morning train
from Rajpipla to Ankleshwar, situated along the southern bank
of the Narmada. Chandod was a charming place, perched
precariously above the river and from the end of the line, I had
to scuttle down a steep, earthen bank to reach the shore where
the ferry waited. To my surprise, the boats were all of the
sea-going variety with elegant, raised hulls and a stout mast that
unfurled a tattered sail to aid the poling. There were broad
sandbanks on the further shore and we had to wait there
patiently until the state bus service arrived. I was told that near
Chandod is a rare temple of Maun Hanuman, and I wondered if
this tied up with Mahatma Gandhi's liking for the talisman of
three monkeys he always carried with him, signifying 'See no
evil, hear no evil, speak no evil'.

Sitting on that sandy shore as the twilight deepened, a
profound air of beatitude settled on both mind and body. It was
as though the pleasure aroused by the sweet motion of the little
train had been heightened by the purposeful sweep of the great
river, now nearing its tryst with the estuary. At such moments,

you know exactly what eternity feels like. Had I been in a less contented frame of mind and cursed the lateness of the connecting bus, the moment would have been lost. Because the mind had been passive enough to see in the passenger's advice some inspirational potential, my journey had been rewarded with an inkling of a consciousness that knew no bounds.

Perhaps because of my brightened mood, I arrived in Rajpipla with a strong sense of its civic oneness. The former state boasted a fine equestrian statue of one of its rulers. The station turned out to be solidly built and it seemed the ruler had originally kept the line at arm's length, across the river Karjan. Only when convinced of its bonafides did he allow it to come into the town, over a sturdy iron bridge made in London in 1906. Optimistically, tubular piers had been sunk to carry a second line, but alas, even the single track did not make it into the new millennium. The station boasted four trains a day to and from Ankleshwar, but the revenue raised was paltry. In 1996 the line ceased to appear in Bradshaw, another victim to the faster bus.

It was in Rajpipla that I experienced the thrill of watching a narrow gauge steamer on the run, as the morning service from Ankleshwar boomed in over the river. ZB 58 reversed on a triangle, then backed in to take the return train. Again, the joy of journeying behind such a smooth-working locomotive remains a lasting memory. I called her *Waltzing Matilda* and everything about her seemed inspired. My heart went out to her as the lady locomotive of my choice. She steamed gracefully to Ankleshwar and out of my life. But I will always recall the silent working of her motion, compared to other classes—a tribute to the love Western zone railwaymen gave to their charges.

Like the rest of the Gujarat narrow gauge railways, the carriages of the Rajpipla line were also of vintage stock and had few frills. First class had ceased to be an option and when it disappeared, it took with it the last hope of revenue. Thus, what had proudly begun as the Rajpipla State Railway in 1897 dwindled as suddenly as the fortunes of its last maharaja and it failed to score a century by a handful of years. In 1993, the Rajpipla end of the line got the chop and this coincided with the last murmurings of my favourite locomotive.

Since this trip had included pilgrim spots along the Narmada, I decided to go from Ankleshwar to Bharuch and thence to Shuklatirth to see the island of Kabirbed with its famous banyan tree known even to Milton. At the Ankleshwar bus station I was jeered at by the bus staff because I could not read the Gujarati destination board. I put it down to the frustration of a backward state having to come to terms with modernity. The government tourist arrangements at Shuklatirth were scruffy and like many visitors to Gujarat, I looked forward to my escape to Daman, a Goan enclave where the humbug levels were as low as the expectations of those Gujaratis queuing up for a drink were high.

I had been away from base for nearly three weeks and this is as much as my constitution can take of daily changes of address and the exacting ritual of packing and unpacking. It was a pleasure to catch steam still on the run in Dabhoi, but sad that I could only snatch at a fraction of the ongoing action in Gujarat. However, in retrospect, I realize that merely to have seen other lines and list interesting facts would not have given the satisfaction of this fragmented tour. Whatever their lack of range, my travels had been blessed with rare moments of railway history and inner harmony.

I recalled Rene Daumal's remarkable guide to the inner realm, called *Mount Analogue*. The gifted mountaineer-author argues that to find eternity you need to be as practical as the leader of an expedition and must sit down and plan your approach systematically. You reach the peak when you are physically fit and in the right frame of mind. Getting these physical and mental coordinates right opens a magical door that carries the seeker through to a state of grace. Paradoxically, this state that we call a gift from a divine source, is locked up within us. Will power is required to get past the little self and to surrender before our real self. Conventional spiritual teaching encourages the seeker to sit passively and still the mind in meditation, whereas Daumal's guru, the modern Sufi Gurdjieff, made his disciples do hard physical labour or dance like dervishes till they dropped from exhaustion. My guru Ashishda also encouraged this method as a means of getting past the smaller self. While in Mirtola, I worked on the ashram farm, in the kitchen and at the temple, from five in the morning till ten at night and know what it is like to drop from exhaustion. This tough regime may not open lotuses in the mind, but it does steel you to face any situation life throws at you thereafter. As a practical aid to a traveller, my time in Mirtola gave me the useful skill of being able to fall asleep while still on my feet. (Also I learned how to make the most delicious marmalade!)

According to this non-passive approach to the inner world, the goal is not a neutral nirvana beyond the concerns of suffering humanity. Eternity involves the breathlessness of desire because the coursing of molecules in the bloodstream is agitated by the mystical polarity of love.

I see my journey to India as a means to narrow down the gap between Daumal's coordinates. You have to put your instincts about the oneness of life to the test. In the same way that I found satisfaction in coming home to the East, many Indians find it in facing and overcoming the challenges of the West. The branching out from one's home turf to find the grail of certainty in a strange country has little to do with names on the outer map. The coordinates ultimately have to be arranged within you.

2001

NAMITA GOKHALE

NAINITAL

For years I was blinded by nostalgia. And then, the last time I went back to Nainital, I saw what it had become: a dilapidated tourist trap; a small lake beached with garbage, and surrounded—incongruously—by a ring of noble mountains. The town was ugly, dirty and depressing; it did not belong to itself anymore. The lake, which I always remembered as a deep mossy green, was viscous and muddy, the colour of a buffalo pond in the plains. The traffic had snarled up into an impossible mess. It was hot, and although it was still only April it seemed as though the season had already begun and the summer tourists had arrived in full force.

I went to visit the house where I had spent my childhood. It was a large, illogically constructed bungalow where my hospitable grandmother had provided refuge to many generations of summer visitors. The overlays of remembrance and memory had coalesced into a dream territory which some part of me continued to inhabit. These were memories made up of brittle things: the texture of sticky summer lychees; the sound of langurs tramping about on the tin roof; the taste of fresh pine and deodar needles which the mali's son insisted tasted 'just like chewing gum'. And our Malju, the mali, the wizard, who fell off Tiffin top chasing an errant cow. We had continued to return to the house every summer, till my grandfather, inexplicably, sold

NAMITA GOKHALE's books include *Paro: Dreams of Passion; Gods, Graves and Grandmother; A Himalayan Love Story; Mountain Echoes* and *The Book of Shadows*. She is also a regular contributor to major Indian newspapers and magazines.

it off some years ago, leaving all of us who had grown up there in a state of permanent exile.

The bungalow had been bought from a widow named Victoria Grant, who had once run it as a boarding house. Victoria had gone back to her little village in England with the money, and died there. Sometimes she would return, at odd hours, to inspect the rooms of her old establishment in Nainital. The ghost of Victoria Grant competed for popularity with the 'twals', the strange green pillars of light that the servants claimed they saw on the dark slopes adjoining the tennis court. A patient uncle explained the twals to be a natural phenomenon, something to do with fluctuating phosphorous levels. An impatient aunt dismissed Victoria Grant's visitations as schoolgirl hysteria. But the hauntings gave an edge to our holidays, and we did not surrender them so easily.

My grandfather had retained the name Victoria Grant had given the bungalow: Primrose. Now, the name on the gate read: Prem Lodge. As I walked up the slight slope that led to the house, past the familiar magnolia tree and the clumps of eponymous and now redundant primrose, a sense of nightmare began engulfing me. What had once been garden, lawn and pebble and neat geometrical flowerbeds, was now a large single surface of concrete. The two symmetrical pines fronting the house had been encircled with cement; they looked as though they were slowly dying of asphyxiation. The new owner of the house appeared before me, flanked by his wife and daughter. He recognized me, although he showed no particular signs of welcome. 'It was difficult to maintain the garden—this is so much simpler,' he said. I had not realized that the accusation in my eyes was so eloquent. To my right, the house had been knocked down altogether. In its place stood a building that looked as though two giant shoe-boxes had been stacked upon each other. 'We decided to convert it into a hotel,' the man continued, following my gaze. There was an apologetic tone in his voice. But his wife and daughter looked at me defiantly.

There was an unspoken solidarity between them. They resented my intrusion; it was their house, they had bought it, it belonged to them and they could do what they pleased with it. I felt ashamed; it was time to retreat. The old lily pond was still there, though slabbed around with concrete. I went up to it on my way out, trying to salvage any small consolation of memory. Goldfish still hovered under the lily pads. They watched me incuriously from the solitude and shelter of their tenuous world. I wished them luck and fled.

In the Mall I met one of Nainital's most regular summer visitors. His name is Shadilal. Shadilal is short, a mere four feet or so, his hands are permanently bandaged to indicate leprosy—a condition from which he may or may not suffer— and he moves around seated on a flat wooden slat mounted on two skateboards. He wears a band of purple feathers around his forehead, like some pygmy tribesman. Sometimes he drapes a row of cowrie-shells around his chest. I am certain he has never been to Africa or even Nagaland. I see him in Delhi sometimes, begging at the Safdarjang hospital crossing, or at Connaught Place. Every summer Shadilal comes to Nainital to beat the heat. He arrives in an air-conditioned bus, and departs only after the rains have arrived. Shadilal knows me by now, as I know him. I suspect that he is rich, and I never give him any money. But today, reassured by the continuity of his presence, I slipped him a ten-rupee note.

Perhaps Shadilal worked a small miracle for me, for soon afterwards the clouds gathered over China Peak. A fog settled over the lake, muffling the din, shutting out the ugliness, and the Nainital which was my hometown reasserted itself against its schizophrenic tourist identity. I remembered a day, many years ago, when I was just nine years old. I decided to go for a walk alone, unescorted by an ayah or grown-up. It was an October afternoon, and the air was clear and sharp. I walked along the lake, by the pebbled shore. The Puja season had not yet begun, and the boatmen had not yet surfaced in search of the Calcutta tourists. I could hear the occasional rickshaw bell on the Mall road, but there weren't too many people around. The gentlest of breezes fluttered over the waves. The indecisive Nainital weather took over, and I was engulfed by a bank of cloud and fog, alone with my little patch of lake. That day I claimed Nainital and made it my own.

For me, Nainital is not a place on a map, it is not even a geographical location. It exists continually for me wherever I go. I live out a part of my life there wherever else in the world I might be.

In the late mornings you can see the schoolchildren promenade in the Mall in their navy-blue uniforms, the girls with tightly braided pigtails, their faces petalled with crisp ribbons. They are led by watchful nuns, or padres from the boys school, or the sports master from the Birla Vidya Mandir. Many years later, they will remember their childhood, and dream of blue skies and a green lake before they wake up to face the day.

The schoolgirls remind me of the days long before I woke up. I had a happy childhood in Nainital, living with my grandparents and a posse of unmarried aunts. I would spend the lazy summer afternoons with my friends and cousins, aiming unripe apricots at anybody walking on the path below our house. I went to school in a dandi, a khaki palanquin balanced precariously on the shoulders of four coolies. The nuns at the school were unusually kind, but the one I remember most clearly is Sister Utah, who would warn me conspiratorially to 'beware of the communists'. I had an uncle called Stalin and a cousin named Lenin, and her misgivings puzzled me.

I had cousins dotting every inch of the landscape. They are scattered around the world now: they have grown up and gone away, claimed by the world. Many of them return every year, as I do, accompanied by uncomprehending children and disdainful spouses exhausted by the long dusty drive through the plains of northern India. They come in quest of their childhood, in search of the things they cannot share with strangers, and are often puzzled and disappointed by what they find here. The official inventory of Nainital's tourist attractions is not dazzling. There are the Flats, near Mallital, which house a dusty pan-Nainital car park; a hockey field which doubles as a cricket pitch; several chaat-stalls which are rumoured to use lake water for their pani-puris; and a Tibetan market where cheap goods from China are on sale. The Naina Devi temple and the Gurudwara front the lake, as does the Boat House club. The boat-walas offer to take you round the lake, past the temple of Pashan Devi and the municipal library. There are pedal-boats shaped like plastic swans for those who are romantically inclined. The horse-walas volunteer to take tourists to China peak, or Snow View if they so desire. There is, of course, a cable-car to Snow View, but it tends to get stalled, leaving the tourists suspended between the lake and the hills, to the amusement of the smug locals.

Every tourist town has a sort of bicameral consciousness. The locals tend to look down on the tourists, but at the same time are quick to exploit them. Living in the rarified heights of the Himalayas gives rise to feelings of spiritual, if not material, superiority. 'The plains people' are referred to rather distastefully, though they are the fodder of the tourist economy. The hotels, the boat-walas, the horse-walas, the shopkeepers, and almost all of Nainital woo 'the plains people'. And when the monsoons arrive and wash the tourists away, a sense of contentment envelops the local population.

Beyond the meagre tourist attractions is another Nainital: the old boat-house, the St. Joseph's boathouse, where the gallows once were; the mysteriously named Smuggler's rock; and Tiffin Top, where lovers and the newly married have killed and died so often that there's a whole mythology of honey-moon crimes associated with the spot. There are the ancient rivalries between the residential schools, between Sem and St. Mary's and Sherwood and the rest. The hermetic Baba from the Pashan Devi temple, who rarely ventured out of his precariously balanced hut that seemed almost to levitate over the lake, is another part of Nainital lore. As are the complex inside politics of the yacht crowd and the annual regatta; and Fredrick Smetacek Jr, the 'Butterfly man', with his collection of Lepidopterae and his doomsday predictions about what happens when the poinsettias start flowering in October.

When I was young, I was in complete awe of a personage known to all only as Girish Gazetteer. His designated function was to relay gossip and newsworthy information from Tallital on the lower Mall to Mallital on the other side of the lake. From here the headlines would distribute themselves at the speed of light. Nainital thinks local and acts local. That is the nicest thing about the town—its incestuous obsession with itself. The Doomsday weed in the lake that heralded the end of the world; the spy from China in Capitol cinema hall; the murders by the Lal Tanki—these were events of far greater importance than Nehru's death, or the Tashkent agreement, or man landing on the moon. When Asha Parekh, the famous actress, fell off a yacht during a film shoot and Sunil Dutt saved her—now that was news. When a villager near Dunagiri was visited by a Goddess who gave him a miraculous herb and almost everybody in Nainital, ill or able-bodied, set off to test the cure—that was news.

That has not changed. Nainital still has its own realities. The rest of the world is out there in the plains where ordinary mortals live. Great wars and feuds are conducted over the most trifling issues involving matters of honour. Eccentrics are loved and given much rope here, and people rarely wear the badge of stress—or perhaps if they do now, it has a different name.

Nainital was 'discovered' by an Englishman named Trail in the year 1841. Before that, it was a place of pilgrimage where the

temple of Naina Devi stood. An annual fair was held in Nainital
every autumn. Apart from that, the hill people, the Paharis, left
it alone, for it was a sacred spot, favoured by the immortals.
There is an interesting account of how Trail and his friend
Baron found access to this forbidden lake. The locals had
guarded their secret well, but a hapless Dotyal labourer with a
rock balanced on his head and a gun to his temple was told to
keep marching until he reached the shores of Nainital. Then the
sons of perfidious Albion took the local land-owning Thakur
for a ride on a boat, the first boat ever to breach the sacred
waters of the lake. The Thakur couldn't swim, and on threat of
being thrown into the water he was persuaded to sign the deed
of ownership gifting the land around Nainital to Trail and his
friend Baron.

Today the lake is one of the most eutropic in India, gasping
for oxygen as the sewage and filth clog its life-force. The
sanitation plant doesn't work, and the rain-water channels
which flow into the lake are choked with waste, refuse and
plastic. Deforestation and over-construction have led to a spate
of landslides. Nainital is an ecological wasteland. The curiosity
and greed which propelled the Englishmen have borne bitter
fruit.

The annual fair dedicated to Naina Devi, the presiding deity
of Nainital, continues to be held in the flats every October. The
original temple of Naina Devi, the spot where Shiva's wife
Parvati's eyes fell to the earth after her death, was buried in the
rubble of the great landslide of 1879. The priest at the temple
once told me the story of how the temple still maintains its
routine of prayer and ritual at the bottom of the lake. Giant fish
guard the entrance, and water-snakes and mermen propitiate
the great goddess in her underwater abode. For the romantics
and the exiles, there is consolation in the thought. Somewhere,
all that was, survives.

Despite the degradation, then, to me Nainital will always
remain the most beautiful lake in the world, a dark, demanding

lake that exacts a bali, a human sacrifice, every year. I have lost my share of friends and relatives to it through suicide and misadventure. Every time a bloated body rises to the surface, usually near the treacherous rocks of Pashan Devi, we locals recognize that the elements are demanding their due. We understand the lake, and forgive it, as we hope it forgives us.

2001

MARK SHAND

MELA MADNESS

Awoken early by the urgent shouts of mahouts and the chanting of sadhus, I walked to the side of the kanat and peered over. Though relatively empty last night, it was now as if an army had moved in quietly during the night and surrounded our encampment. The orchard was alive with elephants, swaying, feeding and dusting, while mahouts, wrapped in blankets, squatted beside fires, watching them carefully over rims of little terracotta bowls containing their morning tea. Arcades, of hastily constructed stalls, like mini-bazaars, had mysteriously sprung up, selling paan, spices, food, cheap jewellery, clothing and medicines.

Behind us, like flowers in a desert, huddled little groups of families. When the sun rose, the women stretched languidly, turning bejewelled arms, ankles and tips of noses and ears bright gold as the first rays filtered through the smoke-filled air. Elephants ridden proudly by young well-muscled mahouts, their teeth a brilliant white against the black of their faces, raced each other down to the river. Like picadors, holding an ankush in both hands behind their elephants' ears, they showed off their skills and their mounts to the best effect. To the casual observer it would seem like a game but it was, in fact, in deadly earnest.

MARK SHAND's *Travels with My Elephant*, from which 'Mela Madness' has been extracted, was the result of an epic journey across India on his elephant, Tara. 'Mela Madness' describes the Sonepur Mela in Bihar, the world's largest animal fair. Other books by Mark Shand include *Skulduggery* (co-authored with Don McCullin), the story of the search for the head-hunting tribes of Indonesia.

Prospective buyers would be watching carefully.

Lallan Singh arrived with an electrician who ran a cable up one of the trees in our camp to connect a large high-wattage bulb. At night it would effectively illuminate Tara and, we hoped, keep the boys awake. I watched shamefacedly, but Lallan Singh consoled me. Three other elephants, he told me, had escaped during the night. It was only a precaution.

Our first buyer offered 70,000 rupees for Tara. This man, a magnificent actor, almost brought tears to my eyes. He told me of the wonderful elephant he had owned for thirty years, which he only rented out on very auspicious occasions. Just last week, tragedy struck when he was away on business. He had instructed his mahout to take the elephant to one of these very special occasions. The mahout, a lazy man, did not carry out his orders and when he returned he gave the mahout a sound beating. A week later the mahout disappeared, not before he had poisoned the elephant, which had just died. I declined his offer.

After Tara returned from her bath, I went shopping. From one of the many stalls specializing in elephant decorations, I bought her a beautiful brass neck bell attached to a bright crimson silken cord. Anklets made of bells and strips of silken material to hang from ears and tusks were also available, but I wanted to keep her looking simple, elegant, like a beautiful woman at a ball, wearing a plain dress, unadorned, except for one astonishing piece of jewellery. She did not need decoration.

I employed a specialist in elephant painting. After drawing a line that sharply demarcated the blackness of her oiled crown from the natural grey of her skin, he created with simple coloured chalks of purple, yellow, white and blue, a series of flowers and lotuses on her ears, face and trunk. In the centre, between her eyes, he traced a dazzling star. Taking down the Union Jack, we draped it over Tara's shoulders and when prospective buyers approached, Bhim and Gokul would dramatically draw it back.

As Don and Aditya had disappeared earlier to take photographs, I set off through the Haathi Bazaar, leaving Tara with the boys. My nostrils were instantly filled with the evocative smells of India—spices, incense, the heavy scent of the tribal woman, mixed with the more pungent odour of urine and excrement, and found myself thinking I never wanted to leave. Passing down the elephant lines, mahouts and owners alike called me over—not out of curiosity but because I was part of them, an elephant man, inexorably entwined with their way of life. I sat cross-legged by little fires and shared bowls of tea and littis, small balls of hot dough roasted over the ashes. I inspected their elephants, checking their backs for tell-tale sores and scars, and chuckled disapprovingly when, opening their mouth, I found patches of black on their pink tongues.

Easily now, I mounted the elephants by way of their trunks and tusks. I sat caressing their ears, and barked commands to make them sit. I watched a big male having part of its tusk sawn off, for a legal sale of ivory. The mahout first carefully measured the distance from eye to lip. After marking a spot which avoided cutting into the nerve, he sawed through it quickly. In India ivory fetches about 5,000 rupees a kilo. Magically, the tusk will grow back, just like a finger nail.

At one encampment stood a huge tusker, excessive in its ornamentation. Richly caparisoned in red brocade, bells hung round its neck and feet, yellow and red silken scarves dangled from its ears and tusks and its tail was braided with silver tinsel. The beast swayed from side to side continuously, its piggy little eyes transfixing everyone who passed, with a stare of pure venom. An old mahout warned me to keep my distance. This was a dangerous elephant, he told me. In the last ten days it had killed three people.

I counted a hundred and ninety elephants; last year there had been more than three hundred and next year probably there would be even fewer. It is inevitable that this way of life will, in time, die out.

Leaving the Haathi Bazaar I moved on to the other animal markets. For the first time, the sheer size of the great mela struck me. At the horse lines I watched a small snow-white arab, its pink eyes heavily kohled to highlight their dullness, its tail dyed the colours of the rainbow, being put through its paces. The rider urged him along at a furious pace, then suddenly pulled him dead on his hocks, whirling him about to perform a kind of 'pas' or, in military terms, 'marking time'. The horses were even more elaborately decorated than the elephants. Some sported headbands worked in gold thread, others had their legs encircled with brass bangles. One wore a necklace of silver and gold, containing verses from the *Koran*. They came from Rajasthan, the Punjab, Afghanistan and even Australia, watched over carefully by their dealers, old men with faces creased like parchment paper, shrewd all-knowing eyes wrinkled against the glare of the sun.

Beyond the horses, stretching for almost two miles, were paddocks crowded with cows, bullocks and buffaloes. Finally, I reached the bull pens, known locally as the 'jewel market'. Apart from the elephants, the bulls fetch the highest prices.

Making my way back to Tara I entered the shopping centres, a maze of streets lined with booths, overshadowed by the giant Ferris wheel of the fun fair and the Big Top of the circus arena. A crowd surrounded a pair of chained, moth-eaten bears. Goaded by their keeper, they shuffled miserably from paw to paw in time to a disco song. For five rupees you could dance with them.

A discordant screeching announced the bird market. Hyacinthine blue macaws from South America sat quietly on their perches, their feathers ruffled, swivelling their heads suddenly, blinking their baleful eyes. Nepalese mynahs chuckled and laughed, and a cage of little rice birds, so gaudy in colour that the owner admitted they had been dyed, hopped nervously from side to side. Outside, a shiny black mynah loaded and fired a miniature cannon, and for ten rupees would play cards.

The inevitable snake-charmers squatted at the sides of the streets, playing their flutes tunelessly to serpents swaying from wicker baskets. One snake-charmer, more enterprising than the rest, advertised 'a fight to the death' between a mongoose and a cobra. I hoped he had an unending supply of cobras, for inevitably the mongoose would win. Or perhaps he waited until he had attracted a large enough crowd to make it worthwhile.

Jugglers ferried their way through the crowds performing with extraordinary skill considering all the pushing and shoving. As I pushed and shoved I noticed an exceptionally tall man with piercing eyes bearing down on me. I tried to move, but it was as if I was hypnotized. Dipping a long large finger in a small jar of vermilion, he stabbed it against my forehead and demanded five rupees. I christened him 'dot man' and over the next few days, whatever preventative measures I took, he always managed to get me. Once, seeing him approach I slipped behind Aditya as the great finger shot out like a sword. I thought I had escaped. Aditya, obviously a seasoned mela veteran, simply ducked and I received it on the end of my nose.

'Your teeth pulled for only 20 rupees. Get a new set. A new look.' Dentists did a roaring trade from padded chairs operating foot drills. Naive patients writhed in agony as the dentists dug into mouths with what looked like pairs of pliers. In intervals between the shops bold placards hung advertising eating houses, their cuisine varied to suit the tastes of every caste and creed. The smell reminded me of the observation of the old planter who wrote in his *Reminiscences of Behar*: 'I cannot say the dishes look tempting while the smell of bad ghee makes you wish you had put a little extra eau-de-Cologne on your handkerchief before you left your tent.'

Passing brassiere shops and signs advertising 'Genuine Siamese Twins' I entered the Bombay Bazaar. The smell of bad ghee disappeared in a wave of perfume. Here was everything for the lady. Women, young and old, queued up at scent booths, in which men sat cross-legged behind a thousand different bottles.

After twirling cotton-wool on to long silver sticks, they dipped them in and dabbed them on the backs of waiting hands. Glass-bangle sellers displayed their incandescent wares on long tall poles. They fought a losing battle to prevent their eager clients from shattering fragile merchandise as the women pulled and pushed them up and down their arms.

In large mirrors, the ladies coquettishly painted on different hues of cosmetics and lipstick and applied kohl to their eyes, while others tried on gold nose and ear ornaments. Baskets filled with brilliant hues of sindoor (the powder used to make the 'tikka') sat in rows of tiny coloured mountains, and gorgeous bolts of gauze, silk and cotton to be made into saris fluttered like butterfly wings as they were gently unfurled.

As I moved on, persistent salesmen pressed me to buy their products: brasswork from Benares, inlaid boxes and trays and miniature Taj Mahals from Agra, enamel objects from Jaipur, beautifully embroidered shawls from Kashmir, and in one rather modern shop a Hell's Angel's leather biker's jacket and a pair of co-respondent brogues.

The ingenuity of the beggars knew no bounds. Beside a man sitting near the temple lay upright in the dust what appeared to be a human head and it was just that. He had buried his colleague up to the neck and rubbed his face with paste to give it the colour of a corpse. Another simply walked around naked from the waist down, with a large padlock clamped through the end of his penis. Yet another had buried himself head downwards to the waist and was managing to breathe through the open ends of two bamboo tubes that just broke the surface of the ground. Unfortunately, he had neglected to hire an assistant. Passersby liberally helped themselves to his begging bowl.

On the other side of the temple, I came across the Naga sadhus, who are fiercely ascetic and protect their privacy zealously. Trained in all forms of fighting they are treated with great respect. Their naked bodies daubed in ash, their faces painted white and vermilion, they resent any intrusion from outsiders, and woe betide anyone stupid enough to try and photograph them. I managed a short conversation with one of them. As a penance, he had not sat down for six years and supported his stiffened and deformed legs by leaning on a kind of wooden swing. He was most indignant when I told him that an elephant belonging to King Louis XIV did not lie down for the last ten years of its life and had worn two holes in the stone buttress with its tusks, on which it supported itself. I beat a hasty retreat.

There were the usual abominable sights of the poor unfortunate cripples. One was more terrifying and heartrending than anything I had ever seen. It was a young boy—or rather what was left of a young boy—just a small torso supporting a head, twisted and contorted by some hideous disease. He was pushed around in a little cart. On it perched a parrot, which took your money in its beak.

As I re-entered the Haathi Bazaar, I witnessed two extraordinary fights. Both had been caused by theft, and both were not without humour. The first was a clash of titans between two female elephants, staked next to one another. One of the females had stolen the other's sugar cane. She turned quickly on the thief and instead of using her head as a battering ram, she tried in the most ludicrous fashion to bite off the other one's tail. They whirled around trumpeting and squealing in a cloud of dust, looking like squabbling schoolgirls pulling each other's hair. Three or four mahouts, armed with spears, waded in quickly and put an end to this farce.

The second fight was decidedly one-sided until an unusual intervention stopped it. A thief had been caught and was being punished in typical local fashion. His hands had been tied behind his back and his feet bound together. Two hefty men wielding long bamboo sticks proceeded to give him a sound beating on his head and the soles of his feet until he was a crying, bleeding wreck. The women, I noticed, particularly enjoyed this spectacle and joined in enthusiastically kicking the unfortunate man's ribs with sturdy feet, their toes encircled by gold rings, like knuckle-dusters. He would have been killed but for the sudden arrival of a tall, pale, sweating Englishman, a camera slung around his neck, wearing a floppy sun hat. I looked more closely. It was a friend of mine, a travel editor for a glossy London magazine. He waded bravely into the melee holding his hands above his head shouting 'Bas, bas,' the only word he knew in Hindi. When this had no effect, he clasped his hands fervently together as in prayer, fell to his knees and cried 'Por favore, por favore!!' Immediately the beating stopped and the crowd became silent. He called the police, who took the bleeding man away.

There was great excitement in the camp when I returned. Tara's price had gone shooting up, from 70 to 90,000 rupees. This offer had come from a man, Aditya told me, who had a dishonest face and apparently owned a hotel in Delhi. The man had said his elephants were well looked after and simply took tourists for rides once a day. Unfortunately, one of them had been hit by a bus.

1991

ROYINA GREWAL

ALONG THE NARMADA

At Amarkantak I find a pastoral world of superlative beauty, the colours as unreal as tinted postcards. Wide golden meadows parted by the narrow blue stream of the holy river are framed by deep-shadowed sal forests. Red laterite soil contrasts with many shades of green. The overcast sky softens the landscape and flimsy wisps of cloud drape the shoulders of forested hills like gauze scarfs.

A small bridge, little more than a culvert, spans the Narmada. She is here a little stream barely six feet wide, sparkling blue and tumbling gently westwards. A river in her infancy. It seems impossible that the water she will discharge into the sea equals the combined volume of three great northern rivers—the Ravi, the Beas and the Sutlej.

A straggling, uninspiring little town, Amarkantak is not as invaded by exploitative commerce as most other religious places are. Shanty shops crowd narrow lanes, selling religious souvenirs, flowers and temple offerings but without the usual hard sell. Many stalls display piles of stones smoothed out by the Narmada into Shivaling shapes, for it is said that men who worship these will have all their wishes fulfilled.

The chief priest of the Narmada temple at Amarkantak, Govind Prasad Dvivedi, is short and sturdy in body, with soft

ROYINA GREWAL's *Sacred Virgin: Travels Along the Narmada*—from which 'Along the Narmada' is extracted—records her journey in 1993 down the Narmada, one of the world's most ancient rivers, which has been the focus of nationwide controversy for almost two decades now over the issues of dams and displacement. Royina Grewal is also the author of *In Rajasthan*.

contours and a formidable double chin covered with dense gray stubble. His family have cared for the river goddess for three generations. The walls of his home are papered with photographs of visiting dignitaries. 'Even the rich and powerful come to seek benediction at Amarkantak,' he says with pride, 'and I have tended to them all.'

Over cups of sweet strong tea Dvivediji tells me the story of the Narmada's birth. 'There was drought on earth and famine,' he explains, pausing dramatically in what is obviously a well-rehearsed recital. 'The devas appealed to Shiva to relieve the dreadful thirst of the land. Shiva meditated for many days. So powerful was his tapasya that a drop of sweat formed on his forehead and fell to the ground. From it arose a maiden so lovely that the devas were smitten. They pursued her, but in vain, for she always eluded them. Shiva, who was seldom given to amusement, laughed. He named her *Nar-mada*, she who gladdens the hearts of men, and commanded her to flow thenceforth for the joy and salvation of mankind.'

'But there are many other versions of the Narmada's nativity,' I interject, eager to show off my newly acquired knowledge.

'Ah,' counters Dvivediji, smiling at such ignorance, 'the Narmada was recreated seven times after the seven dissolutions of the universe. So each story is naturally somewhat different.'

My favourite 'origin' story ascribes the creation of the Narmada to the desire of Shiva for Parvati. The divine couple were resting from their exertions, having made love for a thousand years. Parvati was asleep. The great god watched her lying next to him, content and dishevelled, and became so aroused by her unguarded beauty that a drop of his semen fell to the ground. And from this, it is said, arose the lovely maiden Narmada, characterized forever thereafter by varying inflexions of sensuousness—her joyous flirtation with rocks, her sinuous and undulating passage through hills, her languor in pools, her voluptuousness in the plains of Gujarat.

The priest accompanies me to the Udgam Kund, the spring-fed tank now considered the source of the Narmada. The sacred river splashes gently in through a cowhead spout at one end and settles into the serene pool. White temples clustered around the tank are mirrored in the still water. Floral offerings float with scum at the edges of the tank and coins gleam in the mud at the bottom, a huge sum in small change. A reminder that most devotees are tribals who subsist at the edge of starvation with a calorie intake far lower than anything considered adequate. Each tiny coin, then, represents a major contribution, a true act of love and sacrifice.

'When the tank is cleaned annually after Shivaratri, it takes two to three days to count the offerings which fill many pots,' says Dvivediji.

While there is no doubt that the Udgam Kund marks the beginning of the river's course to the west, there is some controversy about the actual source of the Narmada. The holiness of the source, after all, guarantees a comfortable income.

I stop for a moment at the Narmada temple, one among many others around the source tank. The shrine is uninspiring but the iconography is distinctive. The goddess is mounted on a *makara*—a crocodile, the vehicle associated with river deities. In her four arms she holds objects that reinforce her essence—a chaplet signifying proclivity to prayer, a water jar symbolizing her aquatic element and her fecundity, a lotus, which represents water, fertility and purity, and a Shivaling, which establishes her devotion to her father, Shiva.

From Dvivediji I also hear the legend of the Narmada's unusual direction. The Narmada and the Son—which also rises at Amarkantak and is one of the few 'male' rivers—were to wed. But the groom succumbed briefly to the flirtations of a rivulet that also rose on the plateau. Furious, the Narmada flounced off to the west. She forswore men thereafter and vowed to remain a virgin. And in her virginity rests her supreme sanctity.

The wayward Son begins life as a spring and a tiny trickle shrouded in dense sal. It magically gathers waters from other inlets and within the space of a few yards becomes a sheet of water that roars over a sheer cliff into massed forest below. A mosaic of red mud, black rock, lambent water and enamel green.

A wizened sadhu, his features swaddled in empty folds of skin, has positioned himself at the source spring. He peers at me through cataract-clouded eyes and speaks of the changing pattern of rural life. 'The old tree gods and forest spirits are no longer really venerated,' he says and hunkers down for what is clearly to be a long chat. 'Villagers now worship mainstream Hindu gods. This has led to a diminishing respect for the forest and an increased cutting of trees.'

His pet peeve is the sacred cow. 'Its worship originated in economic necessity.' He pauses, pulling contemplatively at his marijuana-laced hookah. 'Because it was the primary source of food and provided manure for the fields. Today the cow is no longer central to our lives. But it is typical of Hindu hypocrisy to perpetuate its veneration while inflicting unbelievable cruelty on the poor animal.' Apparently a hot rod is pushed up its anus to extract the last drop of milk. And male calves are starved to death.

I linger to talk but Bahadur is restless and anxious to leave as he has heard that the area is infested with bear. Tribals call them *adamzad*, sons of men. A memory surfaces of an encounter with sloth bear not far from Amarkantak over twenty-five years ago. The bear had obviously feasted on fermented flowers of the mahua tree, and three of them walked abreast and upright on a jungle trail, weaving ever so slightly. In the gathering dusk, the white V on their chests stood out and they resembled men in dark suits and white shirts, reeling home after a heavy evening.

This time I see only droppings but give in to Bahadur's persistent requests and retreat to Kabir Chabutra, a small PWD rest house outside Amarkantak. I had chosen to stay there over the more elaborately equipped circuit house with its laminated ethnic furniture and neon lights.

Kabir Chabutra is, of course, named after the fifteenth-century mystic and poet who preached the essential unity of all religions and of all men. Combining what seemed to him the best tenets of Hinduism and Islam, he taught a doctrine of intense personal devotion and love of God. Kabir is said to have meditated here, resting from his travels preaching in the region. Built in the late nineteenth century, the rest house overlooks consecutive hills smothered by forest. The preoccupations of its builders linger in traces of a typical English garden with dahlias, canas and zinnias in carefully laid out flower beds, each contained in neat whitewashed lines of angled bricks that seek to impose order on the Indian wilderness. The local preference takes over in less disciplined clumps of raat ki rani, harshringar, chandni and gainda.

There is no electricity at Kabir Chabutra and as I fry eggs and canned sausages by torchlight, I think back to days when people like Captain Forsythe, who would have travelled here on horseback, dressed for a solitary dinner in the mandatory black tie. The table would have been properly laid with fine linen, crockery and silver, and the meal would have certainly included a soup, some game, perhaps a brace of partridge and definitely pudding, probably caramel custard.

Clouds of fireflies descend on the garden, blinking coded messages to each other. The forest awakens to the night. Insects chitter. A cheetal barks shrilly. Far away a sambhar bells, certain indication that it has sighted a big cat. Much later that night I wake to the faint sawing of a leopard. Till just a few years ago panthers were regular visitors to the rest house garbage. Ten years ago it was not uncommon to see a tiger even in the town.

But felling pushed the prey species away and the great cats followed. Deforestation has also affected the climate. Temperatures have gone up and more rain now falls on fewer days. Naturally, less water is absorbed and more runs off.

A small dam arrests the Narmada a short distance from the source tank, creating a small lake that ripples gently in the sun. People who have worshipped at the tank happily pedal boats here, dropping empty packets of pan masala into the water. Below it, the stream meanders across the plateau, leaping and splashing and gurgling. I sit for a while beside it, entranced by the magic of the tiny Narmada that I could almost leap across. The water takes on the colour of the sky. A small boulder tosses the river up. She tumbles slowly down. A handful of flung diamonds that catch and splinter the sun.

The forest is green. The laterite soil red. The grass tall and gold. A shining black buffalo grazes contentedly. A butterfly pauses at a patch of wild flowers of the palest mauve. A bird sings with piercing sweetness.

A little further, truck drivers stripped to their underpants vigorously scrub mud-encrusted vehicles in the river. Buffaloes wallow in oily water, turbid now with the run-off from the bauxite and ochre mines on the plateau.

The wind whispers through large plantations of pine. A forest ranger who wears Ray Ban dark glasses and gold studs in his ears proudly informs me that in the seventies the forest department conceived of a grand plan to replicate a Himalayan atmosphere at Amarkantak. Acres of prime sal were cleared and replanted with various species of pine. In fact, a forest research institute was set up to study the different types and select the most appropriate.

'Is it not a wonderful idea?' he says. 'We could have had our own Kashmir here.'

Environmental research now opposes the introduction of

exotic plants and favours the perpetuation of local species. So experiments with pine have ceased.

Sal forest closes in again at the Kapildhara falls at the end of the plateau, eight kilometres from the source tank. The youthful river, reinforced now by innumerable springs, plunges off an eighty-foot black basalt cliff and thunders towards the plains with a fine show of maturity. Leaning over the railing (that protects enthusiastic visitors such as myself) to watch the water crash on to jagged rocks below, my skin crawls at the thought of hundreds, perhaps thousands of people who have hurled themselves off from this spot in acts of religious suicide. For the goddess Narmada was known to have a passion for blood. In her feral aspect she is Manasvardhani, the one who demands to be propitiated with the human flesh she has nurtured.

Human sacrifice to propitiate malevolent divinities was common to many ancient societies. But in these isolated regions of India, the gory ritual persisted much longer than in other parts of the world. Today the values of reformed Hinduism prevail at Amarkantak and the eating of meat, even eggs, is strictly prohibited. Bhairav, the ancient tribal deity now regarded as a manifestation of Shiva, however, is still offered a token of blood, but only every three years, when three drops of blood from the ear of a young goat are offered to the deity. . .

I follow the path across the river to the bottom of the Kapildhara falls and pick my way over slippery rocks behind the curtain of water. The wild young river roars a few feet away. A hut near the falls is home to Swami Balwant Ram Puri. He has a serene face and a gentle manner, but his comments are forceful. 'When Kartivir Arjun tried to arrest the virgin Narmada's flow at Maheshwar with his thousand arms she foiled all his attempts. Mankind should beware of her wrath now. The government thinks it is so clever in trying to dam her but it is going to make human sacrifices by the thousands, because eventually the dams will burst. They say that even the construction is substandard. That the steel and cement are all impure.'

'Swamiji is illiterate,' apologizes a visitor, embarrassed by his outspokenness. But Swami Balwant has the bit between his teeth. 'I am telling you now, the Narmada cannot be dammed. And if the dams are built they will burst.'

The rash moment past, we talk philosophy. He puffs at his bidi, looking thoughtful. 'So many great rishis are giving the world advice. But who listens and who cares? The only concern these days is enjoyment. My advice and my concern is that what you say and what you are should be the same. You should speak from the navel,' he says, patting his stomach as he smiles.

He escorts me out of his hut with courtly dignity. My chappals which I had left at the entrance are missing. They are finally discovered being torn to shreds by a pack of puppies who probably enjoyed the sweat-soaked leather.

'It's very auspiscious,' Puriji exclaims. 'Today is *Shanivar* (Saturday), the day of *Shani* (Mercury). It's a malevolent planet. Now *Shani* is associated with the feet and its vehicle is the jackal or the dog. So the fact that your footwear was taken away by dogs means that its possible effect on you has been countered.'

The auguries are good. Perhaps this trip down the river will finally be accomplished.

Hoppers of bauxite ore rumble overhead, returning me to the present and its problems. The dams are far away but the compulsions of modern India have already begun to initiate change. Bauxite mining is the major commercial activity on the plateau. An entire township has been built for mine workers and the management. Lots of little boxy houses, efficient if uninspired. Conversation with the manager, Hussain, inevitably focuses on deforestation in such a valuable watershed and the damage caused by open cast mining.

'Environment has suddenly become so fashionable,' explodes this tall, gaunt man doing a thankless job away from his wife and family who live in Jabalpur where the children are at school. 'Do environmentalists sitting in air-conditioned offices in Delhi or Bombay really understand ground realities? Do they offer employment to the hundreds of tribals we employ? And more importantly, do they not use the products made from our bauxite? Pressure cookers, for example?'

Somewhat taken aback, I spin out the usual rejoinders about least damaging lifestyles and try to retrieve my position by speaking of the growing awareness of the toxics released from aluminium.

He erupts again. 'How elitist can you get? Do you think the poor tribals or any other villager for that matter can afford steel *bartans*?'

I slink away with more questions than answers.

Later, Hussain accompanies me to the mines. Gaping red pits, rather like bleeding wounds that scar the plateaux. He describes new methods evolved to minimize environmental damage, involving simultaneous replacement of topsoil and replanting.

'But sal, the major species, is difficult to replant and grows largely by natural regeneration,' I venture, still smarting from the earlier encounter.

'Why pick on us?' Hussain counters. 'Our operation is small. Sal regeneration is most affected by overgrazing and more so by sal seed collection by tribals.'

I have no answer to this. The tribals do indeed gather the seeds for extraction plants which make sal butter, a cocoa butter substitute. Not only does the collection impair regeneration but tribals also set fire to the forest floor to make their work easier, destroying shrubs and other ground cover.

More relaxed later, Hussain speaks of tribals who gather medicinal plants that help cure constipation and piles. He swears by the product and sends it to friends all over the country. He is undoubtedly a sufferer.

Spumes of foam rise up in a fine mist from Dhuan Dhar, literally 'falls of smoke', as the Narmada pours tumultuously over a thirty-foot ledge. Rainbows shimmer over the thrashing river. Below the falls white frothing water curls furiously against dark rocks and slides into a deep sapphire pool and a marble gorge.

A sadhu in saffron sits in deep meditation near the falls, his chest wide with the contained breath of yoga. Parties of picnickers wade at the river's edge in the shallows above the falls. Men and women bathe in racing water, surrounded by soap wrappers. One young family poses for a photograph on a rock dangerously close to the cascade. A man with his wife and baby daughter who can't be more than three months old. The man leans over to adjust his daughter's large straw hat so that her little face will not be obscured. Later he tells me, with a strange thrill, 'A young woman, mother of two little children, was swept over the falls from this very spot yesterday.' A few minutes afterwards he shows off to his wife, balancing precariously on the slick rocks; confident, as we all are, that tragedy only befalls others.

Children diving into the roaring water for coins are equally confident, but with more reason. They have grown up with the river and treat her with great respect. Five-year-old Raju, small even for his age, works only in the shallows. He swims underwater in a small pool to find a fifty-paise coin I have thrown in, and emerges spluttering, his little brown hand clenched firmly around the coin which he pops into his mouth.

'How much did you make today?' I ask.

A stream of shining coins pours from his mouth. We squat down to count. He has made just under four rupees.

'It's early yet. By the evening I should have made about ten.'

'And do you always keep it in your mouth?' I ask, thinking of the danger of swallowing and matters of hygiene.

He looks at me pityingly. 'Where else would I keep it?'

Since all he wears are skimpy blue shorts, I see his point.

'I have developed a pocket in my mouth, just like a monkey,' he grins.

Several older boys work the deeper water, going further out only according to age and experience. 'We don't take chances,' says ten-year-old Karan, towelling his hair on a piece of rag. 'We know what the river can do.'

'Do any of you go to school?'

There is an embarrassed silence.

Bharati Lal Sen, a flashily dressed young man in his early twenties, supplies the answer. 'All of them should be in school right now. But they are playing truant. The lure of the river is too strong. I should know. I too stayed away from school often and when I couldn't, I would rush here as soon as classes were over. Eventually I dropped out in the fifth standard. It's not the money, though that is nice too, it's the sheer fun of it.'

Bharati Lal has a camera slung around his neck and had earlier photographed the young family in the middle of the river. He started to dive when he was seven. Over the years he became a very strong swimmer and now he dives right into the falls. One look at the fanged rock, the rolling, humping water and I cannot believe it is possible to jump in and survive.

'It's quite easy really,' he explains. 'All a question of timing. See that boulder just below the falls? When it is covered by the water there are dangerous undercurrents. I have to wait till the water recedes for a split second and then I jump. It's important that the water be boiling in great big globs when I hit it, because the moment the bubbling subsides it will pull me down. The water is eighty feet deep here. I go in for about fifteen feet and then surface and swim into a gully on the side of the river.' My disbelief must be apparent for he adds quickly, 'I'll show you if you wait. Tourists are gathering already. I'll be jumping anyway when there are just a few more. Meanwhile let me take your photograph against the falls. A souvenir. Just thirty-six rupees for four negatives.'

I pose obligingly.

The camera has fascinated Bharati Lal ever since he was a young boy. He followed photographers around between dives, learnt a little, rented a Hot Shot camera and started out. Then he graduated to a hired Zenith, now a Minolta. 'It costs sixty rupees a month but is worth it,' he says, fondling the camera as one would a favourite child.

By this time several young photographers are listening in. Around fifteen fledgling photographers work the Bhera Ghat area but only a couple have their own cameras. 'Photography is fun too,' says one of them, 'we get to meet people and talk to them. Otherwise I'd be carving stone like my father, and that's boring.' Daya Ram Yadav, whose father runs a dairy, chips in, 'If it wasn't for photography I'd be a milkman.' Everyone laughs. 'I'm tenth pass,' he says, 'why would I want to waste my education on cows? Besides, I make good money, about thirty to forty rupees a day, sometimes even a hundred, and I've only been a photographer for two years. My father earns 1,500. And that after a lifetime of hard work.'

Noon approaches. Bharati Lal strips, folding his baggy pants and T-shirt carefully. He makes for the rails overlooking the falls with a swagger. All the little divers follow him worshipfully. Curious tourists gather, whispering in horror. Bharti Lal straddles the railing and studies the water intently. Then he jumps, legs curled up under him. He enters the river with a huge splash that is almost lost in the leaping water. It seems to take an impossibly long time for him to surface and the murmur of the crowd rises to a crescendo. Finally his head appears, bobbing in the water. He swims strongly towards the inlet, buffeted by the current.

'See, I told you it was easy. Just a matter of technique.'

I take a photograph of Bharati Lal, and another of him with his friends and we promise to send each other copies.

It has been a long day and I collapse gratefully into a small forest bungalow near Punasa. One of the advantages of being a woman travelling alone is that accommodation at rest houses along the way is usually available. Food is a problem, so Bahadur collects salty snacks from the bazaar—kachoris, pakoras and chewda. Much the same as we had for lunch.

Early next morning we backtrack upstream into forests that will be submerged by the Indira Sagar dam. There is a strange feeling of familiarity. This is the kind of forest I was brought up to recognize as tiger country, an inimitable mix of teak, bamboo, shrub and tall grass with the earthy smell of damp undergrowth. And the feeling of complete unpredictability. You never know what you will see next, what animal is concealed behind the next bush. A lurking tiger perhaps, deer and antelope, or wild boar rooting in the tall grass. There is the delicious spine-chilling feeling that hidden feline eyes could be watching. Almost unconsciously I scan the shrub, watching for the smallest movement, the twitching of ear or tail, that would betray the presence of a tiger.

A haze of smoke drifts somnolently over Dharikotla as the morning meal is prepared. A small hamlet of twelve families, it lies at the end of a triangular valley enclosed by thickly forested hills. A stream curves through fields of lentils towards the Narmada a few hundred metres away.

'The crop has been good this year,' says Kundla bai, an ageing matriarch with weathered skin and sun-bleached hair, actually not much older than I. 'It is the blessing of Mai. Every monsoon she floods our fields, saturating them with water and covering them with silt. All we do is sow and harvest.'

Now she and others in the village are uncertain about the future and fearful. Their lands and the forests where their animals graze will be submerged in just a few months. And no one seems to care. Not even the [Narmada Bachao] Andolan.

Kundla Bai tells me their lands and houses have been measured and mapped for compensation. I ask to see the valuation papers. 'We did get something,' she says, 'but who knows what's written on the paper? I put it away somewhere.' There is a frantic search in all twelve houses. Eventually she emerges triumphant, waving a little booklet. It turns out to be the bank pass book of the family savings account showing a balance of twenty rupees. Everyone returns to search again. This time a stack of propaganda pamphlets are produced which list the benefits of the dam.

'So many papers,' she sighs. 'What difference can they make to us? None of us can read.' The valuation papers are never found.

Closer to the river, at a temple high above the Narmada a young sadhu clambers up a champa tree to collect flowers for the morning puja. Outside the temple I am terribly impressed to see a solar panel tilted towards the sun. A twelve-volt battery in a box below powers a street lamp. 'It was put in two years ago,' says the pujari who has the thickest lensed spectacles I have ever seen. 'But it doesn't work any more.' Bahadur takes a closer look and discovers the cells are dry. He explains the need to top them up with water. 'I don't know all about that,' the priest grumbles peevishly, peering at the contraption. 'How am I expected to take care of these new-fangled things. The government put it in and the government should take care of it.'

A steep flight of steps leads to a beach of white sand. The river is fast and clear. Leaping and gambolling among rapids, noisy in her sport, carefree and almost girlish. The sun slides off rocks which glisten like molten metal. Black rock, blue water and white sand—a triumvirate of great beauty against a dark green backdrop of forest. The rivulet from Dharikotla joins the Narmada nearby. Maize ripens in the bed of the stream inches thick with silt. A fire burns brightly in front of a hut precariously perched on the hill above. Cows meander up a steep path into the forest to forage. Two men walk slowly by, carrying an inflated truck tube. They are on their way to the rapids where they will spread their net and catch the fish tumbling downstream. They stop from time to time to study the water, taking their time.

Rows of white stones over forty feet above the river in the forest indicate the level of submergence. They remind me of tombstones.

1994

M.J. AKBAR

THE LAND OF SEVEN HUNDRED HILLS

A sizeable proportion of India's population consists of Adivasis (aboriginals) who still live in the jungles. These children of the forest had little contact with urban civilization until various groups of people—timber contractors, missionaries, government functionaries— came looking for them, each with its own motives. Today the tribals have begun to fight back.

Saranda Forest: Our guard of honour is made up of five small blue and yellow birds. They appear just a little after we enter the forest. They are sitting on the road when we near them and then for quite a while they fly in front of our car, hopping back on to the ground when they go too far ahead, and then again flitting through the air ahead of us as we catch up. A peacock, disturbed while pecking for food, looks up, pauses a little, and then walks away with quiet dignity. The dry, brown, crumbling leaves crunch with a loud crackling sound under the wheels, disturbed for the first time perhaps since they have fallen from the sal trees: not much traffic passes this way. The silence is broken by a noisy waterfall. It is getting dry now, with the onset of winter, but in the monsoon the hills echo and re-echo with the song of

M.J. AKBAR has been editor of the magazines *Onlooker* and *Sunday*, and the newspaper *The Telegraph*. He is now the Editor-in-Chief of *The Asian Age*. 'The Land of Seven Hundred Hills' is from *Riot After Riot: Reports on Caste and Communal Violence in India*, a collection of essays that deal with incidents of violence that occurred in various parts of India in the 1980s. M.J. Akbar's other books include *India: The Siege Within*.

tumbling water. The evening sun sparkles through the branches of the tall sal trees. We are in the heart of Asia's biggest sal forest, Saranda, the Land of Seven Hundred Hills, and the protected home of the tribals.

Earlier on in the journey, a tree trunk slung across the road, and then locked to a stump, had stopped us at the edge of the forest, and we had to show our written permission before we were allowed in. *Nature's loveliest poem Is A Tree and Tree Plantation Combines the Goodness Of All Religions*—different ideas merged into single sentences by some poetic bureaucrat and painted on boards for public nourishment. These had become victims of time and lay broken in a corner. The caretaker at the barrier had smiled in relief at the written note from the sahib (he had got word of our imminent arrival, but there was no guarantee like the written word), informed us that he had heard from a truck driver that one kutcha bridge had broken along the way, and wished us luck on our thirty-kilometre trip to the Kholkabad forest bungalow in the centre of seven hundred hills draped with the graceful sal.

Sal is the tree of life, the sustainer. Its seed is medicine and revenue; it cures dysentery, the killer disease; and when converted into fat it is sold to big factories which, among other things, produce Cadbury's chocolates with its help. The sal is the tribal's spirit and culture. When the Government once tried to develop teak plantations in the forest, the tribals protested, and one day, men from about twenty villages gathered and simply devastated every tree in the area where teak had been sown. Broken trunks piled one upon the other in a sudden clearing in the jungle bore testimony to tribal anger and tribal veneration of nature's loveliest poem. The high point of the year for the tribal is the festival of Sarhul in spring, when the sal flowers; the festival must be held before the first touch of rain falls on the flowers and the date is determined by those who understand the sky. This year (1986), the tribal weathermen have determined that Sarhul will be early, before the end of February.

When the administration mounted its last campaign against her, among the things they accused her of was working with the CIA to destabilize India and create a country of the tribals, Kolhanistan. If such indeed are her motives, then Jyotsna has disguised them well. On the walls of her office it might have been reasonable to expect pictures of Jesus Christ and the Pope, in respect of the faith she was born into, or perhaps Queen Elizabeth, in honour of the land which gave her part of her education, and her teenage sustenance. Instead, there are large portraits of V. I. Lenin and Karl Marx.

Perhaps the best thing about her personality is that she is free of the ultimate sin of the reformer—pomposity. She takes her work seriously, not herself. She was born a Syrian Catholic in a small town in Alleppey, Kerala—Kuttanad. 'On the seventh day they baptize you with happiness and joy,' she says with a wry smile that suggests that one's options at that age tend to be somewhat limited. The family was devoted to the Church, and early in her teens she decided to become a celibate and dedicate her life to the service of the poor. 'I would work for the poor, at least as I understood it then.' Instinctively she thought of Bihar; after all, poverty and Bihar have been synonymous for some time. 'We used to learn about Bihar through mission Sundays, when collections would be made; we began to believe that the poor only lived in the north, not Kerala.' A short laugh. 'I was fifteen or sixteen when I decided to join the Notre Dame mission.' She was sent to Britain to be a help to the delegation there. She learnt catering in Northumberland, and then taught in Liverpool. But it was not the poor of England she was going to dedicate her life to. After nine years she came back to Bihar, and started teaching in Patna. This was now 1970.

The mission school was useless, she says; it only concentrated on teaching the children of the elite, who in turn were only interested in learning how to eventually go abroad. She tried to awaken the consciousness of the children by taking them to visit slums, but everyone protested: the children did not want to go there, their parents were shocked, and the school administration angry. The school was happy to let her and four or five friends with similar ideas go. After three months, Jyotsna took leave of absence from the mission and went to live in a tribal village called Sonya near Chakradharpur. She was nervous and afraid, she recalls. But the people accepted her with love. The moment her leave of absence was over she resigned from the mission and continued her individual work. 'I had no longer any fear. I was living with the people.'

Did she turn against the Church? 'Just then I was not taking a position against the Church. The Second Vatican had given hope, and I thought things would change. I had become anti-institution but not yet anti-Church . . . Later I discovered that the Church was itself anti-poor. The students of St. Xavier's Church did not want to disturb the status quo. I lost whatever faith I had in the Church, or in any kind of institution for that matter.'

But not the institution of marriage? I point to the simple gold ring on her finger. 'Oh that! When we were in the Church, we used to wear a silver ring, so I put on a gold one after we left . . . And you know when you go back home to Kerala they feel a woman must wear some ornament. And I am married now. Raj and I had been working together for so long, I felt, why not get married!' The laughter tinkles across the courtyard.

You pays your money and makes your choice. Singbhum derives its name from the Singh Rajas of Porahat who ruled the tribals, says one version, hence the bhumi (land) of Singhs. The second interpretation says Singhbhum is a corruption of Singh Ponga, the main god or spirit of the tribals of the district. The Singh came over from Orissa to rule this neighbouring district through the classical syndrome—tribal jealousies led to division, and anger led to an invitation to the neighbouring feudal who soon took over every village. There are more than fourteen lakh tribals now living in this forest-and-hill-strewn district; not even one-fourth of the more than four-and-a-half-thousand villages have drinking water; and only 218 villages have electricity (thanks to their proximity to mining centres). The only real variation is in the levels of poverty. Get your measuring rod and find who is how far below the line. There are some who still live in the trees. *Birhor* literally means man of the jungle. About a hundred people of this tribe have been settled, thanks to the Tata Steel Rural Development Society, in a small colony about twenty miles from Jamshedpur, but most of them still live in the trees or in rudimentary huts that barely last a rainy season. Life determines what we become most proficient in. They make their huts out of leaves, and their skill is such that if a roof leaks then the man who has made the hut is excommunicated for a month. He must show that he can build a perfect roof of leaves before he is allowed in society again.

The dam on the Koyna river catches the water in a pretty valley tucked in the middle of rising, wooded hills. The sun is just above the curving line of trees on the slope, mellow and tired after a long day's work. The sun—the single source of light—shapes the nature of the day. The moon and the stars and the kerosene lamp provide just enough light for a drink of rice wine, song, dance or a last conversation with a friend before it is time to sleep. As the sunlight thins and the cold breeze picks up, the women, as usual harder working than the men, begin the walk back home with bundles of kundi leaves on their heads, the result of a full day's work. They have been brought here to the middle of the jungle from Manoharpur by the contractor, to pick these large kundi leaves. After the leaves have been dried and the weight of the moisture has evaporated, these leaves will be weighed and the women paid one rupee for every kilogram they have plucked. The money spent on the food they are given is deducted. They have pitched camp on open space beside a running brook; and built huts of leaves.

Public Carrier MPA 6581 is standing there when we reach, ready to take some women back to Manoharpur and perhaps replace them with others for the next day's work. The contractor's name, we learn, is Iqbal Hussein, and these leaves will eventually reach Madras where they will become plates on which food will be served. Who says we are not a secular country: a tribal picks the leaf and is exploited by a Muslim so that a Madrasi Brahmin may eat his vegetarian lunch in pristine purity!

Is one rupee per kilogram (less the money on the food) an average rate? No, even Orissa, not particularly famous for its benevolence towards tribals, has raised the wages for the same work to one-and-a-half rupees per kilogram. Why could not Bihar do it too? Ministers decide these things . . . There are committees. And is it really wise, the man in power tells me, to suddenly raise wages so steeply? Might it not hurt the trade?

Fifty paise may be just a cup of tea in Calcutta or Bombay or Delhi; in the jungle it is a fifty per cent rise in wages. But where is the Government in Bihar to whom the woman plucking the leaves is more important than the contractor?

The Civil Procedure Code does not apply in tribal Singhbhum; it is still governed by the Wilkinson Rules. When the British finally subdued the Kohl tribals' revolt in 1832, the man sent to ensure future peace was Captain Wilkinson, and he guaranteed the tribals that their way of life would be protected, that their systems of independent governance would be retained. So it is still.

The first proper administrator to rule from Chaibasa came, in fact, only in 1850. Lt J.S. Davis, a junior assistant agent to the

Governor General, was given the job. The position gradually grew in importance. The second District Commissioner was Lt. J.C. Haughton, a principal assistant rather than a junior assistant. By the ninth DC it was a Lt. Col who was the chair, and by the twelfth a full Colonel. The Indian Civil Service proper came only with the arrival of the Right Honourable T.H. Renny on 8 November 1887, and the first Indian as late as in 1906 when Hira Lal Sen, a deputy magistrate, was put in charge, followed by Maulvi Saiyed Karam Husein in 1907 and Hira Lal Banerjee in the same year. The first Indian ICS was B.C. Sen who was posted here in 1913. And then we have to wait till 1928 before Rai Bahadur K.C. Sarkar arrives for precisely four months. Babu M.L. Dutta is even less enamoured in 1933, and gets his transfer in just three months. National integration begins with K.V.B. Pillai in 1936, but our man from Madras does no better than our men from Bengal, and is in office for just fourteen weeks. Khan Sahib G.Z. Abdin in 1937 can't take Chaibasa for more than ten days, while Rai Bahadur A.D. Banerjee in 1938 lasts out a full twenty before returning to the charms of Calcutta. N.P. Thandani goes six full months in 1938, but Rai Bahadur Rameshwar Singh restores the average by lasting only twenty-four days in 1939, and G.M. Ray creates some kind of a record by an official tenure of just four days in May 1944. K.N. Singh sees through independence and our first IAS officer turns up in 1952, B.P. Prasad. Mr Prasad stays four years.

Chaibasa, to put it mildly, was not a place where the Indian sahibs of the ICS cared to spend their youth.

The discussion in the background, as I stare at the roll of honour, deals with how to govern tribals. The secret, says one babu, is that one should not show one's face too often, otherwise these illiterate tribals begin to lose their awe of Government. One has to keep them properly afraid. 'Ghar ki Murgi, daal barabar!' he points out—the officer must be the occasional feast of chicken, not the daily daal.

Later, the present DC, a fine example of the IAS, a little cynical about good intentions, but with reasonable commitment to liberalism and progress, describes the rationale of the Wilkinson Rules and the psyche of the tribal. 'When a child cries, and its mother does not hear, it will cry louder and louder until its mother responds. The tribal will not cry. He will keep his resentment pent up until one day it bursts.'

One small story:

The dispute between the workers and the management of the mine began, ironically, over the distribution of sweets. But all that is unimportant. We will limit our story to what Deepak Varma, the District Superintendent of Police of Kiriburu, did to teach some 'errant' tribals a 'lesson.' He whipped them in public and then dragged them on the streets after tying them to the back of a police jeep.

All right, another story:

Ganga Ram Kalundia was given a medal for bravery by the President of India for his services in the army. Upon his retirement he involved himself in work among his people, and became a leader of the resistance to the dam over the river Kharkai which is part of the Rs 350-crore Subarnarekha Project. In the early hours of 4 April 1982 the police knocked on Kalundia's door; he tried to escape; the police fired, a bullet hit his leg; the police bundled him up and threw him into the van, destroyed and looted his house. On the way, near the village Soso, they bayoneted Kalundia to death in the van.

The first thing you see upon entering Chaibasa is a dramatic advertisement for *Jaan Ki Baazi,* showing at the Jain Movie Palace. (You would never suspect it, but the Jain family of Chaibasa is one of the biggest taxpayers in the country.) This is Tuesday, the day of the haat (market) and the city is alive with the din of commerce. Tribal women have brought sacks of rice, the men wood and woodcraft. This is their Sunday, and they are in their Sunday-best: the hair oiled and the one sari or dhoti in their possession freshly washed. Down the road from the market is the stadium of the Singbhum Sports Association. On the 21st, says an announcement, the semi-final match between the Damoria Block and the Khunitpani Block will take place; tickets, 50 paise. Almost five years back, in March 1981, Narayan Jonko, Ashiwini Sammaiya and Christ Anand Topno held a public meeting at this stadium at which they demanded a separate country for the tribals, the State of Kolhanistan. Some of the promises made were fascinating; the proposed University of Kolhanistan, it was said, would be directly affiliated to Oxford (Topno and Jonko had just come back from a visit to England and Geneva where they had appealed for help from the UN and the Commonwealth Conference). Nobody took them very seriously to begin with, neither Delhi which had issued them passports, nor Patna. There were a few scattered reports in the papers. But then suddenly one day the Government awoke. Topno and Sammaiya were arrested; Jonko was discovered to have gone underground.

The cry was an exaggeration of a child long denied a mother's attention, and it did not achieve more than passing impact. Jonko was the brain, and perhaps he was partly sponsored by those who would like to see a fragmented India. But the Topnos and Sammaiyas were manifestations of a long frustration, men fuelled by anger rather than mischief. Of course everyone dipped their hands into the current to see what flotsam would come their way. The mine-owners and the moneylenders who had robbed tribals turned every protest movement into a CIA den; the political parties turned it into electoral games. But there was a residual benefit too. Suddenly there was recognition that some glint of development had to be taken to this bhumi. A simple decision like the mobile Government shop can mean an enormous amount. Kerosene is sold by the mobile shop at Rs 2.30 per litre; the local shopkeeper charges Rs 5 or more in the interior. (Since there is no possibility of proper weights and measures, the soft drink bottle, with its measured capacity, comes in very handy.) The anger has provoked a trickle of change. And when you have not ever seen the miracle of clean water, the tubewell can be a wondrous sight.

One leg. A beautifully clean, cylindrical body, lean and straight. A neck which is a rod. On its head a metal walking stick, curved at the top and curved at the tail. This is the Goddess of Water. The tubewell. If gods and goddesses are symbols of need and fulfillment, fear and its containment, then perhaps the new deity of the tribals should be the tubewell. Wherever it has reached, its impact has been stunning. It is now the difference between the lifestyles of two villages. Kholkabad, the village at the foot of the hill on which is our bungalow, does not have a tubewell yet, but Gope, our guide, is confident that a sanction will come soon. That is his ambition before he retires as chowkidar of the bungalow in three years; to persuade the big sahibs who come to stay there to grant a tubewell to the village at their feet.

They make the stars differently in Saranda forest: in such thick and bright clusters that you feel that they might spill out of the sky at any moment. There is no moon that night as we walk down to the village, and the pool of shifting light formed by the torch seems an intrusion. We move towards the sound of the drum. A forest officer is with us, and doing all the talking. 'Want to see a dance?' he asks, hardly hiding the leer. Then adds regretfully, 'Hum log ka Ranchi main hiyan say jyada advanced naach hota hai.' What he means is that the women in the tribal villages around Ranchi show more of their breasts than here. I ask him if he could organize the sleeping arrangements back in the bungalow; he goes back looking very busy and useful.

When the sun was rising
And the moon was large and beautiful in the sky
At such a wondrous moment were you born...

There is great fun in their singing and dancing. The young people hold hands behind their backs, linking with one another in an affectionate, strong chain that goes back to the beginnings of their existence. Rice wine, warm and heavy and languorous, is being passed around. The presence of our guide, Gope, helps ease the tension which strangers bring to a family gathering. With some hesitation and then excitement we are offered the rice brew, the handiya. A lantern is placed beside me on a wood log. A woman comes and sits down a little beyond the lantern: the light falls on her face and on the faces of her young children, the flame swaying slightly and forming patterns on the five faces: it is one of the most exquisite compositions I have ever seen. An old woman brings another leaf-cup of handiya, and teases, a little high herself, 'You should have come twenty years ago when I could have held you in my arms.' Gope translates and laughs. The banter is warm and wonderful; it is the ease of a confident culture that will always be outside the understanding of those who confuse 'advanced' learning with happiness.

I did not see you in the village
I did not see you in the market
Should we go ahead and fall in love, stranger?

The young man with the flute joins us. He has been standing outside the line of young dancers. 'No, no, he cannot join them,' Gope says: he is from another village, and if they ever hear that he has joined the dance here, it will be difficult for him to get married in his own village. We move away, and in the darkness meet a second group of young people. Just outside the line is a man with a transistor, tipsy and jovial. 'Jugri is drunk,' Gope hears from his friend. Jugri sees us and shows off the transistor

radio that he is holding and trying to tune (the batteries have
clearly run out). 'This is a tape,' he suddenly shouts. 'I am going
to tape this song.' Everyone laughs. 'Look at Jugri; he says he is
going to tape!' Jugri is teasing us—men from the world of the
tape recorder. He shouts again: 'Disco!' He looks slyly at us
amid the renewed laughter. Then he runs into the dancers and
begins flirting outrageously with one of the girls. His wife is on
the other side of the dancing line. She steps out, takes firm hold
of Jugri and walks off. 'That is the end of Jugri's adventures for
the night,' Gope laughs.

The beauty only adds to the pain: that there should be poverty in
the core of so much that is so gloriously beautiful, the sky, the
forest, the land, the laughter, the heart, the sharing, the
openness. Everything becomes the victim of hunger and disease.
The mother pointed proudly to her daughter, about six years
old, and said, 'Today she had medicine!' Doctors from Tata
Steel had come that day on one of their periodic missions and
checked everyone; and that medicine was like a feast, a sudden
opening of the heavens; it was not something that the mother
could ever take as her right from a modern society. *There is no
real conflict between the human being and wildlife in their
claims to the environment,'* one of the rusted boards had said at
the gates of the forest, this time quoting Mrs Indira Gandhi. Yes,
but the vicious conflict was surely between the co-aims of man
and man. What was the difference between man and animal?
That man could laugh? Or that man could be both poor and
rich, while every animal was equally rich or equally poor. Or
should the analogy be different? Was it a conceit to call animals
by different names and treat man as a single species? Was it not
more accurate to admit that there were the same differences in
the human race too; that some were the vegetarian, huge
brahminical elephants, jovial and learned, the laddoo in their
palm, extremely equable when given their demanded place, and

violent and roguish when angry; that some were lions among men, who had usurped, with their acquired might, the resources of the environment, who ate the flesh of others and proudly called themselves warriors and Singhs; that there were yet other men who were poisonous snakes, hissing their way through life, injecting the spittle of poison in communities, spreading lies and propaganda and their gospel of hate. And a caste of jackals, and then castes of the oppressed and the forgotten, denied by history and destiny their right to live as equals and as human beings, kicked, killed, smashed or simply spat upon, taunted and derided by the aggressors at the top . . .

Too much philosophy? Perhaps. But maybe one should be pardoned for a journey into thought when one reaches a forest where they make the stars differently.

1986

ANEES JUNG

GODS AND GOD

To seek knowledge men and women should travel and explore, said the Prophet. They were partners in life, in war, in a home. My father in his own way pushed the ideal. Stand on your feet, do not stretch out your hand in front of a man, work with men but do not forget that your strength is your own, that of a woman. He trained me to live in a world of men like a woman. You don't look like a Muslim woman, people say. My religion has no face, I tell them, and move on. Faith is an energy, which along with other forces, lends a dimension to my life. It is not as integral to my life, though, as it is to most women around me.

I travel to Bidar, the stronghold of Muslims who, I am told, continue to live as they did in Bedouin times. Driving three hours from Hyderabad is like driving back across three centuries. I go to meet Jalaluddin Changezi, keeper of the Muslim faith that he has ringed around with dogma in the manner of the massive fort walls that hem in the town. He shuffles out of the shadows, holding in his hand a hurricane lantern that sheds light, vaguely revealing his face and form. It is unmistakably one of a man of religion—saffron robes, a long reverent beard, kind eyes. What brings a Muslim woman without a veil to him? 'A search,' I tell him, as he looks away unconvinced. Women from long distances, hidden behind veils, come on Sundays to hear him preach. He brings to them the

ANEES JUNG was editor of the magazine *Youth Times*, and has written for several Indian and foreign newspapers. 'Gods and God' is an extract from her best-known book, *Unveiling India: A Woman's Journey*. Her other books include *Night of the New Moon* and *Peace in Winter Gardens*.

word of God and tells them how to be a dutiful wife, a good mother, a good neighbour.

'Times have changed but the written word has not,' he begins, in the manner of an oration. 'Look around you. There is more greed, more want. Man struggles shamelessly to fulfil these wants, though his needs are few. He can meet them with what he honestly earns. If he can fulfil his wants with ten rupees why does he want to earn fifty? Why does he seek from a wife a dowry that his religion prohibits? What did the Prophet give his daughter when he married her? A wooden bowl, twelve small clay bowls to serve guests, a camel skin, a pillow of grass and a chakki to grind the grain. God grants the children and provides the bread to feed them. No one can interfere with the will of God. Interference accelerates the degradation of man. And of woman. Today you see women walking down streets with their heads bare, their faces revealed. A woman's place is not in the street but in the home. She is made different from man. If a man stays at home he loses his vitality. A woman does not. She is like a diamond. If you have something precious you don't wear it on your cap and show off. You preserve it, guard it. And if you have a wound you don't expose it. You bandage it, look after it, hide it. That is the way a woman is. In the Koran she is described as a *fitna*, one who tempts man and brings trouble. She should stay where she belongs, within the walls of her home.'

But haven't times changed? Does woman not need to step out, see and understand the complexities that are now part of a world in which she too lives? Isn't this the world in which she makes a home, raises a family, makes friends? If this world has begun to surround others will it also not impinge on her? 'Yes, the world has changed. But the word of God has not,' repeats the reverent old man. His voice is friendly but noncommittal. The essence of his teaching is solely religious, based on the precepts of a book that, according to him, is changeless. Though he lives in a time that has changed, he continues to live outside it. The large white house, seemingly sturdy in the shadows, is the root of his world. He was born in it, has aged in it and will probably die in it. Like his forefathers. But the veiled women who come to him on Sundays have begun to live in houses whose walls have begun to crumble. Their courtyards have shrunk. Their children have been pushed to play in streets that have other sounds. The words of God though continue to be recited in the madrasas of every mohalla in Bidar. The Koran was first spoken, not written. When recited from memory it had power; it conveyed not just the meaning but the vital energy of the person reciting it. The speaker's personality and his tone altered the meaning of the text. Today, when it is read, not recited from memory, the text is less alive, more literal.

For maulvi Karamatullah neither the tone has changed nor the meaning. He kept alive the word of God in madrasa Mahmud Gawan, built 500 years ago, until he was driven out by the archaeological department which was more keen to preserve the monument than the word of God. Gathering his brood the respected teacher retreated into a tin shed that became one of the twenty-five madrasas donated by the city to the community. On its paint-peeled wall hangs a tarnished frame that encloses an image of Kaaba, the holy shrine in Mecca. In a corner amid a cluster of worn-out sandals and shoes rests a well-used earthen pot that cools water for the thirsty young. Young boys wearing round, white caps on their heads squat on the mat-covered ground and chant the Koran in small, shrill voices. Young women, their heads draped, crowd the other half of the room. Their eyes move from right to left over the ornate Arabic script that flows into their lives like an eternal poem whose beginning they have yet to fathom. The maulvi's pride in this class of hundred is a young girl who is blind. Conscientiously she chants the holy verse in the manner of a divine performer. Like the other girls she too comes to the madrasa in a curtained rickshaw. But she is blind, I tell myself. 'But the world is not,' says the maulvi, as if he has read my thoughts. For she has the body of a woman. And like a diamond, or a wound, she should be hidden, not exposed, as said Jalaluddin Changezi in the light of the half moon.

At the edge of Golasangi village in Bijapur, an ancestral kingdom of the Bahmanis, the women continue to hide themselves as if they were diamonds. Ragged in discoloured saris, they are gathered in the bare veranda of a stone house, one that belongs to the most important Muslim family in the area. They are the former jagirdars to whom the village was gifted by the Mughal Emperor. The jagir entitled the family to land, money and privilege, isolating them from the life of the village. The jagir was sold a long time ago but the aura it once bestowed on the recipients continues to cling. In the small stone houses that tumble into each other live the descendants of the feudal overlords—six greying brothers and their wives with forty children and relatives. No man is allowed beyond the door on which hangs a burlap curtain.

'The women of our household observe strict purdah. None of them has stepped out of this house, not even to vote,' says the eldest brother as if he is recording a feat. I feel I have achieved another by taking my photographer in, the first man and outsider to enter these guarded premises in a hundred years. Our entrance does not stir the women out of their entranced condition. With heads draped and bodies garbed they move in a monotonous rhythm, reciting verses in praise of a saint whose tales of miracles have acquired the sanctity attached to the word of God. An elderly woman takes me aside and tells me a tale of the saint's miracle as if it has happened in her lifetime. 'We may not go out of our houses but we are educated women,' she says, in the manner of an assertion. 'We can read the Koran and the *hadith*, understand Arabic and Persian. Everything that needs to be known is in these books.' She withdraws when she realizes that I am a Muslim who does not swear by the Book. 'Who is the man with you,' she asks, looking suspiciously at the photographer. 'He is my brother,' I lie, putting her mind at rest.

'Do you go around without a veil?' she questions.

'Purdah is a state of mind', I tell her, repeating my father's words.

In Islam, the veil is not just meant to hide a face but cover a woman's body in a modest fashion—leaving the face, the hands and feet exposed. 'The Book,' I tell her, 'allows a man to see a woman's face before he marries her. Even the Prophet saw Khadija and, later, Ayesha, whom he married. Does the woman cover her face when she goes on the Haj pilgrimage?'

She stares and says nothing.

I then pull out of my bag a copy of the Koran and read out to her a verse that pertains to purdah. 'The rule of modesty applies both to men and women. A brazen stare by a man at a woman is a breach of refinement. Where sex is concerned, modesty is not only good form, it is not for the good of the weaker sex but also to guard the spiritual good of the stronger sex. The need for modesty is the same both in men and women.' That is in English.

The word of God is in Arabic, she says, in the manner of a dismissal. 'Why were girls buried among the Arabs?' she asks.

'Because of dire poverty, because of their inability to earn, because there was compulsion to sell them as slaves and because they could not be married,' I tell her. At a time when women were treated as chattel, the Prophet endorsed the view that women should seek knowledge, go with their men to war and help nurse the sick and the wounded.

The woman listens and looks blank.

'Why so many children?' I ask, as a trail of unkempt, unwashed children circles me.

'Can anyone stop nature? It is God who gives and God who takes. To tamper with one's body is against the word of God,' says the woman.

Why then did she pierce her nose, her ears, and have her sons circumcised? Did that not amount to tampering with the body?

'But sterilization is another matter,' she rejoins. 'It amounts to killing life.'

'Azal, or *coitus interuptus*, was practised even in the days of the Prophet, and at a time when the Koran was being revealed to him,' I tell her. 'The Prophet and his four Caliphs advocated *azal*. Nine hundred years ago Imam Gazali preached that *azal* was good for the health and beauty of a wife, for safeguarding children and the slave girl from getting pregnant. The Prophet blessed a family with children only when they were not a burden on the parents. If a man recognizes his inability to support his children and decides not to have them, he is doing the right thing, according to Islam. After your prayers, go and look for a job, a way to live. Work according to your ability. Only then does God bless you, said the Prophet.'

'Our times have changed,' say the greying brothers. 'What work can we do in a place where we once ruled?' It is time for me to withdraw. I leave them clustered behind the burlap curtain of their house, cloister kept intact by the inspiration of a Holy Book. Wrapped in a heavy velvet cover, that has lost its colour and texture with time, the Book embodies a God who for this family is changeless in a changing world. Within this ghetto they live trapped by God, not inspired by Him.

The pattern repeats itself. The great traditions of religion that thrive across the land appear to have closed their doors to the free movement of gods. I seek out Bhalchander shastri in a dark, forgotten building behind the main bazaar of Dharwar. Guardian of an ancient lore, he has been teaching the shastras in this Sanskrit *pathshala* that prides itself on having kept alive a tradition for more than a hundred years. Women do not come to him to seek knowledge. The learning of the shastras is confined to men. When I ask him why women are barred from his school, he looks away, seeking a distant focus.

'A woman does not have the necessary detachment to commit herself to a goal, a discipline or a journey. She is blessed to bear life, to nurture and sustain it whatever its form or shape; be it good, evil or indifferent. She cannot renounce that life. A man can separate himself from the world. That is his nature. That does not make him superior to a woman. Each has its nature. Each is important. Young men who have divorced themselves from the world come here to live and learn, to look upward; not to die into life but afterlife.'

His voice is friendly but impassive, reminiscent of the old maulvi in Bidar contained and secluded by his own faith. They speak different languages but project a sensibility that has decided not to bare itself. Unlike the maulvi, the shastri seems to be a man who has reflected on the nature of experience, though his lifestyle has not varied much in forty years. The shastri, a tall, trim man, has walked one way, a kilometre each day, from his home to the school and back. He has not seen a modern university nor felt the need to read a newspaper, listen to a radio. The building where he spends his days wears a deserted look: one of majestic quiet, almost impenetrable. The pace inside is unhurried. A dark wooden staircase leads one up the school's tiered heights—a level for astronomy, a level for logic, a level for poetry and the roof, open to the heavens, for meditation. This is the world of Bhalchander shastri, one that has contained him and given him his peace.

'I do not have enough time to understand what is in front of me. Why should I clutter my life with things that only confuse and distract?' His voice is calm, his manner unperturbed. Keeping out the world, it seems, is the price of his serenity. The shastri, I learn, is a married man.

What is his ideal of a family?

'One in which a man lives a life of dharma, a woman is a good housekeeper and the children are pious,' he propounds. 'The first son is *dharmaputra*, the one who keeps the family line. The rest are born out of lust. It is essential to have a daughter in the family. It is she who perpetuates it. If there is no son, a daughter has the right to perform the last rites of the parents.'

Who is more important of the two?

'In a train, is the guard more important than the driver?' asks the learned man.

Do the shastras endorse a planned family?

'All life is sacred. At no point should life be tampered with,' he pronounces gently. 'Life enters the foetus during the seventh month. Until then it is a body waiting for life. If you kill the foetus you are destroying the house in which life would have dwelt. That amounts to violence. After the seventh month it is a total manifestation of life. It starts from the cloud in the sky. It then rains on earth and a flower blooms. Its seeds become the grains which man eats. There is life in every grain that in turn nourishes the semen, the life force. At no stage is there no life.'

The words of the shastri return to me in a field of mustard where I meet a ploughman joyous in song:

> With a pure heart a peasant sweats
> the drops fall on earth
> the rain clouds burst
> the land turns green
> the flower blooms
> the grain ripens
> I knead my bread
> that gives me life

What the teacher preaches, the peasant sings. The teacher's god evolves out of books. The peasant's god is everywhere—in land, in cloud, in rain, in sun, flower and grain. His is a daily worship that stems from the earth, is groomed by the seasons.

For a sanyasi who lives by the river, God lies in renunciation. In a sanctum on a hill, where he has raised his own temple, he lives divorced from a family, friends, attachments. A sadhu does not get attached to anything. When asked about the place where he was born he looks away, says nothing. For twenty-five years he has lived on fruit. He will not allow anyone

to cook for him lest he gets attached to their service. 'Like the
lotus that has its roots in water and yet remains above water, a
sadhu remains detached from life, is in life but is not immersed
in it.' The words of the Dharwar shastri return and reinforce
man's ability for renunciation.

I meet women, on a desolate hill in Palitana, who too have
renounced a home, a family, a past. They are sadhvis of the Jain
faith. Their dress is white, their heads bald, each hair has been
plucked out meticulously. All that they own, they carry in their
two hands—a walking stick and a red lacquered pot, in which
they receive the food they beg for daily. During the day they
move like the wind. As the sun sets they withdraw into ashrams
that have no light—wisps of white crouched in darkness, some
in silence, some in song. They call me in, question me about my
home, my city. Night permeates their life. Their eyes, though,
betray a buoyancy which one associates with other women,
with caring, with love. Though detached, these women, it
seems, have not shut themselves out from a world where there is
light and colour, where journeys have goals. A Jain sadhvi's
journey is like water. If it stops, it stagnates. In its movement lies
its essence.

1987

SARAYU AHUJA

THE KOYAL AND THE GUAVA

The stewardess welcomed us aboard the Jet Airways flight to Madras, her English corrugated by a Tamil accent. A fifty-plus woman sat next to me on the aisle seat. Her greying hair was well-oiled, tied into a knot at the nape of her neck. Chandan dotted her forehead, an ashline underlined the dried blob. Two diamond studs shone on the sides of her nose like clots of mercury. Her silk sari was wood-coloured; she smelled of sandalwood and incense. She rummaged through her handbag. She fished out a framed photograph of Murugan, the popular peacock-loving childgod of the South. She made pious gestures to him, touched the photograph to each eye, *touch, touch*, dunked it into her handbag. She shut her eyes, waited for the seatbelt sign to be switched off.

When it was, there was a slight commotion. A number of people rushed towards the back of the plane. The old woman turned, asked the passenger behind her what it was about. '*Aiyoo, ma*, it's that Rajnikant,' she told me in a conversational way, 'that South Indian film villain. Also Prabhudeva and Nagma, that north-Indian actress. Now she acts in South Indian films also.'

I studied her as she put on her spectacles, unfolded the newspaper. She was the prototype of an elderly South Indian woman: conservative, inquiring, knowledgeable, disapproving and terribly sharp.

SARAYU AHUJA trained as an architect and planner at Madras and Tokyo universities. She is the editor of *Indian Architect and Builder*, and is the author of *Where the Streets Lead*.

When the crowd dissipated I got a glimpse of the three thespians: Rajnikant, dark-skinned, beady-eyed, in a flaming orange silk kurta worn over a pair of jeans. In the seat in front of him was Nagma, a voluptuous woman in a short, red dress with long leather boots. On another seat, in a denim shirt and jacket was Prabhudeva, the dancing sensation, the liquid-bodied marvel—the South's own Michael Jackson. It was rumoured that Jackson had invited Prabhudeva to perform with him in the US.

The air-hostess deposited two breakfast trays on the tables in front of the old woman and me. The hostess was South Indian; she was dressed in a tight navy blue skirt, a printed silk blouse, dark nylon tights. The old woman surveyed me and my clothes from under her spectacles. 'Nice sari, *ma*,' she said appreciatively. 'They used to wear nice saris before, *ma*,' she said pointing to the hostess as she moved away. 'Now they wear these horrible skirts,' she said. 'Salwar-kamiz, *oo-oo* okay. It covers the whole body. If you ask me, *ma*, it's better than a sari. Also so convenient. Many South Indians are wearing salwar-kamiz now. But, I am telling you, nothing like our South Indian sari, *ma*.'

She peeled the aluminium foil off from the hot dish of idli and sambar. Took short sniffs at the newly liberated steam from the dish. She distrustfully jabbed the fork into an idli, ate a small piece, made a face. 'Very sticky,' she complained. 'Don't touch the idlis, *ma*, they're not fermented properly. You'll get a stomach-ache.' She was wheat-skinned, kohl-eyed, frail and wiry; her lush eyebrows, a startling ink-black, curved like crow-wings.

She turned back to look at the actress. She click-clicked with her tongue. 'See, that Nagma behind,' she said turning back, 'such a short skirt she's wearing. Muruga-Muruga, from here also her thighs can be seen. *Aiyoo*. These north-Indian actresses and these airlines are spoiling our girls, *ma*.'

She shook her head. 'Job, job, that's all. Our girls are now only interested in their jobs. They will wear anything, say anything, do anything because of jobs,' she said. 'But it's not even easy to get jobs today. Now young people from good-good families like ours join films. They join TV, modelling to make quick money. So many films now, *ma*. In our time, very few, only religious films. People would love to see their hero singing to Krishna, Vishnu, and the gods singing back. What heavenly music, *ma*. Now villains are heroes. Now villains are singing, *ma*. That Rajnikant,' she pointed to the back row, 'he acted in many films as a villain, now he is a hero, *ma*, and people think he's such a noble fellow. So much violence, so much sex, *shi*, this is what these young people want to see today.'

She started to read the paper again. I picked up the latest magazine from the front pouch. An interesting report caught my attention: the younger Japanese were fed up of serious Samurai films or the aesthetic ones like those of Kurosawa. The young Japanese liked South Indian films, because they were so funny and fantastic; because they were about family values and dreams coming true.

The old woman touched my arm. Smiling gently she said, 'You remind me of Radha, *ma*. My daughter in Chicago, you look just like her. About your age, she is.' She asked me my name, I told her.

'You are Tamil?' she asked. I smiled, nodded. 'You speak Tamil?' She asked me the question as though to test me.

I replied in Tamil.

'*Aiyoo*. You speak like a Brahmin,' she said with a pat on my arm, 'a *papati*, are you?'

'Yes,' I said. My mother had told me that the Shudras called the Brahmin *Parpannan*, the Brahmin woman, *papati*. 'Yes, I'm a *papati*.'

'I am also,' she said. With clucking sounds she added, 'What this world is coming to, *ma*, Muruga-Muruga, now these Shudras are telling us not to call them Shudras, that we must call them Dravidians.

'My God, I tell you, Madras has changed so much, *ma*. Not at all like the old Madras. But—but, you know what is the biggest change here?' Her eyes turned big and rough: 'people are believing even more in religion now, I say.'

I remarked that people in the South were always very religious.

'No, *ma*, no. Not at all like that, *ma*. You don't know,' she said removing her glasses and rubbing the sweat that collected on the top of her nose. 'In 1967, people were against religion. Because of Periyar and his speeches. His real name was something else. The Dravidians called him Periyar, the great prophet. Periyar made fun of the Brahmins, *ma*,' the old woman said screwing her nose, 'he ridiculed Hindu gods. He talked and talked about *this* society and *that* society, *this* science and *that* science. He said they would solve all problems. What solve? He said the North Indians with fair-fair skin were very bad; they looked down upon the dark-dark people of the South. Such rubbish he talked. That Periyar, he ate like a pig. Do you know he even ate beef? Muruga-Muruga! He was not even properly educated. He wrote in the newspapers that why should South Indians suffer because of the Aryans from the north? He blames us Brahmins. He called us Aryans because of our fair skins. Periyar even burned Rama's effigy on the Marina beach to prove that Rama's victory and capture of Sri Laṇka was an Aryan control of the South.'

'But if you go to Mylapore—' the old woman said leaning towards me, 'the strict Brahmins live there, I also live there— they will tell you that Periyar was thrown out of the Congress party. Like that,' she waved her arm across, 'because he robbed some funds, *ma*. Muruga-Muruga, see all the things he preached, *ma*, what happened to all that, no? Also not belief in God and all!'

She was quiet for a minute. 'But, what I'm thinking, *ma*, is that all this belief in God is also to do with jobs only. In the end, I think,' she said, her hands clenched below her chin, 'everything has only to do with jobs. Communal. Tension. Rioting-fighting. Crime. Violence. Sex-sex. Why? Because of jobs only. If good jobs were there, tell me, would it be like this? No. So many people went to the Middle East for jobs, my son also went. They were not against Muslim religion or Muslim countries, ye? They simply went there to earn more money.'

She dusted idli bits from her sari. She sighed; it was an elongated hiss. 'You must come to my home, *ma*, in Mylapore.' She looked into her bag for a piece of paper, wrote down her phone number on it. 'You will come?' she asked touching my arm.

I looked at the slip of paper she gave me, she had put down her name on it: Meenakshi Balakrishnan. 'Yes,' I promised.

She retrieved a variety of framed gods from her bag, bestowed pious gestures equally upon each of them, mumbled nervously.

I looked up at the airshaft ejaculating cool, antiseptic jets into the plane-body. A few minutes later, the old woman was fast asleep. I looked at her, eyes tightly shut, a crease on her brow. I smiled; she reminded me of my mother.

Meenakshi transported me to those post-acne-ravaged pubescent, reflective years I spent in Madras, when I mused over the light in the mornings which seemed to roll off the back of the clouds and ignite the water drops on the leaves. The wafer air and sky over the city as I remember it carried a muted echo of both religious space and spirit broken only by the pneumatic honk-honks of the milkman on his cycle at dawn or, in older areas, the moo-moos of cows. Also heard was the swish-swish of the broom on the cemented floors outside houses as non-Brahmin servant maids with round-round *pottus* sprinkled water, swept the floors, drew large flour diagrams on them. Breakfast odours of soured ricebatter filled the air. The chanting had begun in nearby temples; and I could hear the sounds of prayer bells in every other house.

I left Madras in 1975 to study in Japan. When I revisited it almost a decade later, it was the same: vacuous as a long afternoon. Cities grew through successive superimpositions, but Madras remained untransformed. It chug-chugged, with its fierce dependence on religion, astrology, arranged marriages, the love for silk saris and music and dance. Madras ambled on, inside houses, behind closed doors demarcating clearly the public and the private realms. Within their cocoons of privacy people lived with a vision of a nice, happy, pious family life.

Almost a decade later, on this trip to Madras, as I drove from the airport to my old house, I noticed many changes in the city. Roads and plots were dug up for new buildings. Large hoardings announced new products and politicians. Old Heritage buildings were replaced by modern glass towers. There were more hotels, shops, restaurants, boutiques and beauty saloons. There was No Prohibition in Madras: there were more wine shops. Working women wore salwar-kamizes. People were not averse to speaking Hindi; Hindi films were popular. Hindi film actresses in large numbers acted in Tamil films. Tamil film actresses were slender and tall—not as buxom as before, they now resembled the Hindi actresses. Tamil films were remade in Hindi.

Later in the day I drove to an older, poorer part of Madras to meet Vidyakar. People on the streets were generally neat but poorly dressed. Young women were either plain and dishevelled or brightly made up, their pancake make-up forming a shore-sea boundary under their chin. Corpulent men with bandit moustaches, in dark T-shirts several sizes small, strolled down the road, flashy handkerchiefs tied around their necks. This part of the city appeared as though it had its own terminal keyboard: one touch of the key would burst the hot tarry bubble of city-evil, spread it like gas, rapidly. In the evening backwash of sunlight I suddenly felt a nervous apprehension.

Vidyakar was a social worker. He had founded a centre,

Udavam Karangal—Helping Hands. I waited in a small office room. Time had a different count here. Tiredness had a different shape here. Patience extended languidly like a long yawn. On the wall were posters asking for contributions, particularly of rice and baby food. Then (with cynical humour perhaps) they stated that anything at all would be accepted.

Several minutes later one of the workers led me to another room. As I waited, Vidyakar came out of a bathroom. His body was damp, and his hair and moustache wet. He had just bathed. He was wearing a black singlet and a green lungi.

Vidyakar told me he was from Karnataka, but educated in Madras. He studied sociology and law. 'Let me tell you how it started,' he said about his present occupation. 'One day, you see, a baby of eleven months was left, totally abandoned, in a theatre. It was a night show. Then a cycle-rickshaw man, he brought the baby to me. I didn't know what to do, so I took it to an orphanage. They said, no, they wouldn't take it. What to do? So I decided to keep the child. What I did was take up another hut in the slum. The child was lonely, you see, so I got more children to live with me. All abandoned. Then I went, door to door, door to door, shop to shop for food and money. This centre is now fifteen years old. Over the years, I have picked up babies from—where? From garbage dumps, railway compartment toilets, manholes and even from my own doorstep.'

Vidyakar also helped destitute women who wandered about the streets, homeless, without family. 'One day I got a call from a psychiatrist,' Vidyakar said. 'He said that a mentally deranged woman had given birth to a child on the street. That was five days before the call.'

By the time Vidyakar found her the baby had died. And the woman had been raped, shortly before the call from the psychiatrist. She was with the Centre now. 'HIV positive, she is, tch tch,' Vidyakar said. He closed his eyes for a full minute. He seemed tired—exhausted and in despair.

'I had taken a mentally retarded thirteen-year-old girl to the hospital. She was six months pregnant, you see. How could she look after the baby? So we took the baby to the Centre and sent the girl back to her home. Her family threw her out one night. Again she became pregnant. I am so tired now. You know what I am running here? A dustbin. Illegitimate children, destitute women—all that is not useful to society lands in my dustbin.'

Vidyakar was silent, almost meditative. 'Be a Proud Indian, Be a Proud Indian, those advertisements say, *ma*,' he said pointing outside his window at a hoarding of a beautiful village, with children smiling. His voice broke: 'How? How can I be a Proud Indian? I am forty-four years now,' he held up his palms, each with four fingers up, 'and I am tired, I want to run away. But I see the children in the Centre every day. They seem happy. Can I just leave them and run away?'

Much of Vidyakar's bitterness and gloom had rubbed off on me. The streets I passed through were mirrors of what he described. I drove back in silence. Closer home the surroundings appeared familiar, affluent, assuring, like the glowing, advertised India: Be a Proud Indian.

Mylapore is a religious neighbourhood. It is well known for the orthodox Tamilian Brahmins who lived there for many years and for the Kapalishwaran temple and tank. I passed the temple on my way to Meenakshi's house. She lived in a small, typically Brahmin house behind the lane facing the temple. Her house, like many others in Mylapore, had a small veranda in front of the living room and an open courtyard behind it. The other rooms were arranged around the courtyard.

Meenakshi seemed pleased to see me. An old man sat reading the newspaper on a long easy chair in the living room. Meenakshi took me to the courtyard. She spread out a *pai* on the raised verandah; we sat on it. 'My husband,' she said pointing to the old man. He looked very old, at least ten years older than

Meenakshi, perhaps twenty.

The living room walls were painted green and full of pictures of gods. But on the side wall facing the old man was a bright calendar; a cheap, shiny sort which came free with a large box of detergent. On it was a lurid picture of a buxom starlet. She was dressed like an apsara, like popular film stars in dream sequences. Her melon-breasts were suggestively covered with sequinned magenta tissue. A dazzling green garment was tied tight around her hips. Her face was creamy white; her neck, arms and the rest of her body were strawberry pink. Under the picture was a pile of square sheets with the date written in bold red.

The old man stared at the calendar. I presumed he was staring at the semi-clad apsara. Suddenly he arose, walked to the calendar, tore off several sheets until he came to the number '8'. It was 8th July. He looked up, satisfied, at the apsara, then at each of the gods hanging beside her. Gods and apsaras, both pink and smiling, kept each day safe for him. He returned with incense sticks, which he lit, then muttering shlokas he inserted one stick in the frame of each of the gods' pictures.

Meenakshi talked about her husband. During the gulf boom, he left to work in Muscat, she told me. 'It was a good job,' she said, 'we needed the money; my youngest daughter had to be married and my younger son to be sent abroad for his masters in engineering.'

'Sha! What nonsense, Meenakshi!' Her husband spoke abruptly from the hall. His voice was raspy. 'You tell her why I really left,' he said, shaking a finger at Meenakshi. 'Tell her it was because I didn't get my promotion. Tell her it was because I am a Brahmin.' He beat his chest hard several times. 'Tell her, because of DMK. Bloody Rascals! Now these politicians, these rascals, say Brahmins have nothing to do with Tamil culture. Even Sanskrit has nothing to do with Tamil culture. And they claim their Dravidian culture is Tamil culture. Tamil culture, I say, is here, here,' he pointed to the floor, 'here, in the Brahmins in Mylapore. In us!' He beat his chest again. 'I am tired. I am so tired now.'

Meenakshi nodded silently, tapped gently on my lap. 'It's okay, okay, *ma*,' she said. 'Yes, I'll tell her,' she shouted to her husband. 'He was so dejected, *ma*,' she whispered. 'Night and day he worked, all for his promotion. He would have been the assistant general manager. He was rejected, poor man, just because he was a Brahmin, *ma*!' She rolled a newspaper, swatted a fly with it, her anger directed towards killing the casteless insect in one swat.

'So he left the job, *ma*. Very difficult time then. I prayed each day to God Kapaleshwaran to do something. I broke so many coconuts at the temple. See, it is not so easy for a metallurgical engineer to get job. So he went to Dubai. Lots of money he made, but he was so unhappy there, *ma*. Then he came back. After that he has not worked at all.'

She sighed as she looked at him, wiped the sweat from her brow. He was asleep. His lower jaw had dropped, his mouth was wide open. A line of saliva slimed down to his chin.

Suddenly he let out a yell, 'Meenakshi-Meenakshi, that sparrow is pecking at the guava again. Wretched birds. Soon no fruits will be left. I am so tired now, with these birds.'

Meenakshi walked to the window and clapped hard. 'I'll tie a cloth on the fruit,' she replied, 'all the guavas are ripening now. Many birds will come. Don't worry. Go, go to sleep.'

I visited Meenakshi again before I left Madras. Her husband was fast asleep on the easy chair, a newspaper folded over his face. On the wall in front of him the pink apsara's melon-breasts were covered with sequinned magenta tissue. Below it, the date read '14'. I looked out of the window at the guava tree. A koyal sat on one of its branches. Coo-coo-coo, it cooed. It looked like it was going to rain. The guavas were wrapped in red cloth.

2000

JONAH BLANK

AYODHYA

When Guru Baba Raghunanden Das last saw the world beyond his door, George VI was the emperor of India, Mahatma Gandhi had temporarily given up politics for weaving, the Japanese ruled most of eastern China, and German panzers were preparing to roll over Poland. Guru Baba Raghunanden Das did not care. He was nine years old.

For the past half-century Guruji hasn't set foot outside his home in Hanuman Cave. From visitors he hears bits of news mixed with village gossip, everything from the Soviet Union's disintegration to the latest scandal of the postman's lascivious daughter, but he doesn't particularly care. It is all unimportant to the hermit. Just more talk of busy people running about in furious circles. They never get anywhere, he laughs, so they try to run faster.

The guru wears a dirty white robe and a dirty white beard. He doesn't bother to wipe away the flies that are crawling all over his face, in and out of his nostrils, across his lips and eyelashes. Why should he? If he shooed them off, others would come in a moment or two, and are not flies living creatures? Outside the mouth of his cave a troop of monkeys sits chittering. A young acolyte shakes a stick at them when they try to steal the rotting pieces of fruit left as oblations on the makeshift altar.

I kneel to touch the old man's sandals, and he pours sour

JONAH BLANK is former editor of *Asahi Evening News* in Tokyo. He has also reported for several newspapers in USA, Sri Lanka, Sudan, the Philippines, Burma, Thailand and India. 'Ayodhya' has been extracted from *Arrow of the Blue-skinned God: Retracing the Ramayana through India*.

curd into my palms as a blessing. When I look up, he has shuffled into the dim recesses of the room to prepare a simple meal of stewed vegetables. Guruji personally cooks the food he serves to every guest. Each day his routine is exactly the same: ten hours of private worship, seven hours of public ministry, four hours of meditation, an hour for meals and bathing, and two hours of sleep. Doing the math, I find that he's spent less time asleep in his sixty years than I have in my twenty-five.

What does he ponder in his predawn yoga, while all the rest of Ayodhya lies dead in sleep? Lord Rama, the old man says with a chuckle, as if any other answer would be faintly absurd.

From all over the state of Uttar Pradesh, devotees come seeking advice. Guru Baba Raghunanden Das gives them guidance on life—he, whose knowledge of life comes from books written two millennia ago. At noon, two dozen men and women file into the dank little room, reverently kiss the guru's feet, and deposit their offerings before a big picture of Rama and Sita. It is the only ornament there.

The cave's air is thick with the greasy smell of a dozen oil lamps, whose flickers illuminate the guru as he speaks. In a patient, paternal voice he admonishes his disciples to work hard at their jobs, show kindness to others, and be diligent in their worship of the gods. Just do this, he says, and all else will follow.

Outside the cave, I talk to a teenager who had been fidgeting during the sermon. He's an apprentice auto mechanic from bustling Allahabad, out here in the boondocks to visit relatives. A pious aunt dragged him to the guru for a blessing, he says, and his knees are still stiff from sitting so long. He hasn't much time for theology and the like—his is a world of carburetors and movie houses and flirtatious cigarette girls. When I ask him who serves as his model in life, the answer comes almost automatically:

Lord Rama, the young man says with a chuckle . . .

Rama's hometown today is no imperial capital, no seat of a

world empire. It is a sleepy little village like thousands of others, its twisty, unpaved alleys full of flounder-eyed goats, creaky bullock-carts, and emaciated dogs with yellow teeth. There are maybe half a dozen cars here, and the telephone numbers have only two digits.

The pious have long flocked to Ayodhya. The town typically draws four million Hindu pilgrims a year—almost twice as many visitors as the Taj Mahal. But recently the outsiders have not all been pilgrims. Ayodhya today seethes with political intrigue just as venomous as that of Queen Kaikeyi and her dwarfish servant. The wrangling has sown rancour between Hindus and Muslims all through India.

Hari Prasad, a market vendor in Ayodhya, doesn't like Muslims. They're violent people, he says, untrustworthy people, people who kill cows, people who will cheat you any chance they get, people who never bathe. And at that lumpish grey mosque, they defile sacred soil with their arrogant prayers.

'They want everyone to worship *their* god,' he complained as he pushed his cart of cooking utensils to sell in the bazaar. 'Why can't they just live quietly? We do not insist that they become Hindus, but this is *our* country. If they don't like it, they should leave.'

Hari Prasad doesn't personally know any Muslims. There are almost none left in Ayodhya.

Babri Masjid, the mosque at the centre of the maelstrom, was built for the Mughal emperor Babur in 1528. Did it actually rest on Rama's birth site? Who's to say? Can a mythical figure whose incarnation is a matter of faith rather than history really be said to have a birthplace at all? It's rather like arguing over the location of the Garden of Eden. But until the end of the nineteenth century Westerners, from Richard the Lionheart to 'Chinese' Gordon, searched long and earnestly for the grottoes of Adam and Eve. I do not know whether we are better or worse off for giving up Eden as nothing more than a legend.

For four and a half centuries, the land deed of Babri Masjid was a question only for pandits and scholars. But in 1986 the politicians came. After a court order unchained the mosque's doors for the first time since Independence, Hindu militants and Muslim mullahs drove in from Delhi to stake out their rival claims. All over the country, from Hyderabad to Aligarh, blood was spilled in the name of a little grey temple. The people of Ayodhya could only sit back and watch as their town became the national symbol of religious strife.

'We didn't ask for this fight,' said Gayan Das, a resident of Ayodhya since birth; I'd struck up a conversation with him while asking directions to the temple. 'We didn't ask for it, we didn't look for it, we don't want it.' He ran his hand over his tonsured scalp—Gayan Das has been an ordained swami virtually all his life. 'Any good Hindu tries to avoid discord, works for social harmony. This is a holy place. It is not right to make it a battleground.'

Gayan Das himself is no stranger to combat. He used to be the heavyweight wrestling champion of all Uttar Pradesh. At forty-six, he still has a pugilist's build. His arms are a pair of billy clubs, his chest a keg made of oak. He has one cauliflower ear, and a nose mashed flat by an illegal sucker punch twenty years ago. The stubble on his chin has more salt than pepper, but he still looks like he could eat you for lunch.

'Wrestling has nothing at all to do with violence,' he said. 'It is physical, yes, and people do get hurt sometimes, but there is no anger, no malice. You always respect your foe, treat him honourably, try to minimize his pain. *That* is the proper way to fight.'

He sent a boy to fetch his scrapbook, a collection of brittle yellow clippings from the local papers. There were even a few from the national press: the *Times of India,* the *Hindustan Times,* the *Indian Express,* real big stuff, man, have a look. A much younger Gayan Das, still with the cauliflower ear and mashed nose, lifts trophy after trophy above his head and mugs for the shot.

'No matter what your opponent's caste,' he continued, 'no matter what his faith, always you compete as equals. And after the bout you salute each other like gentlemen and live as friends. If you get hurt, what of it? People often get hurt in life, that is nothing to be upset about. Certainly no reason to get angry at your foe.'

Gayan Das still enters wrestling competitions, still trains almost daily. 'Only now,' he said with a grin, 'I don't win *every* match.' Like most wrestlers he has particular reverence for the Monkey God, Hanuman, the loyal servant of Rama who helps rescue Sita from the abode of demons. What better inspiration could a grappler want than the Prince of the Apes? Gayan Das's monastery, even, is named after Hanuman. It has a reputation for being a rough-and-tumble place, a temple where monks train in ancient weaponry and all manner of martial arts. In the dusty courtyard several sadhus were practising their holds as we spoke. 'Our wrestling is a symbol,' said the former champion, 'a mark of our commitment and our will. This is how we keep our minds and our bodies sharp for the defence of the faith.

'But these, these . . . *politicians*,' added with a snort, 'what do they know about faith? They stir up the ordinary people to fight their battles for them, then sit back and watch in safety. '

That evening I saw an impromptu wrestling match in a public park. A crowd of fifty or sixty was gathered in a tight circle around a barker who offered 150 rupees to any man who could beat the champ. That is not an enormous amount of money, and for some time nobody stepped forward. The champ wasn't particularly big or muscular, and I thought of having a go myself, but fortunately a friend shook his head. 'Look first,' he said. Once the prize money was raised to 200 rupees, several challengers lined up. Each stripped off his shirt, dropped some crumpled bills into a hat, and was promptly hurled to the ground. The champ did it for pocket change. I realized then that for Gayan Das wrestling was not just a symbol, it was a joy.

But Gayan Das, unlike Ayodhya's newer brawlers, knows

the difference between a good fight and a bad one.

A few minutes' walk from Gayan Das's monastery is a little cold-drinks stand owned by the Sodhi family, the only Sikhs in town. They are relative newcomers to Ayodhya, having arrived a mere two hundred years ago. On a hot day (and in late March every day is hot) each passerby stops in for a bottle of Limca, and a bottle soon becomes three or four. Nowadays the afternoon talk generally turns to Rama, politics, and Babri Masjid.

'Foolish, *yaar*,' said Gurjit Singh Sodhi, the proprietor. 'So much foolishness, so much to-do.'

'You see the news last night?' asked Sunil, a village headman. It was an unnecessary question, since nobody else there owned a television set. 'They say more MPs will come "fact-finding" next month.'

'Just what we need, eh?'

'Yes, just what we need.' Like almost everybody in Ayodhya, Sunil has little use for meddling outsiders. If pressed, he vaguely supports plans for the new temple but, like his neighbours, he seems to wish the whole matter would just go away.

'What I say is, let them build the temple to Ram,' said Gurjit, using Rama's Hindi rather than his Sanskrit name. 'Let them build it as big and beautiful and fine as they like, but build it right *near* the mosque, without tearing it down.'

'Good, good,' said somebody else.

'No, man, no,' another voice answered, 'Ram's temple must be in the right place, eh? Got to be there. Let the Muslims move *their* building.'

'Perhaps the best solution,' said Gurjit with thought, 'would be if the Muslims did move it voluntarily.' He brought out four more bottles of soda that would have been refreshingly cold had the ancient refrigerator been functioning. 'But you can't just tear it down, can you? I mean, it is a house of worship.'

'One way or the other,' said Sunil, 'voluntarily or not, there *will* be a temple soon. As there should be.' He turned and pointed his empty bottle at me. 'You should not think we have a problem here between Hindus and Muslims. At least, we didn't used to. Muslims used to study Sanskrit right alongside us at my father's school. We Hindus still hang garlands of flowers at the graves of Muslim saints. '

'I never do that,' said a man at the back.

'Well, I do,' Sunil continued. 'Why not, eh? What can it hurt? Maybe you get some good luck—maybe your girl will find a husband one of these days, eh?' A round of chuckles. 'Just last week,' he said, turning to me again, 'two of my Muslim friends came to celebrate the festival of Holi with my family. We don't need trouble here, everything is just fine.

Sunil, Gurjit, and most of the other people of Ayodhya know something that the outsiders seem to have forgotten. Perhaps living so close to the source of the epic has given them a better understanding of the *Ramayana's* meaning. What they know that the politicians do not is this: Rama, the earthly avatar of God the Sustainer, would never have been a purveyor of hatred.

Three bullocks ambled lazily by the storefront, leaving three steaming piles of dung in their wake. A few minutes later an old woman waddled along, dropped to her knees, and scooped up the fresh patties with her chapped hands. She slapped them onto an already laden tin plate, and shuffled down the alley. In any small town one can see women and children picking up cow dung, kneading it with straw, shaping it into small bricks, sticking it onto the sides of their houses to bake dry in the sun. These bricks are a peasant family's most common source of fuel, but that is not the only reason the old women scrape the pavement. To an orthodox Hindu, even the cow's excrement is holy.

Is it illogical to kill and die for a myth? Is it any less illogical to have reverence for cow dung? For a phallus-shaped Shiva lingam? For the dead body and dead blood of a beggarman nailed to a cross? 'It is ridiculous,' wrote the second-century Christian theologian Tertullian of his own faith, 'and therefore it must be true.' All religion is shot through with illogic. Otherwise it would be mere science.

Anything that can be proven cannot last. We laugh at the 'science' of yesterday, the Ptolemaic spheres of the universe, the balancing of choler and phlegm in the human body, the reading of a person's character by the shape of his skull. Even a hypothesis conclusively proven true soon loses its relevance: does anybody care that the earth really is round instead of flat? Facts falter, only ideas survive.

The Ramayana is not a fact but an idea. That is why it will continue to dominate India in a way no objectively verifiable chronicle ever could. It is beyond corroboration. It can never be confirmed, so it can never be denied.

Around the corner from the manure collector, another old woman hung a string of dried cow patties outside her door for luck. A large mound of dung sat at the step, stuck each day with newly plucked flower stems. Had I been rude enough to tell her that the custom was unhygienic, she would assuredly have laughed at my science.

The woman's name is Ramvati, and her home is a temple. Her family are pandits, hereditary priests, and have little patience for the controversy engulfing their village.

'Of course we all serve Lord Ram,' said Ramvati. 'We love God just as much as any big man from the city—my family doesn't need anyone to tell them about religion.'

Her son, the current pandit, shook his head vigorously in agreement.

'Certainly we'd like to see a temple built,' the woman continued, 'but it is just not worth all the anger and the fighting. In Ayodhya there are already 8,500 temples—do we really need one more?'

On my second day in Ayodhya, I went to the heart of the matter. To the spot where it all happened, or did not happen, or happened in a mythical sense if not a physical one. I went to the most celebrated spot outside of Bethlehem where God did (or did not) incarnate as Man.

At Babri Masjid, pilgrims clad only in loincloths were being searched for concealed weapons. Ancient yogis who wouldn't know how to operate a telephone walked through airport-style metal detectors to prove they weren't harbouring high explosives. The plain, unassuming building had fences tipped with razory tangles of barbed wire.

'Belt, belt!' a man in some sort of semi-official uniform called out to me. 'You! Belt, here!' He put out his hand.'

I took off my belt and gave it to him. Leather—the hide of butchered cows—was not permitted beyond the gate.

The inside of the mosque had already been turned into a Hindu temple. There were no Qur'anic verses painted in scribbles of gilt Arabic, no prayer-clocks, no men in Abraham Lincoln beards bowing in the direction of Mecca. In their place were icons of the pudgy blue baby Rama, candles, bells, incense sticks, and bald-headed sadhus prostrating themselves before the graven images of the infant god. The site was already Ramjanam Bhumi, the temple of Lord Ram at his birthplace, in fact if not yet in name.

Soldiers were on patrol everywhere. They carried heavy Sten rifles, Second World War-vintage guns inherited from the British army at Independence. The massive wooden stock on the weapon makes it awkward for firing, but ideal for bashing heads.

One young infantryman refused to give me his name, rank, or serial number, but quite cheerfully answered any other question.

'These precautions are here to safeguard the public,' he said.

'Safeguard them from what?'

'Riots, bombs, any type of insurrectionary mischief.'

'Have there been any riots yet?'

'No, not here yet. But the Muslims are always threatening.'

'Do Muslims ever come here?'

'Oh, certainly they are free to come here.'

'But *do* they?'

The soldier stomped some dust off the sole of one foot. He was dressed in full combat gear—khaki fatigues, helmet and all—but since this is holy ground his feet were bare.

'They are free to come,' he said. 'If they wanted to come, nobody would stop them.'

I asked who was in charge of the town.

'The legal government, of course,' the soldier replied. 'Not the VHP. Most assuredly not. Good day.'

A few months later Babri Masjid would indeed be the site of riots, bombs, and insurrectionary mischief. Hundreds of thousands of marchers would overwhelm the security forces, push through the accordion wire without noticing the pain, break down the chain-link barriers, begin physically tearing the mosque to pieces with their bare hands. The army would restore order with lathi-poles and lead, with bamboo and bullets.

In all likelihood, a few months after our conversation this very soldier had a hot day's work. In all likelihood he spent several sweaty hours fracturing rib cages with the butt of his splintering Sten, terrified at every moment that he might be torn apart like the bricks of the mosque at his back. Perhaps he was pummelled to death, perhaps he was promoted for valour, but either way the sacred soil of Rama's birth must have taught him something about tolerance: the mob clamouring for his blood was made up not of Muslims but of his fellow Hindus.

Right next to the temple, inside the steel perimeter with its knife-edge spirals, was a large-scale model of the temple-to-be. It was under the display tent of the Vishva Hindu Parishad, as the VHP is called on those rare occasions when Indians forego initials for full names. Whatever anyone may say, the VHP was very much in charge of Ayodhya. Here at their recruiting pavilion, hundreds of visitors stopped to marvel at the mockup of a lavish architectural fantasy. If the Ramjanam Bhumi temple is built anything like its model, it will be by far the most extravagant temple in a town full of temples, perhaps the most spectacular in the entire state. Pilgrims pressed their noses to the glass case and dropped coins in a box to become part of the dream.

The man who really ran Ayodhya was asleep when I arrived. Mahesh Narayan Singh, the secretary of the Ramjanam Bhumi Committee of the VHP, was taking his mid-afternoon nap. An aide brought me tea, and time passed. When it became clear that the secretary would not be waking up unprompted, the aide ushered me into his room.

Mahesh Narayan Singh, a big, beefy man with hair prematurely white, sat up in his bed and rubbed his bleary eyes. The heavy curtains were still drawn, so there was little for him to see. He took a cup of tea from a tray at the foot of the mattress and told me of his plans.

'Ram is the most important god in the Hindu faith,' he said. 'And this is the very spot where he was born. How could we *not* give him every due honour?'

I asked why, with all the mandirs already standing in Ayodhya, he needed another. Couldn't there be some compromise, some way of honouring Rama on the site without humiliating the Muslims by razing their mosque?

The new temple, he replied, would be far more than a place to worship Rama. It would be a beacon to guide all Hindus back to their faith. 'Look at the splendours of India's past,' said the secretary, 'Khajuraho, Ellora, Somnathpur, Kanchipuram, the list goes on and on. Each one strengthened the people's spirit, reminded them of what a wonderful thing it truly is to be a Hindu. And when was the last such temple built? Not for many hundreds of years.'

He poked a pillow into a more comfortable shape and wedged it under his back.

'You see,' he said, 'India is our mother. That, plain and

simple, is the essence of Hinduism. You must honour and
cherish your parent, always. You would sacrifice anything to
defend your family from harm, would you not? Of course you
would. Well, our nation is our parent, and we must defend her
status.'

It is filial obedience that sends Rama into exile. The prince
of Ayodhya places his father's command above his duty to his
wife, his subjects, his own birthright, even right and wrong.
When the modern-day prince of modern-day Ayodhya honours
his parent, he is following an illustrious example.

'But aren't the Muslims Indians as well?' I asked. 'Aren't
they your brothers and sisters, children of the same Mother
Soil?'

'Yes, they are, but they seem to forget this. After all, who
were their ancestors, these Muslims, eh? Their ancestors were
Hindus just like mine. Back when the Mughals invaded our
country, they forced so many good Hindus to convert to Islam
at the point of a sword. So many. Not just here—everywhere in
the world the Muslims gain converts by force. They are a
warlike people, it is bred in the bone.'

The VHP is still battling against Islamic warriors long dead.
When a television serial on the eighteenth-century Muslim ruler
Tipu Sultan was aired in 1990, the Hindu group staged a hunger
strike in protest.

'Our Indian faith was in existence since the beginning of
history,' the secretary continued. 'That is not dogma, mind you,
that is historical fact. Hindu worship goes back two thousand
years before this Prophet of theirs was even born.'
Undeniable—if one stretches the definition of Hinduism a bit to
include archaic Brahminism. 'We do not force others to accept
our belief. We are the only faith that truly practices
non-violence. But simply because we eschew killing and hurting
people does not mean that we're pushovers.'

There are two other Mughal mosques that the VHP is
pressing to take over. Babri Masjid is far and away the most

celebrated, but it is only one of many sites where, fundamentalists say, Muslims destroyed existing Hindu temples over the centuries. 'There are mosques on top of a Shiva temple in Varanasi and a Krishna temple in Mathura,' said the secretary. 'All we are demanding is the return of three holy places that originally were ours. It is not a lot to ask for.'

Not a lot, or perhaps far too much. Like most things in India, it depends on your point of view.

All hatred, it has been said, comes from fear. Despite a long tradition of mutual atrocities, it is hard to believe that 735 million Hindus feel truly threatened by 97 million Muslims. I asked the secretary whether the fundamentalist revival might stem from a different fear entirely, a fear that always smoulders but can never burn hot enough to enflame a people's spirit: a fear of modernity.

The secretary leaned forward on the bed to take a biscuit from the tea tray, and nibbled on it as he spoke.

'Yes indeed, we have much to worry about quite apart from the Muslims,' he said. 'Hindus, more and more, are forsaking their own traditions freely, without anybody forcing them. More and more, all the time, they would rather go to the movies, wear Western clothing, study abroad and move to the United States. They forget to worship the gods—how can you call yourself a Hindu if you don't worship the gods? For them the great epics *Ramayana* and *Mahabharata* are merely television programmes.

'Those television programmes have made the VHP successful.'

'Yes, they have helped stir up interest in the grand epics. But the Indian nation must be reminded that its days of glory are not all in the past. This is why we will build a new temple. We must be reminded not merely with pretty words, but with monuments in immovable stone.'

Mahesh Narayan Singh is a Kshatriya, of course—just about everyone with the name of Singh is either a Kshatriya or a

Sikh, and the secretary wears neither a Sikh's turban nor a
beard. His father was a 'farmer', most likely in the same sense
that a landed English baronet may refer to himself as an
'agriculturist'. As a member of the caste entrusted with the
defence of faith, Mahesh Narayan Singh sees his work as a
sacred crusade. 'It is,' he said, 'my religious duty to wake my
countrymen up.'

Rama himself is a Kshatriya. He too is duty-bound to
protect Hinduism from any attack. But the epic tells us that he
goes far out of his way to avoid every battle, fights only as a last
resort, never takes up arms without regret. I couldn't help but
admire Mahesh Narayan Singh's pious convictions, his
commitment to uphold traditions that too many consider
old-fashioned. But I also couldn't help but wish that his fervour
were tempered with a healthy streak of Rama's righteous
restraint.

Was Babri Masjid actually built by tearing down an older Hindu
shrine? The question is of vital importance to Ayodhya and of
vital importance to India. The answer (like so many answers in
India) is maybe, maybe not . . .

Certainly the Mughals rode roughshod over their Hindu
subjects and destroyed an incalculable amount of irreplaceable
art. But was a temple in Ayodhya one of these casualties? The
town itself was settled by 700 BC, four hundred years before the
Ramayana was written down, but scholars still don't know
whether this was the Ayodhya referred to in the epic. In
Valmiki's day it was a Buddhist centre called Saketa—Gautama
the Buddha himself lived and preached there for a time. By the
fifth century after Christ, the wandering Chinese monk
Fa-Hsien reported that the village boasted one hundred
Buddhist monasteries by the banks of the Gogra River.

The worship of Rama as a major deity did not arise until the thirteenth century. Guru Swami Ramanand soon made this new cult one of India's most popular, but any Rama temple that Babur's army found in Ayodhya could not have been much more than two hundred years old. If a mandir was standing (there is no contemporary record for or against), it dated back not to Rama's birth or even to Valmiki's writing, but only to Swami Ramanand's preaching a millennium and a half later.

Tulsi Das, the author of an immensely popular Hindi version of the *Ramayana*, lived his whole life in and near Ayodhya at the very time Babri Masjid was constructed; in none of his writings is there any mention of the demolition of a venerable shrine, an event he'd hardly be likely to pass over. Still, devout pilgrims (not to mention the editors of *Encyclopaedia Britannica*) have believed Babri Masjid to sit atop Rama's birth site for as long as the most ancient of the bazaar gossips can remember. When the facts are inconclusive, truth is what you declare it to be.

For one bazaar gossip named Mrs Sahia, the truth has never been in question. 'The Muslims don't know their place,' she said. 'They act like they own this country. They should just be happy we let them stay here.'

Mrs Sahia is a shopkeeper on Ayodhya's central street. She came to the village ages ago, sent here as a terrified bride barely out of childhood. Now she has four sons, four grandsons, four houses, four general goods stores, and (she notes with pride) two television sets.

'Back in '47,' she said, 'the Muslims got all of Pakistan for their state, and we got India for ours. Do you think Hindus are welcome in Karachi or Lahore? Of course not. Yet we let Muslims live here in peace, and they do nothing but stir up trouble. If they don't like it here they should go back to Pakistan where they belong.'

'Yes, yes,' said her son, 'send them all back.'

In the street outside, two pariah dogs fought listlessly over a chicken bone. One had the aristocratic black-and-gray markings of an English harrier hound. All over the northern part of India these uniquely speckled descendants of pampered hunting dogs scavenge along with mongrels. It was not only humans that Partition left homeless. But the dogs have shorter lives and shorter memories.

'Our whole family hates the Muslims,' Mrs Sahia said proudly. 'They want special treatment—what special treatment did *we* ever get?

'None!' said her son. 'None at all!'

I asked if she had felt this way before the VHP and the politicians of the Bharatiya Janata Party came to town. Her Highness the Maharani of Gwalior, now seated as a BJP member of Parliament, has made Ayodhya's temple her own pet project.

'The politicians are just windbags,' Mrs. Sahia huffed. 'All of them, just in it for their own purposes. They don't really care about us at all. But the VHP we support. Before they proposed the temple, we'd never really thought about it much. They made us aware of the problem and started to do something about it. Why shouldn't good Hindus from other parts of the country help build a temple? Ram is not just for Ayodhyans, he is the god for all Hindus everywhere.'

What about tolerance, I asked her, and the tradition of Hindu non-violence.

'I know nothing of theology,' she said with a dismissive toss of her hands. 'What do I look like to you, a pandit? I am an ordinary woman, not some city-educated girl like today. If you want to know about theology, go ask a sadhu. There are certainly enough of them around in this town.'

A small boy came up and tugged at her sari. She brushed him off without looking down.

'I will tell you this,' she added, looking me straight in the eye, 'if the government does not stop its foolish talking and allow the temple to be built very soon, the ordinary people will not wait. There will be a revolution.'

A revolution of bitter shopkeepers, of sour-hearted matriarchs, of angry, jealous, ungenerous souls, a revolt of intolerance and bile, an uprising born not of righteousness but of hatred. It does not seem the sort of revolution that Rama, the embodiment of charity, harmony, and all human virtues, could ever inspire.

It took me several days of hard searching to find any Muslims at all in Ayodhya. They were cloth merchants, six of them, huddled together in a small textile stall. Five were travelling salesmen from Maharashtra, just in for the week. The other was Muhammad Latif.

'My family has lived here for nine generations,' he said, 'ever since the time of my great-great-great-great-great-great-grandfather. Was that six "greats"? Good. We have been here for a very long time, and we will not be forced out.'

'Never,' said one of the men from Maharashtra. 'We Muslims from all over the nation will defend our brethren.'

'If we give in here,' said another of the cloth merchants, 'what will be next? Maybe they'll try to close our schools, maybe take away our voting rights, who knows? You must make a stand.'

I asked how many Muslims were left in town.

'Not so many,' Muhammad Latif conceded. 'More than a few have gotten fed up and left. We are not physically threatened, you understand, but the constant struggle is sometimes too much. Still, we have enough here to defend what is ours.'

'And they do not fight alone,' said the first merchant.

'Couldn't there be a way to compromise,' I asked, 'perhaps to move the mosque or—'

'Never,' said Muhammad Latif. 'Never. The house of God must remain a house of God, always.' His hard, angry stare softened a shade. 'We are not unreasonable people,' he said, 'we are quite willing to talk. If all the outsiders on both sides went away, I am certain we Ayodhyans could resolve the problem among ourselves. But the mosque must never be torn down . . .'

On my last evening in Ayodhya, I sat on the roof of Guru Baba Raghunanden Das's compound next to the hermitage at Hanuman Cave. Around five o'clock each day any friends, students, or visitors of the guru climb the crumbly mud-brick steps to savour the refreshing cool breeze. They lounge about, talk, sip tea, and bask in the mellowing rays of the setting sun. Guru Baba Raghunanden Das, the half-century hermit, cannot come up here from his home below. He can see the sun and hear the wind, but he will never again feel them on his face.

Those of us on the roof were discussing, naturally, Babri Masjid.

'What really matters,' said Dr Lohtia, a mathematics teacher in nearby Faizabad, 'is not the place where you pray.'

'The place?'

'Yes, the temple, the mosque, what-have-you. It makes no difference. Any filthy alleyway can be a mandir if your mind is right.'

A woman who had been sitting quietly clucked her tongue. 'Praying in an alley?' she said. 'Surely you cannot mean that, baba.'

'Yes, yes, in an alley, I tell you. Why not? Do you think that God will not hear?'

The woman shook her head but didn't presume to question. Dr Lohtia is not only one of the guru's oldest pupils, he is also a close friend.

'What matters,' he said, turning to me, 'is how you treat others. Plain and simple. And it is the very same for Hindu, non-Hindu, even for those who have no belief in God at all. Be kind to others. Not very difficult, eh?'

'What about Babri Masjid?' I asked.

'You know, for the thirty years that the mosque was locked

up we would worship Lord Ram right outside—quietly, side by side with the Muslims, without turning the place into a mandir all our own. Not just me, almost everyone in Ayodhya. Nobody seemed to mind until the VHP told them to stop it. After all, a house of God is a house of God.'

The tongue-clucker broke her silence. 'Guruji supports the temple,' she said triumphantly.

'Yes, indeed he does,' Dr Lohtia replied. 'But Guruji has helped each of us learn how to think. What sort of students would we be if we merely parroted his words?'

I had no standing to make a judgment, but I felt that Guru Baba Raghunanden Das had trained his pupil well. The militants on both sides of the Babri Masjid controversy are so caught up in the minutiae—whose shrine was built when and under what circumstances—that they forget the essence of their respective faiths. Love God and treat all humans with kindness (the guru preaches)—the rest of theology will follow from that. The *Ramayana* is not the stuff of petty bickering. It is an epic of self sacrifice, of unbending morality, of trust, and of love.

In the courtyard down the crumbly mud steps, three old women sat with their backs to the brick wall. They did not care about religious disputations. For most of the afternoon they had been lazily singing a simple refrain to the idle beat of a slow drum. It helped to pass the time of day. The song had only two words, two names that encapsulated every bit of theology the old women needed to know. One name was Sita, the other Ram.

'SitAA-RaaaaAAAm, SitaaaaaaAAAA-Ram! SitAAA-Ra AAAaaaAAAm.'

1992

SEEME QASIM

KUTCH TOUCH

I went to Kutch in December 1995 to write and photograph its people, its cultural and artistic traditions, seen through the perspective of a traveller bearing witness, recording the narratives of everyday life. In the earthquake in January 2001, many parts of Kutch including Bhuj were devastated. This travel account now has taken on a dimension of the Kutch that was.

The only sounds are the rattle of the sleeper bus coach mixed with snores emanating from the shadowy huddled shapes sprawled on bunks. It is rather like being in a train compartment. I am on the night sleeper, halfway to Bhuj (Kutch) from Ahmedabad. Outside, the dark is thick with fog.

I reach Bhuj during that hour just after dawn, when only the service industry is awake—hotels, lodge-owners, auto-rickshaw drivers. My address to the auto-driver, of a hotel I have read about in the old city, is met with an incredulous gasp. He mumbles, 'No, no, you can't stay there. That's only for foreigners.' And then he proceeds to drive me to places which are either too expensive or cloaked in a tired, slovenly respectability—rooms that reek of stale papads and dry flush systems; proprietors who stare relentlessly at me, their entire demeanour questioningly distrustful of this lone Indian

SEEME QASIM is a freelance writer and journalist based in Delhi. She is the author of a book of poems, *Beyond October*.

woman's gall to ask for a room in a strange town.

Finally I refuse to leave the auto and am reluctantly sped down narrow gullies with broken pillars from another time, passing schoolchildren in crisp uniforms laden with books, and numerous yapping street dogs.

The hotel is spotlessly clean and comfortable in an austere kind of way, with a friendly management. The auto-driver was right. Barring myself and a resident Khan Saab, there are only foreigners here—backpackers from America, Australia, Japan, Israel, though the majority are Europeans. I now understand the driver's reluctance, since Indians often associate foreigners with immorality. Here they are even compared with the flamingos who arrive every year to breed in the Great Rann of Kutch and then fly away.

Khan Saab is here on government transfer. He introduces me to the nearby dhaba for a cup of strong hot chai. It takes me some time to get used to drinking tea the Gujarati way in an overflowing small white cup and brimming saucer. The dhaba is full of locals out to grab their early morning tea and read the newspapers, as bleary-eyed foreigners gaze into their cups.

I explore Bhuj, Kutch's most prominent town and district headquarters. Kutch is also the largest district in Gujarat. Even today, Bhuj has the medieval appearance of a desert town. Chosen by Rao Khengarji I as his capital in 1548, it is studded with old buildings and history. The five gates provide entry into the city which is tightly packed with residences, work places and bustling bazars. In his book *The Black Hills: Kutch in History and Legend*, L.F. Rushbrook Williams writes: 'During all the long rule of Maharao Khengarji III, the keys of the five gates of Bhuj were delivered to him every night; every morning they were obtained from him so that the citizens could go about their business beyond the walls . . .'

And within the walls of the Old Quarter, most distances can be covered on foot down the winding streets in the midst of people, overladen carts, traffic, cows and dogs. Outside the town's walls are the Maharao's *chhatris* (memorial tombs) of sandstone with a ruined splendour about them—their funeral slabs called *palias* scattered at curious angles, etched with intricate symbols in memory of heroic warriors. Some of the *chhatris* suffered major damage in the 1819 earthquake. Maharao Lakho, commonly called Lakhpatji's *chhatri*, built around 1770, is the biggest and has a fine carved roof supported by pillars in every corner. There is an image of him on horseback, and the memorial stones of fifteen dancing girls daubed with an orange pigment: they followed him to the pyre as satis, since he had been their patron and protector.

Yvette Spicher, who works for Television Suisse Romande in Geneva, joins Khan Saab and me for a day trip to Dhordo village in the northern Banni area. It is a long arduous journey in desert conditions, and we are soon covered from head to foot in talc-like dust since our wheezy cab's windows cannot be wound up. The area was once renowned for possessing Asia's richest grasslands where the *maldharis* bred fine cattle. Now, only thorny acacia trees can be seen across the undulating yellow sands; grasses grow only following a heavy monsoon. But the rain floods entire villages and their population is forced to migrate onto dry roadside patches.

Gulbeg Mian, headman of the forty Banni villages, is weather-beaten, with gentle eyes. He shows us the area's famous leather embroidery, the sepia albums of another time when his word was law. 'I'm of Arab descent,' he tells us, 'originally from Sindh and used to breed horses here.' And sitting in his *bhunga* (circular mud house) Gulbeg Mian speaks about the past and his community's history, about decades ago, when climatic conditions were more favourable and the Banni people flourished with their cattle herds. Being a hardy group, they survived mainly on milk, while selling enough butter and ghee to buy clothes, tobacco and opium.

On our return journey to Bhuj we stop at Nirona, a crafts village. Everywhere, young children follow us shouting,

'European, European'. We meet Khatri Arab Hasam, one of the country's last remaining master-craftsmen of Rogan art—the intricate process of painting on cloth with a mix of coloured powder and castor oil. He shows us his work done on covers, bedspreads, wall-hangings. Further down, a lacquer worker is engrossed in his craft.

They are used to tourists here—as in the *bandhani* (tie-and-dye) village of Bhujodi near Bhuj or even in faraway Tundavan with its *bhungas* facing the sea. The Rabari tribals watch us with a practised commercial eye while displaying their wares. Yvette is shocked at their hard-sell approach as she searches for the pure ethnic India. 'Does it even exist?' she wonders aloud, dodging demands to pay for taking pictures. I have to admire their scepticism for outsiders like us from strange places who arrive often only to capture them on fast film like animals in a zoo.

Everywhere in the bazaar near my hotel there are thriving barber shops open well into the evening and sweet shops piled with *laddoos* and *burfis* behind smudged glass counters. Maulana Idris' 'Omlet' Centre specializes only in eggs made in different ways. Some Americans are intrigued by his menu on the blackboard. They want to know the difference between *desi* and farm eggs. The Maulana replies, 'Farm eggs by hens, *desi* eggs by cocks!' The Americans look dazed. He laughs and settles the matter by saying, 'Therefore farm eggs vegetarian eggs.'

I am rudely woken up at 3 a.m. by six policemen standing outside my door. They want to conduct a room search, see my identification papers. Their leader strides in arrogantly and demands, 'Journalist, huh? Why are you here?'

They have come minus a search warrant, minus a policewoman. I am shocked to be confronted by something like this. I notice none of the sleeping foreigners are woken up. After I explain, the leader abandons search plans, remarking quickly, 'This is routine. Sorry to bother you.'

The next day I confront ASP Malik, the officer of the raid party. After profuse apologies about their 'mistake' the truth finally comes out. 'We saw your surname in the hotel register and thought you were a spy from across the border.'

The news spreads like wildfire. Many stories emerge. Even the Gor brothers who run Annapurna Guest House and a restaurant serving delicious Kutchi food say they have often been at the receiving end of officialdom. 'They would come in large numbers, polish off our food and leave without paying.' Matters reached such a state that they took the authorities to task.

Perhaps the saving grace in Indian small towns lies within the people themselves, who like Zaheera Siddiqi, vegetable seller, or Deepak Bhai, auto-driver, nonchalantly go about their business—with things like even the Collector's name remaining a perpetual mystery. And they explain away their ignorance by remarking, *Woh badal gaya hoga* (He must have changed).

JAMES CAMERON

REFUGEES

The town of Shikapur was roughly on the frontier. I left the car in the Border Security Forces' compound and got a lift to the edge of East and West Bengal, to a township where the Pakistanis were pouring into India like a river through a broken dyke, a beaten, ragged, penniless, plodding line, drained of everything but the compulsion to stay with the herd.

The township normally held some 20,000 people; in the past week about 200,000 more had flooded in. They were still arriving at the rate of about 50,000 a day. They were camped in schools, temples, cowsheds; they had thrown up little matting shelters in stretches of marshland; hundreds of the elderly were merely lying immobile by the roadside where they had found that they could walk no more. The columns never ceased, long unsmiling exhausted lines of gaunt people, their shreds of dhotis and saris in mud-matted rags, heavy bundles of everything on their heads. The rain poured down in a thick pitiless torrent, as it had done for days. All the great Gangetic delta was now a swamp.

A grey-faced official wrung out the tail of his soaking shirt in a futile gesture.

'Strange how we long for this monsoon every year. Bengalis would die without it. And now they're dying because of it.'

JAMES CAMERON started his lifelong career in journalism in Dundee, Scotland in 1928. He travelled widely as a foreign correspondent in almost every part of the world. 'Refugees' is an extract from *An Indian Summer*, the record of a year he spent in India in the early seventies. James Cameron wrote several other books, including *Point of Departure*. He died in 1985.

Because, I suppose, of the age in which I lived I had been obliged to engage myself in so many situations involving refugees. 'Refugees'—the word itself had almost a generic sound, as it were: Animals, Cripples, Jews, Latvians, Hindus, People. Refugees of one kind or another had been a semi-permanent factor of the world society ever since I could remember. When I was a boy of three we had in our home what were called Belgian Refugees; they were the class of 1914, inconspicuous and individual; as far as I can remember they were those exceptionally out of luck; they were not Social Problems, let alone instruments of massive politics. A generation later came the refugees swarming westwards over Germany; Palestine refugees most ironically dispossessed by those themselves dispossessed; Hindu and Muslim refugees by the hundred thousand crossing each other's paths in the Punjab after Partition; Korean refugees, Vietnamese refugees, all presenting their own variant aspects of exile.

I had seen them all, written about them all in various manners of easy professional pity or wholly useless anger; I had never really *done* anything for them except, perhaps, make known a slender part of their sorrow. It is a disturbing thing for a journalist occasionally to consider how far unhappiness and want and martyrdom had become, despite himself, part of his stock in trade; the facts of disaster a kind of raw material for the manufacture of a momentary emotion in people far away, somewhere between the stock market and the sports page.

If that were not so, why was I here at all? Was it possible that I was only responding to some ingrained impulse, like a voyeur or a boy who follows fire-engines? I would reproach myself forever if that were true, but it might have been. If so I was to be well repaid.

Of all the mass-migrations I had seen, none had been like this.

These were early days, yet already the influx of refugees was counted in five million?—six million?—nobody knew for sure.

How could they? Nobody knew for sure the population even of West Bengal in normal times, whatever they were; nobody even knew the population of Calcutta. It is presumably not for nothing that the major unit of Indian counting is the lakh, which is 100,000, and the crore, which is ten million. In the calculations of Indian calamity, as in the days of princely riches, this would seem to be an inevitable convenience.

All one knew was that in the sudden frantic desolation brought about by the soldiers of President Yahya Khan one certainty emerged: the ten million Hindus who had, in their optimism, decided to stay on in the Muslim state after Partition—committing themselves in their ignorance to twenty-four years of harassment and injustice—had finally realized that their only hope lay in India. (Since in those early days the prospects of an independent Bangladesh were, to say the least, speculative.) For a time, in the past year, the Hindus of East Bengal had responded to promises of Sheikh Mujibur Rahman and his Awami League, defying the army of Yahya Khan and offering equality to all. That, it seemed, had been another bad bet, for now the Pakistan Government had ordered in the soldiers to crush all these preposterous democratic pretensions with all the military machinery their American armoury could provide. With every little group in flight across the border came tales of murder, rapine, the burning of crops, destruction of villages. In the nature of such stories many may have been true, many half-true, some apocryphal; the important thing was that everyone believed them to be true, and in consequence the hungry multitudes pouring into India were in a state of high desperation. In any case in the fifty-mile stretch between Krishnanagar and Shikapur one had to believe no more than the evidence of one's senses: the smell of death from the ditches, the sight, beloved of cameramen, of babies suckling at dead breasts and dogs devouring the almost-dead. The even more important thing was that the Indian Government of West Bengal, itself forever on a knife-edge of political crisis, itself the archetype of economic insecurity, was now confronted with this unprecedented and almost unmanageable situation. It could not, as they say, have happened to a more unlucky people.

So I found myself in this township, which I believe, without any certainty, was called Barsat, in the remorseless rain, watching the refugees move in like an incoming tide, filling the rockpools, overflowing them, filling the saturated fields and overflowing them. There was a Reception Centre where, incredibly, they were supposed to register. The queues stood there patiently in the rain, drained of everything. The inoculations were first; without an inoculation card they did not get a ration card. The ration card entitled them to four hundred grammes of rice and two hundred of pulse. Some had been waiting in line already a day and a half for the medical shots; about two were dying every hour. There was a kind of a hospital, already more than a hundred per cent overcrowded. A building behind had already been turned into a cholera ward; it was awash with the faeces and vomit of choleric diarrhoea. Porters with cloths tied across their mouths brought the bodies out and heaved them over a low wall. In this quagmire it was impossible to find a means of Hindu cremation; their week-long struggle to safety would end in the indignity of burial in the sodden ground.

In the months to come there was time to reflect on all this. Pakistan was a nation conceived in fear, born in bitterness, and broken in folly. It took less than twenty-five years to prove to the world, if not to itself, that a nation created out of negatives was founded on sand. In Simla and Delhi back in the forties we had, indeed, been thinking so already.

A nation came into being wholly, and solely, to institutionalize Islam in the subcontinent, in what Mohammed Ali Jinnah argued was a gesture of defence of the Faith against the pre-eminent Hinduism of India. To the creators of Pakistan, nationalism was an instrument and a vehicle of religion; to the leaders of India religion had, and has, no constitutional place in an avowedly secular state. There was a certain amount of humbug in both these attitudes; nevertheless therein lay all the difference in the world between the concepts of the two nations which would otherwise, and certainly should, have grown as one.

Now even in those early days when I was dismally wading through this slough of despond in Bengal, we were already thinking of Pakistan in obituary terms.

The world's reaction to this sorry mess of Bangladesh was initially as confused as the events themselves. The United States, which had provided President Yahya Khan's Army with most of the weapons with which to whip the Bengalis, decided that the debacle was a matter of Pakistani internal politics. The British swithered and equivocated.

The Chinese perversely came out on Yahya Khan's side, to the consternation of most Bengali Communists who had prematurely jumped on to the Bangladesh bandwagon as a textbook exemplar of the People's War. India wholly disproved Pakistan's allegations of conspiracy by being herself manifestly caught on the wrong foot by the appalling load suddenly thrust upon her, and even in her deepest difficulties could not shake off her impenetrable and mercenary bureaucracy. A month after I had gone a British voluntary medical team were unable to release their mobile hospital and its vaccines and equipment, flown in by the RAF, because it was held up at the airport by the Customs for days, for want of either an excise payment or an unobtainable official signature.

At the border township I had had enough—of rain, of sorrow, of eating other people's rations, of sleeping in the slime, of debates that ended in despair, of the realization of total uselessness. I asked if I could find a lift back to Shikapur so that I could go back to Calcutta; even Calcutta offered some sort of improvement on this.

The Indian Colonel who had been patient and considerate with me for so long was considerate again; his jeep was ready to leave and there was room for me. We would at least, he said, have a goodbye drink in the Mess. It seemed in the circumstances a callous ambition, but I greatly shared it.

For a few miles our road led us along the refugee trail, against the prevailing stream of the people. The coming of evening seemed in no way to diminish the columns of empty-eyed, stumbling Bengalis, they still trudged into India with their bundles on their heads and their rags in the rain.

'The problem is clearly insoluble,' the Colonel was saying as the bus truck appeared up the road ahead of us, apparently about a half a mile away. It was rolling slightly from side to side, sending up a bow-wave of brown water from its front wheels. From the moment it became visible I knew we were in trouble. Neither the bus nor our jeep was travelling very fast; ordinarily there would have been just room to pass in a chancy safety. But the refugees had narrowed the highway, such as it was, and the surface of the road was now a sequence of pools linked by skid pans of greasy mud. Indian drivers make it a point of honour never to give way until the last moment, and I knew that this could not be many seconds off.

I said: 'We're cutting it fine, Colonel.'

He grunted: 'Take it easy, driver.'

'Thik hai, sahib,' said the driver, but he suddenly tensed as he swung the wheel of the jeep and it did not respond. We hit the bus exactly head on. The horn, too late, began to howl.

After a while I became aware that we were embedded under the bonnet of the bus, and that the soldiers on either side of me were gravely hurt. Nobody moved for some time, except the refugees who plodded slowly round our debris; it meant no more to them than anything else; this was someone else's calamity, and they were too numbed to trouble.

By and by a police truck came by and found me sitting in the red slime on the roadside, and helped me into Krishnanagar, and by then I had really had enough.

It was not a good road back to Calcutta and the driver was

not anxious to dally through ninety miles of Bengal in the darkness; after a while of jolting the pain became quite bad. I do not recall talking about anything on the way. Finally we rolled up the silent Chowringhee past the closed cafés and the pavement-sleepers and reached the hotel about three in the morning.

The driver covered me with an old macintosh to hide my appalling clothes; I was so soaked and matted with the soldiers' blood that I feared the night-clerk at the desk would invoke some regulation and refuse to admit me. As it was I must have appeared grotesque enough, blundering and stumbling in supported by the driver's shoulder, and the hotel clerk slid my key across the desk with obvious distaste; at that time in the morning he must have concluded that I was very drunk. Somehow or other I got manhandled upstairs to the room. I cut off my filthy clothes with a razor-blade, very slowly and painfully, and lay on the bed to consider what might next be done. I fell asleep at once.

When I woke up in daylight I simply could not move at all. I felt as though I had been jumped on by an elephant. It seemed clear enough that I had broken one leg and not improbably both; one kneecap seemed to be on the wrong side. The left of my ribcage appeared to be one immense soggy bruise, and my back from the buttocks to waist had no feeling at all. The situation presented a dilemma.

For nearly twenty-five years I had had a singularly haunting horror of being ill in Calcutta. Of all places in the world it would be the worst nightmare for personal sickness; Calcutta, dedicated for generations to the maintenance of suffering, is necessarily the most indifferent to it, quite apart from the fact that in all of West Bengal there is scarcely one hospital bed for every thousand people. Moreover I feared being ill in Calcutta because once it had happened to me.

Long before, some time in the late 1940s, I had come to Calcutta from South India, travelling by stages up the eastern coast. In those days there was much primitive accommodation; by night one shared it with clouds of winged things, and the thin whine of the mosquito then was often that of the anopheles. By the time I reached Calcutta the malaria had incubated well; as we jogged along in the wooden bus from Dum Dum airport through the dusk, through the flaring lamplit squalor of the suburban slums, through miles of flickering clamorous streets, through banks and strata of turbulent sounds and smells, the ride took on more and more the quality of my own fever; we seemed to be threshing wildly deeper into the core of some surrealist delirium.

I walked in a heavy daze into the gaunt hotel—the same in which I found myself today, now so transformed—which made no impact on my mind but the throb of what seemed to be many unrelated dance-bands of blaring dissonance, into a wooden room, on to a rocking bed.

Only one incident remains: as I dripped into the deeper confusions of the fever I was further distracted by two realizations, or rather one that was concomitant to the other. First that I was going to die, which seemed of little consequence except for the fact that I had omitted to register in the hotel, nor had I been able to send a routine telegram. Therefore no one in the hotel, indeed no one in Calcutta, nor for that matter anyone anywhere, could possibly know who I was. They would find me, and after some desultory enquiry would shrug me off and heave me incognito on to one or another of the congested burning ghats of this starving city. I tossed around resentfully at the thought of this ultimate anonymity, but I did not appear to have the resolution to do anything about it. I began to dream of gallons of soda-water, oceans of it lapping to my chin and down my burning throat.

The doctor who eventually arrived—I never learned exactly how or why—recounted sardonically how he had come into the bleak room of the hotel and found it littered, scattered wildly everywhere with sheets of copy-paper, on the bed, the floor, the table; on each sheet were scrawled only the two words of my name.

'Something of an egoist,' he had suggested with professional good humour. I had found it impossible to explain how wholly wrong his theory was, how completely contrary an emotion had been involved.

And now I was back in the same place, and in rather worse case. This was evident because Calcutta itself was clearly in worse case. At best one needed all one's health and strength to cope with the wretchedness of this hopeless place; now its concentrated unhappiness was even more compounded and congested by the demands of the uncountable refugees, it seemed truly unpropitious, not to say churlish, to impose an extra unimportant demand on the overtaxed medical resources. In any case they were becoming very edgy about the likelihood of the spreading cholera, and I had no wish at all to get involved in that.

So I decided to get myself splinted up and sellotaped together in a do-it-yourself way to see if I could make it back to London on my own.

1974

KHUSHWANT SINGH

PHOOLAN DEVI, QUEEN OF DACOITS

For over six months after this article was written, Phoolan Devi continued to evade capture. Then, in February 1983, she surrendered to the police. She was released from Gwalior jail in 1994 after spending more than ten years in remand. In 1996 she was elected to the Parliament from Mirzapur, UP on a Samajwadi Party ticket.

It was the afternoon of Saturday, 14 February 1981. Winter had given way to spring. Amidst the undulating sea of ripening wheat and green lentil were patches of bright yellow mustard in flower. Skylarks rose from the ground, suspended themselves in the blue skies and poured down song on the earth below. Allah was in His heaven and all was peace and tranquillity in Behmai.

Behmai is a tiny hamlet along the river Jamuna inhabited by about fifty families belonging mainly to the Thakur caste, with a sprinkling of shepherds and ironsmiths. Although it is only eighty miles from the industrial metropolis, Kanpur, it has no road connecting it to any town. To get to Behmai you have to

KHUSHWANT SINGH has been editor of *Yojna*, the *Illustrated Weekly of India*, *National Herald*, *The Hindustan Times* and *New Delhi*, and is today India's most widely read columnist. His novels include *Train to Pakistan* (Grove Press Award for the best work of fiction, 1954), *I Shall Not Hear the Nightingale*, *Delhi* and *The Company of Women*. Among his other works are *A History of the Sikhs*, translations from the Guru Granth Sahib, and books on Delhi, nature and current affairs. 'Phoolan Devi, Queen of Dacoits' is from *Not a Nice Man to Know: The Best of Khushwant Singh*.

traverse dusty footpaths meandering through cultivated fields, and go down narrow, snake-infested ravines choked with camelthorn and elephant grass. It is not surprising that till the middle of February few people had heard of Behmai. After what happened on Saturday the 14th, it was on everyone's lips.

There was not much to do in the fields except drive off wild pig and deer: some boys armed with catapults and loud voices were out doing this; others played on the sand bank while their buffaloes wallowed in the mud. Men dozed on their charpoys; women sat in huddles gossiping as they ground corn or picked lice out of their children's hair.

No one in Behmai noticed a party dressed in police uniforms cross the river. It was led by a young woman with short-cropped hair wearing the khaki coat of a Deputy Superintendent of Police with three silver stars, blue jeans and boots with zippers. She wore lipstick and her nails had varnish on them. Her belt was charged with bullets and had a curved Gurkha knife—a *Khukri*—attached to it. A sten-gun was slung across her shoulders and she carried a battery-fitted megaphone in her hand. The party sat down beside the village shrine, adorned with the trident emblem of Shiva, the God of destruction.

The eldest of the party, a notorious gangster named Baba Mustaqeem, instructed the group how to go about their job. A dozen men were to surround the village so that no one could get out; the remaining men, led by the woman, were to search all the houses and take whatever they liked. But no women were to be raped nor anyone except the two men they were looking for, slain. They listened in silence and nodded their heads in agreement. They touched the base of Shiva's trident for good luck and dispersed.

The girl in the officer's uniform went up on the parapet of the village well, switched on the megaphone and shouted at the top of her voice: 'Listen you fellows! You *bhosreekey* (progenies of the cunt)! If you love your lives hand over all the cash, silver and gold you have. And listen again! I know those *madarchods* (mother-fuckers) Lal Ram Singh and Shri Ram Singh are hiding in this village. If you don't hand them over to me I will stick my gun into your bums and tear them apart. You've heard me. This is Phoolan Devi speaking. If you don't get cracking, you know what Phoolan Devi will do to you. Jai Durga Mata!' She raised her gun and fired a single shot in the air to convince them that she meant what she said.

Phoolan Devi stayed at the well while her men went looting the Thakurs' homes. Women were stripped of their earrings, nose-pins, silver bangles and anklets. Men handed over whatever cash they had on their persons. The operation lasted almost an hour. But there was no trace of Lal Ram Singh or Shri Ram Singh. The people of the village denied having ever seen them. 'You are lying!' roared Phoolan Devi. 'I will teach you to tell the truth.' She ordered all the young men to be brought before her. About thirty were dragged to her presence. She asked them again: 'You motherfuckers, unless you tell me where those two sons of pigs are, I will roast you alive.' The men pleaded with her and swore they had never seen the two men.

'Take these fellows along,' she ordered her men. 'I'll teach them a lesson they will never forget.' The gang pushed the thirty villagers out of Behmai along the path leading to the river. At an embankment she ordered them to be halted and lined up. 'For the last time, will you tell me where those two bastards are or do I have to kill you?' she asked pointing her sten-gun at them. The villagers again pleaded ignorance: 'If we knew, we would tell you.' 'Turn around,' thundered Phoolan Devi. The men turned their faces towards the green embankment. 'Bhosreekey, this will also teach you not to report to the police. Shoot the bloody bastards!' she ordered her men and yelled: 'Jai Durga Mata!' There was a burst of gunfire. The thirty men crumpled to the earth. Twenty were dead; others, hit in their limbs or buttocks, sprawled in blood-spattered dust.

Phoolan Devi and her murderous gang went down the path

yelling: 'jai Durga Mata! Jai Baba Mustaqeem! Jai Bikram Singh! Jai Phoolan Devi!'

The next morning the massacre of Behmai made front-page headlines in newspapers all over India.

Dacoity in India is as old as history. In some regions it is endemic and no sooner are some gangs liquidated than others come up. The most notorious dacoit country is a couple of hundred miles south-west of Behmai, along the ravines of the Chambal river in Madhya Pradesh. In the Bundelkhand district of Uttar Pradesh in which Behmai is located, it is of comparatively recent origin and the State police suspect that when things became too hot around the Chambal some gangs migrated to Bundelkhand where the terrain was very much like the one they were familiar with. The river Jamuna, after its descent from the Himalayas, runs a sluggish, serpentine course past Delhi and Agra into Bundelkhand. Here it passes through a range of low-lying hills covered with dense forests. Several monsoon-fed rivulets running through deep gorges join it as it goes on to meet the holy Ganga at Allahabad. It is wild and beautiful country: hills, ravines and forests enclosing small picturesque hamlets. By day there are peacocks and multi-coloured butterflies; by night, nightjars calling to each other across the pitch black wilderness flecked by fireflies. *Neelgai* (blue bull), spotted deer, wild boar, hyena, jackal and fox abound. It is also infested with snakes, the commonest being cobras, the most venomous of the species. Cultivation is sparse and entirely dependent on rain. The chief produce are lentils and wheat. The peasantry is amongst the poorest in the country. The two main communities living along the river banks are Mallahs (boatmen) and Thakurs. The Thakurs are the higher caste and own most of the land. The Mallahs are amongst the lowest in the Hindu caste hierarchy, own little land and live mostly by plying boats, fishing and distilling liquor. Till recently dacoit gangs were mixed: Thakurs, Mallahs, Yadavs (cattlemen), Gujjars (milkmen) and Muslims. But now more and more are tending to become caste-oriented. There is little love lost between the Thakurs and the Mallahs. Behmai is a Thakur village; Phoolan Devi, a *Mallahin* (boatwoman.)

No stigma is attached to being a dacoit; in their own territory they are known as *bagis* or rebels. Hindi movies, notably the box-office hit of all times *Sholay* (Flames), in which the hero is a dacoit, has added romance to the profession of banditry: It is said that a song entitled 'Shall we kill you or shall we let you go' is Phoolan Devi's favourite.

Dacoit gangs are well-equipped with automatic weapons, including self-loading rifles mostly acquired through raids. A police note on anti-dacoity operations records that Jalaun district which includes Behmai has fifteen gangs of between ten to thirty members each operating in the area. Phoolan Devi and her current paramour, Man Singh Yadav, have fifteen men with them. In the last six months the police have had ninety-three encounters with dacoits in which they killed 159, captured 137; forty-seven surrendered themselves. Four hundred and thirty-nine still roam about the jungles and ravines, hunting and being hunted.

I sat on the parapet of the village well at the same spot from where Phoolan Devi had announced her arrival in Behmai a year-and-a-half earlier. In front of me sat village men, women and children and the police escort provided for me. An old woman wailed: 'That *Mallahin* killed my husband and two sons. May she die a dog's death!' A man stood up and bared his belly which showed gun-shot scars; another bared his buttocks and pointed to a dimple where a bullet had hit him.

'Can any of you tell me why Phoolan Devi came to this village and killed so many people?'

No one answered.

'Is it true that Lal Ram Singh and Shri Ram Singh were in Behmai?'

A chorus of voices answered: 'No, we have never seen them.'

'Is it true that a few months before the dacoity they had brought Phoolan Devi with them, raped her for several weeks before she managed to escape?'

'Ram! Ram!' protested some of them. 'We had never seen the Mallahin in this village before the dacoity.'

'Why then did she ask for the two brothers? How did she know her way about this village?'

No one answered.

'You will not get anything out of these fellows,' said the inspector of police to me in English. 'You know what these villagers are! They never tell the truth.'

I gave up my cross-examination and decided to go round Behmai. I started from the village shrine with the Shiva's trident, came back to the well and then to the embankment where she had killed the twenty men. I went up a mound where the police had set up a sentry-box from which I could get a bird's-eye view of the village, the river Jamuna and the country beyond. The police sentinel on duty who had been in the village for several weeks volunteered the following information: 'Sir, I think I can tell you why Phoolan Devi did what she did. You see that village across the Jamuna on top of the hill? It is called Pal, it is a Mallah village. Mallahs used to come through Behmai to take the ferry. Thakur boys used to tease their girls and beat up their men. I am told there were several instances when they stripped the girls naked and forced them to dance. The Mallahs appealed to Phoolan Devi to teach these Thakurs a lesson. She had her own reasons as well. Her lover Bikram Singh had been murdered by Thakur Lal Ram Singh and his twin brother Shri Ram Singh. And they had kept her imprisoned in this village for several weeks, raping and beating her. She managed to escape and rejoin her gang. She also suspected that these fellows have been informing the police of her movements. It was revenge, pure and simple.'

'For every man this girl has killed she has slept with two,' said the Superintendent of Police in charge of 'Operation Phoolan Devi'. The police estimate the number of men slain by her or one of her gang in the last year-and-a-half to be over thirty. If that is so, Phoolan Devi could claim mention in the *Guinness Book of World Records* for sex without payment. There is no way of finding out the exact number of men she murdered or she was laid by. But it is certain that not all the killings nor the copulations were entirely of her choosing. On many occasions she happened to be with bandits who went trigger happy; and being the only woman in a gang of a dozen or more she was regarded by them as their common property. She accepted the rules of the game and had to give herself to them in turn.

I was able to reconstruct Phoolan Devi's past by talking to her parents, sisters and one of her lovers, and cross-checking what they told me with a statement she made to the police on 6 January 1979, the first and the only time she was arrested. This was in connection with a robbery in the house of her cousin with whom her father had a dispute over land. Some stolen goods were recovered from her. She spent a fortnight in police custody. Her statement is prefaced by a noting made by the officer. He describes her as 'about twenty years old; wheatish complexion; oval face; short but sturdily built'. Phoolan Devi stated: 'I am the second daughter of a family of six consisting of five girls. The youngest is a boy, Shiv Narain Singh. We belong to the Mallah caste and live in village Gurh-Ka-Purwa. At the age of twelve I was given away in marriage to a forty-five-year-old widower, Putti Lal.' Then she talks of her second 'marriage' to Kailash in Kanpur. The rest of her life-story was given to me by her mother, Muli. 'Phoolan Devi was too young to consummate her marriage and came back to us after a few days. A year or two later we sent her back to her husband. This time she stayed with him for a few months but was unhappy. She came away without her husband's permission, determined not to go back to him.' It would appear that she had been deflowered. Her mother describes her as being 'filled up'—an Indian expression for a girl whose bosom and behind indicate that she has had sex. It would appear that she had developed an appetite for sex which her ageing husband could not fulfil. Her parents were distraught: a girl leaving her husband brought disgrace on the family. 'I told her to drop dead,' said her mother. 'I told her to jump in a well or drown herself in the Jamuna; we would not have a married daughter living with us. Putti Lal came and took away the silver ornaments he had given her and married another woman. What were we to do? We started looking for another husband for her; but it is not easy to find a husband for a discarded girl, is it?' she asked me. Phoolan Devi kept out of her parents' way as much as she could by taking the family's buffaloes out for grazing. She picked up a liaison with the son of the village headman. (In rural India such affairs are consummated in lentil or sugarcane fields.) The headman's son invited his friends to partake of the feast. Phoolan Devi had no choice but to give in. The village gossip-mill ground out stories of Phoolan Devi being available to anyone who wanted to lay her. Her mother admitted: 'The family's *pojeesun* (position) was compromised; our noses were cut. We decided to send her away to her sister, Ramkali, who lives in village Teonga across the river.'

It did not take long for Phoolan Devi to find another lover in Teonga. This was a distant cousin, Kailash, married and with four children. Kailash had contacts with a dacoit gang. He gives a vivid account of how he was seduced by Phoolan Devi: 'One day I was washing my clothes on the banks of the Jamuna. This girl brought her sister's buffaloes to wallow in the shallows of the river. We got talking. She asked me to lend her my cake of soap so that she could bathe herself. I gave her what remained of the soap. She stripped herself before my eyes. While she splashed water on herself and soaped her bosom and buttocks she kept talking to me. I got very excited watching her. After she was dressed, I followed her into the lentil fields. I threw her on the ground and mounted her. I was too worked up and was finished in no time. I begged her to meet me again. She agreed to come the next day at the same time and at the same place.

'We made love many times. But it was never enough. She started playing difficult to get. "If you want me, you must marry me. Then I'll give you all you want," she said. I told her I had a wife and children and could only keep her as my mistress. She would not let me touch her unless I agreed to marry her. I became desperate. I took her with me to Kanpur. A lawyer took fifty rupees from me, wrote something on a piece of paper and told us that we were man and wife. We spent two days in Kanpur. In the day time we went to the movies; at night we made love and slept in each other's arms. When we returned to Teonga, my parents refused to take us in. We spent a night out in the fields. The next day I told Phoolan Devi to go back to her parents as I had decided to return to my wife and children. She swore she would kill me. I have not seen her since then. But I am afraid one of these days she will get me.'

'What does your Phoolania look like?' I asked Kailash. 'I am told her sister Ramkali resembles her.'

'Phoolan is slightly shorter, lighter skinned and has a nicer figure. She is much better looking than Ramkali.'

'I am told she uses very bad language.'

'She never spoke harshly to me; to me she spoke only the language of love.'

Phoolan Devi had more coming to her. A few days after she had been turned out by Kailash, at a village fair she ran into Kailash's wife, Shanti. Shanti pounced on Phoolan, tore her hair, clawed her face and in front of the crowd that had collected, abused her: 'Whore! Bitch! Home-breaker!' What was known only to a few hamlets now became common knowledge: Phoolan was a slut. As if this were not enough, the village headman's son who was under the impression that Phoolan was exclusively at his beck and call heard of her escapade with Kailash. He summoned her to his house and thrashed her with his shoes. Thus at the age of eighteen Phoolan found herself discarded by everyone: her parents did not want her, her old husband had divorced her, her second 'marriage' had come to naught, she had been laid by men none of whom was willing to take her as a wife. It seemed to her that no one in the world wanted to have anything to do with her. She had only two choices before her: to go to some distant city and become a prostitute, or kill herself. There were times she considered throwing herself into the well.

Unknown to her there was someone who had taken a fancy to her. This was young Bikram Singh, a friend of Kailash and member of a gang of dacoits led by a man called Babu Gujjar. Bikram Singh had seen Phoolan about the village and heard stories of her performance in the lentil fields. One afternoon he came to Gurh-Ka-Purwa with some of his gang and bluntly told Phoolan's parents that he had come to take away their daughter. Phoolan was adamant. 'I will talk to you with my sandals,' she said spitting on the ground. Bikram hit her with a whip he was carrying. Phoolan Devi fled from the village and went to stay with her other sister, Rukmini, in village Orai. It is there that she heard that there was a warrant of arrest against her and Kailash for the dacoity in the house of her cousin. The man who took her to the police station raped her before handing her over. She spent a fortnight in jail. When she returned home, Bikram came to she her again. He threatened her: 'Either you come with me or I take your brother Shiv Narain with me.' Phoolan was very attached to her only brother, he was just eleven years old and studying in the village school. After some wrangling, she agreed to go with Bikram.

Kailash describes Bikram Singh as fair, tall and wiry. Bikram was obviously very taken by Phoolan. He had her long hair cropped. He gave her a transistor radio and cassette recorder as she was inordinately fond of listening to film music. He bought her a khaki shirt and jeans. He taught her how to handle a gun. She proved a very adept disciple and became a crack-shot.

For the first time in her life Phoolan felt wanted by someone. She responded to Bikram's affection and began to describe herself as his beloved. She had a rubber stamp made for herself which she used as the letterhead in the letters she had written for her. It reads: '*Dasyu* (dacoit) *Sundari* (beauty), *Dasyu Samrat* Bikram Singh *Ki Premika*' (Beloved of Bikram Singh, emperor of dacoits).'

Being 'the beloved of Bikram' did not confer any special privileges on Phoolan. Whether she liked it or not, she had to service the rest of the gang. At the time the leader happened to be Babu Gujjar, a singularly rough customer. He had his own way of expressing his superiority over his gang. He liked to have sex in broad daylight and in front of the others. So Phoolan Devi had to submit to being ravished and brutalized by Babu Gujjar in public. When her turn came to be made love to by Bikram, she complained to him about the indignity. By then Bikram had developed a strong sense of possession over Phoolan Devi. He did not have the courage to admit it, but one night while Babu Gujjar was asleep, he shot him in the head. Bikram Singh became the leader of the gang and at Phoolan's insistence forbade others from touching her. There wasn't much resentment because the gang soon acquired another woman, Kusum Nain, who happened to be better-looking than Phoolan Devi. Kusum, a Thakur, attached herself to the Thakur brothers, Lal Ram Singh and Shri Ram Singh. The two women became jealous of each other.

Despite her many unpleasant experiences with men, Phoolan Devi, according to some male dacoits of her gang, did not give up her habit of cock-teasing. She sensed that her full bosom and rounded buttocks set men's minds aflame with lust. Nevertheless, say the dacoits, she persisted in bathing in the presence of the men of her gang. One gangster, now in police custody, who had known her as well as Kusum Nain and Meera Thakur (other female dacoits since then slain) vouches for this: 'The other girls were as tough as Phoolan but they observed certain proprieties in the company of men. They would go behind a tree or bushes to take a bath. Not Phoolan; she took off her clothes in front of us as if we did not exist. The other girls used language becoming to women; Phoolan is the most foul-mouthed wench I have ever met. Every time she opens her mouth she uses the foulest of abuse: *bhosreekey, gaandu* (bugger), *madarchod, betichod* (daughter-fucker).'

The Inspector of Police has in his files a sheaf of letters written to him on behalf of Phoolan Devi. They are a delightful mixture of the sacred and the profane, of high falutin Hindi and sheer obscenity. The one he read out to me began with salutations to the Mother Goddess, under her printed letterhead: 'Jai Durga Mata. Dacoit Beauty, Beloved of the Dacoit Emperor Bikram Singh.' The text ran somewhat as follows:

> *Honourable & Respected Inspector General Sahib, I learn from several Hindi journals that you have been making speeches saying that you will have us dacoits shot like pye-dogs. I hereby give you notice that if you do not stop bakwas (nonsense) of this kind, I will have your revered mother abducted and so thoroughly fucked by my men that she will need medical attention. So take heed.*

It is more than likely that Bikram Singh, besides keeping Phoolan Devi exclusively for himself, claimed his right as the leader to enjoy the company of Kusum Nain as well. This irked the Thakur brothers. They left Bikram's gang and looked out for an opportunity to kill him. On the night of 13 August 1980, they trapped and slew Bikram Singh. It is believed that the murder was committed in Behmai and the Thakurs unceremoniously kicked Bikram's corpse before it was thrown into the river.

Lal Ram Singh and Shri Ram Singh kept Phoolan Devi in Behmai. They brutalized and humiliated her in front of the entire village. One night, on the excuse of wanting to relieve herself, Phoolan Devi managed to vanish in the darkness. She crossed the Jamuna to the Mallah village, Pal. From there she got in touch with the Muslim gangster Baba Mustaqeem and pleaded with him to help her avenge the murder of Bikram Singh. Mustaqeem agreed. This is how she came to Behmai on the afternoon of 14 February 1981.

Gurh-Ka-Purwa is idyllically situated on hill slopes that dip into the None river on one side and level out on the sands of the Jamuna on the other. The headman's double-storeyed house overlooks the None. Alongside it are rows of mud huts with brick-tiled roofs which face the Jamuna: One of the meanest looking is that of Devi Deen and Muli—Phoolan Devi's parents. Apart from cooking utensils and charpoys, all they have is a pet partridge in a wicker cage. At the time I went to see them they had their younger married daughter, Ramkali, visiting them and two unmarried girls with them. Their only son Shiv Narain was at school. The family have got used to the limelight that Phoolan Devi's exploits have focused on them. 'One crowded hour of glorious life,' is to them 'worth an age without a name.' They have been visited by pressmen, photographers and many others who come to whet their curiosity. Old Muli now varnishes her nails and when a visitor comes, wears whatever silver jewellery she owns. Ramkali wears lipstick and rouge and knows how to strike poses like a film star. She is an uncommonly attractive young woman with large almond-shaped eyes which she uses like side-winder missiles, a full bosom and slender waist. If Phoolan Devi is anything like her—and most of those who have seen both the sisters are of the opinion that she is better-looking than Ramkali—she must be something.

I could not take my eyes off Ramkali during the hour I spent in their hut. She was aware of the admiring glances she received from our party. 'Everyone who comes wants my photo,' she said saucily to our photographer. He turned to me and asked: 'Isn't she worth a crime? If Phoolan looks anything like her, I am willing to join her gang.'

When we left Gurh-Ka-Purwa, it was high noon. We went through its narrow lanes, stepping gingerly, avoiding the slimy ooze that ran in the middle and the blobs of cowdung strewn everywhere. A large black cobra slithered out of a hole and went along the base of the wall. A herd of buffaloes coming down the lane came to an abrupt halt. The cobra raised its hood and looked angrily around. Seeing that neither the buffaloes nor we meant any harm, it continued its journey and disappeared into a mound of drying cowdung cakes.

The police net is closing round Phoolan Devi and her current lover, Man Singh Yadav. They are believed to be hiding in an area of some fourteen square miles along the Jamuna. The police have grounded all fishing and ferry boats to prevent her crossing over. They have announced a Rs 10,000 prize for anyone who gets her dead or alive. She is reported to be ill and in need of hospitalization. The police have arrested some villagers suspected of having taken medicines for her. They keep a watch on the movements of her brother Shiv Narain whom she is reported to have visited last raakhi, to tie a string bracelet on his wrist. She has narrowly escaped capture. Once on 31 March 1981, only a few weeks after Behmai, she almost walked into a police trap and had to shoot her way out. It was a close shave which she herself ascribed to providence. Since then she always carries a silver figurine of her patron goddess Durga on her person. How long Durga will protect her is anyone's guess.

'The average life of our Indian dacoit is about thirty years,' said a police officer to me. 'They usually join these gangs when they are seventeen or eighteen years old. Most of them are captured or shot within ten or twelve years. Phoolan is now thirty. Her career of crime is about to come to an end.'

'It is you press people who have made a common criminal who has the blood of innocent men on her hands into a heroine,' said S.K. Datta, DIG Police. He gave me many examples of how journals (mainly Hindi) had cooked up all kinds of romantic stories about Phoolan Devi's favourite film songs and her dare-devil escapades. His Superintendent, Vijay Shankar, who is in charge of the district in which Phoolan has been operating, added: 'All our normal police work has come to a standstill because of these dacoit gangs. We must clear them out of the countryside before we can attend to other duties. The longer we take in nabbing them, the more acute other tensions become. And how is it that the press has seldom anything to say of the heroism of the policemen who give their lives fighting these gangsters or of the widows and orphans of men slain by these thugs?'

I had no answers. Besides, the atmosphere was Phoolan-charged. We were sitting on a balcony overlooking the Jamuna. Soft breezes, the river shimmering like quicksilver under a full moon, fireflies flitting about among frangipani: 'A savage place! As holy and enchanted as ever beneath a waning moon was haunted by a woman wailing for her demon lover.' One could almost hear Phoolan wailing for Bikram. My reply to the charge against the press was very tame: 'It is human nature: Phoolan Devi has such a beautiful name—Flora, Goddess of flowers; and she may soon be dead.'

'I don't want to kill her; said Vijay Shankar. 'I don't look upon her as a dacoit but as a child that has lost her way. We will find her and put her on the right path.'

I don't know what that 'right path' can be for one who has taken so many lives except one that leads to the gallows.

1982

VIKRAM SETH

KATHMANDU; DELHI

I get a cheap room in the centre of town and sleep for hours. The next morning, with Mr Shah's son and nephew, I visit the two temples in Kathmandu that are most sacred to Hindus and Buddhists.

At Pashupatinath (outside which a sign proclaims 'Entrance for the Hindus only') there is an atmosphere of febrile confusion. Priests, hawkers, devotees, tourists, cows, monkeys, pigeons and dogs roam through the grounds. We offer a few flowers. There are so many worshippers that some people trying to get the priest's attention are elbowed aside by others pushing their way to the front. A princess of the Nepalese royal house appears; everyone bows and makes way. By the main gate, a party of saffron-clad Westerners struggle for permission to enter. The policeman is not convinced that they are 'the Hindus'. A fight breaks out between two monkeys. One chases the other, who jumps onto a shivalinga, then runs screaming around the temples and down to the river, the holy Bagmati, that flows below. A corpse is being cremated on its banks; washerwomen are at their work and children bathe. From a balcony a basket of flowers and leaves, old offerings now wilted, is dropped into the river. A stone image of a Nandi bull sits firmly between two competing sadhus, each muttering his

VIKRAM SETH is the author of the novels *The Golden Gate: A Novel in Verse*, *A Suitable Boy* and *An Equal Music*. He has also published four volumes of poetry, including *All You Who Sleep Tonight* and *Beastly Tales from Here and There*. 'Kathmandu; Delhi', the last chapter of his travel book *From Heaven Lake: Travels through Sinkiang and Tibet*, describes his homecoming.

mantra, each keeping a careful but hopeful eye on the passers-by. A small shrine half protrudes from the stone platform on the river bank. When it emerges fully, the goddess inside will escape, and the evil period of the Kaliyug will end on earth.

At the Baudhnath stupa, the Buddhist shrine of Kathmandu, there is, in contrast, a sense of stillness. Its immense white dome is ringed by a road. Small shops stand on its outer edge: many of these are owned by Tibetan immigrants; felt bags, Tibetan prints and silver jewellery can be bought here. There are no crowds: this is a haven of quietness in the busy streets around.

In Kathmandu I wind down after my journey. I luxuriate in my tiredness; drift deliciously along, all energy spent, allowing sight to follow sight, thought to follow thought, for now (apart from the easily fulfillable intention of returning to Delhi) there is nothing, no intermediate step that I must perform: there is no lift to look for, no hill to climb, no load to carry, no town en route. There are no papers that I have to obtain. For a person of fundamentally sedentary habits I have been wandering far too long; a continuously wandering life like Sui's would drive me crazy. I marvel at those travellers who, out of curiosity or a sense of mission, wander through unfamiliar environments for years on end. It requires an attitude of mind more capable of contentment with the present than my own. My drive to arrive is too strong. At many points in this journey, impatience has displaced enjoyment. This tension is the true cause of my exhaustion. When I am back in Delhi I will not move for a month, just sit at home, talk with my family and friends, read, rewind, sleep.

Kathmandu is vivid, mercenary, religious, with small shrines to flower-adorned deities along the narrowest and busiest streets; with fruitsellers, flutesellers, hawkers of postcards and pornography; shops selling Western cosmetics, film rolls and chocolate; or copper utensils and Nepalese

antiques. Film songs blare out from the radios, car horns sound, bicycle bells ring, stray cows low questioningly at motorcycles, vendors shout out their wares. I indulge myself mindlessly: buy a bar of Tobler marzipan, a corn-on-the-cob roasted in a charcoal brazier on the pavement (rubbed with salt, chilli powder and lemon); a couple of love story comics, and even a *Reader's Digest*. All this I wash down with Coca Cola and a nauseating orange drink, and feel much the better for it.

I discover that Indian currency is accepted on the Kathmandu streets at an exchange rate of 1.45 Nepalese rupees per Indian rupee. The Chinese exchange rates at the bank in Zhangmu were 0.149 yuan per Nepalese rupee and 0.162 yuan per Indian rupee. It occurs to me that the disparity in cross-rates could enable any habitual border-hopper to realize a tidy profit.

Using Indian currency to pay for a map of Nepal makes me feel quite dislocated. I consider what route I should take back home. If I were propelled by enthusiasm for travel per se, I would go by bus and train to Patna, then sail up the Ganges past Benares to Allahabad, then up the Jumna, past Agra to Delhi. But I am too exhausted and homesick; today is the last day of August. Go home, I tell myself: move directly towards home. I enter a Nepal Airlines office and buy a ticket for tomorrow's flight.

I look at the fluteseller standing in a corner of the square near the hotel. In his hand is a pole with an attachment at the top from which fifty or sixty *bansuris* protrude in all directions, like the quills of a porcupine. They are of bamboo: there are cross-flutes and recorders. From time to time he stands the pole on the ground, selects a flute and plays for a few minutes. The sound rises clearly above the noise of the traffic and the hawkers' cries. He plays slowly, meditatively, without excessive display. He does not shout out his wares. Occasionally he makes a sale, but in a curiously offhanded way as if this were incidental to his enterprise. Sometimes he breaks off playing to talk to the fruitseller. I imagine that this has been the pattern of his life for years.

I find it difficult to tear myself away from the square. Flute music always does this to me: it is at once the most universal and most particular of sounds. There is no culture that does not have its flute—the reed *neh*, the recorder, the Japanese *shakuhachi*, the deep *bansuri* of Hindustani classical music, the clear or breathy flutes of South America, the high-pitched Chinese flutes. Each has its specific fingering and compass. It weaves its own associations. Yet to hear any flute is, it seems to me, to be drawn into the commonalty of all mankind, to be moved by music closest in its phrases and sentences to the human voice. Its motive force too is living breath: it too needs to pause and breathe before it can go on.

That I can be so affected by a few familiar phrases on the *bansuri*, or by a piece of indigo paper surprises me at first, for on the previous occasions that I have returned home after a long absence abroad, I have hardly noticed such details, and certainly have not invested them with the significance I now do. I think it is the gradualness of my journey that has caused this. With air travel the shock of arrival is more immediate: the family, the country, the climate all strike with simultaneous impact so that the mind is bewildered, and the particular implications of small things obscured.

As evening comes on I walk to the Maidan, the open grass-covered common in the centre of Kathmandu. Goatherds drive their goats between the football players and the goal. The last overs of a cricket match are interrupted by a group of elder citizens taking a stroll across the pitch. I walk back to the hotel.

At 3.30 at night I am woken by insects. At five I am woken by the cooing of pigeons outside my window. At six I am woken by my alarm clock. I take a taxi to the airport. The plane is delayed, but by eleven o'clock we are airborne. Below lie the green hills of Nepal; in an hour I will be home. It will be the first time that my parents, my brother, my sister and I have been together in seven years. The family does not know where I am: I later discover that the telegram from Lhasa never did get to Delhi.

As I sit in my seat sipping tomato juice and adjusting my watch to New Delhi time, the whole of the last two months takes on a dreamy quality. I can more easily see myself standing outside the police station at Turfan than travelling through Anduo or Shigatse. Even having been to Tibet, it still strikes me as 'somewhere I would like to travel to', a place I feel I still know next to nothing about; yet I cannot imagine, once I am no longer a student, that I will ever have the means to return.

Almost to reassure myself that this journey did take place, I recite an incantation of names: Turfan, Urumqi, Liuyuan, Dunhuang, Nanhu . . . —the images regain substance— . . . Germu, Naqu, Lhasa, Shigatse, Nilamu, Zhangmu, Lamasangu, Kathmandu. But alongside these names there are others—Quzha, Sui, Norbu—that mean even more to me. I recall Quzha's comment: 'I'm glad things have improved in our relations.' It is a curiously innocent remark in a world where foreign relations are determined by little other than realpolitik.

If India and China were amicable towards each other, almost half the world would be at peace. Yet friendship rests on understanding; and the two countries, despite their contiguity, have had almost no contact in the course of history. Few travellers have made the journey over the Himalayas, and not many more have made the voyage by sea; trade, while it has existed, has always been constrained by geography. In Tibet and South East Asia we find a fusion of the two cultures; but the heartlands of the two great culture zones have been almost untouched by each other. The only important exception to this is the spread of Buddhism.

Unfortunately I think that this will continue to be the case: neither strong economic interest nor the natural affinities of a common culture tie India and China together. The fact that they are both part of the same landmass means next to nothing. There is no such thing as an Asian ethos or mode of thinking.

The best that can be hoped for on a national level is a respectful patience on either side as in, for instance, trying to solve the border problem. But on a personal level, to learn about another great culture is to enrich one's life, to understand one's own country better, to feel more at home in the world, and indirectly to add to that reservoir of individual goodwill that may, generations from now, temper the cynical use of national power.

We touch down in Delhi at noon. The customs officer looks dubiously at the rice sack I am carrying over my shoulder and at the bottle of Glenfiddich I hold in my hand.

'Anything to declare?' He looks at the bottle.

'No. I got this at the duty free shop in Kathmandu.'

'Please open that . . . thing.'

I place the gunny bag on the counter, and take out the objects inside, one by one, like Santa Claus. He passes his hand gingerly over the stone with '*Om mani padme hum*' inscribed on it. He taps my soap-box thoughtfully. The photographer-bear goes through his paces, raising his camera and flashing away at the other now perturbed passengers. The customs officer looks at the bear with distaste.

'All right. You can go.'

I am home in half an hour.

1983

AMIT CHAUDHURI

SMALL ORANGE FLAGS

*This piece was written after my winter holidays in early
1993 when I had come back to India from Oxford. I
encountered a changed world which would also lead to
the seed of the idea for* Freedom Song.

We have read all about Hindu revivalism in newspapers, and
seen the pictures on television; one's personal feelings about it
cannot be separated from the information the media give us.
When I returned to Calcutta for two months in mid-January, I
listened to all the arguments given by people one had always
thought of as 'liberal', a category as vague as 'normal', for and
against Hindu fundamentalism. I listened to the various ways,
small and big, in which middle-class Hindus had been infuriated
by Muslims—the recitation of prayers five times a day on
loudspeakers; the Shah Bano case, where a Muslim woman
pleaded to be divorced under civil rather than Muslim law (her
plea was upheld by the Supreme Court, but overruled by the
Rajiv Gandhi government in the face of widespread Muslim
protest, and against the advice of 'secular' Indians, both
Muslims and Hindus); the way in which Muslims supposedly
support Pakistan at cricket matches. Hindu fundamentalism
was only an extreme reaction to years of 'pampering' Muslims, I

AMIT CHAUDHURI's novels include *Freedom Song, Afternoon Raag*, and *A
New World*. He has won the Betty Trask Award, the Commonwealth Writers
Prize, the Encore Prize, the Southern Arts Literature Prize and the Los Angeles
Times Book Prize for Fiction. 'Small Orange Flags' first appeared in the *London
Review of Books* (10 June 1993) as 'Diary'.

heard; but then I heard about its disturbing consequences as well: many innocent people were killed, mainly in the slums, during the riots in Bombay, the city where I grew up; militant Marathi Hindus—the Shiva Sena—even invaded the exclusive, inviolate upper-middle-class areas where my parents and I had once lived.

Visiting a building in Cuffe Parade where we had lived before my father's retirement, I noticed that the metal nameplates on the ground floor, on one of which my father's name had once been inscribed, now were all blank—this had been done, apparently, to protect the Muslims living in the building. Small, accidental sensations, too small to be called incidents, told me I was now living in a slightly altered world, where certain signs and words had changed imperceptibly in meaning. Taking a stroll down a quiet lane near where my parents live in Calcutta, I noticed the usual political graffiti on the walls, and among other things the symbol of the North Indian Hindu revivalist party, the BJP—the lotus. Yet the sign, or the emotions I registered on seeing it, had changed in some way from two months ago; it inhabited a new world, and I would have to find new words to describe it. Similarly, people had changed, and I mean the everyday, recognizable people who form one's friends and family. Everyone speaking for and against the Muslims, and sometimes doing both at once, seemed to have discovered a faculty or talent that they did not know they had had before.

In Calcutta, news came to us of what was then happening in Bombay from the National Programme—although these days even Calcutta has satellite television, with stations like Star TV and Zee TV and the greatly revered BBC Asia. Satellite dishes multiply on terraces where clothes used to dry and servants bathed, and still do. A small industry has spontaneously grown up around them; boys who were bad at studies but good at 'fixing things', and who once would have become motor mechanics, have now become fixers of antennae and tuners of satellite frequencies. When Star TV first came to our building, the picture our set received was very poor. It soon got better, though the general consensus on the quality of its programmes was that, as a Third World country, we had been cheated again—not only were banned drugs and obsolete guns being dumped on us, but also, now, a huge mountain of television programmes that the Americans no longer wanted to watch. However, BBC Asia—in fact, anything with the letters 'BBC' appended to it—continues to be trusted, as something natural and whole, in the way that preservative-free orange juice is trusted these days in the West: as something that has the ring or the flavour of that old-world thing, 'truth', about it. And it was BBC Asia that had first flashed the news, to Indian audiences, of the demolition of the Babri Masjid. Yet during my visit, I often found myself seized by a great nostalgia to return to that forgotten giant, the National Programme, to watch its numbing series of documentaries, news programmes, historical dramas. Compared with the liberating and anarchic fun of Star TV, the governmental, bureaucratic world of the National Programme served as an anodyne to the muted panic of what was happening now in India; it muffled, numbed, took me back to my grumbling adolescence, when we hated television, politicians, the Hindi language, longed to see adult films without the crude cuts, but took for granted the immortality of our parents and the existence of the nation.

The National Programme showed us thousands of people crowding the Victoria Terminus railway station in Bombay, nearly all of them from the working classes, anxious to leave the city. Not only Muslims, but Tamils, Bengalis, Gujaratis had been attacked or threatened; and I remembered the servants we had had, people who had arrived in Bombay from different parts of the country and quickly been absorbed into its world of part-time jobs as cooks or bearers, people from villages in Kerala or flood-hit Midnapore who learnt how to make a perfect cheese-toast or twist napkins into flowery shapes and put them in tumblers. I remembered James, an honest, ebony-coloured Keralite, who called himself 'butler' and who had a weakness for only one thing—coconut oil. One day, more than twenty years ago, my mother found the lid off a tin of coconut oil in her bathroom—and in the afternoon, she found James, bathed and fresh and smelling of it. He was the one who told me that the Marathis wanted the Madrasis (as all South Indians were then collectively called) out. In much of the next two decades, however, Marathi chauvinism went underground and remained hidden, only to resurface a few years ago in Bombay as Hindu fundamentalism. James retired and went back to his village long before that happened; his life as a 'butler' had been a distinguished and unendangered one; and we received letters from him, one of them asking for money for, as his letter-writer put it, 'the affection of his body', until we heard from him no more.

And I remembered the Shiv Sena as well, vague images from a protected childhood. One day, in the mid-Sixties, I first became conscious of them, in the strange new way that I was then becoming conscious of things, as a shadowy but noisy procession of men that caused our car to become immobile for forty-five minutes in Breach Candy one evening when we were returning home from the suburbs. Who were they? My own life had its certain and fixed co-ordinates: soon my mother would get off at Breach Candy and buy a few hot 'patties' from a hugely popular confectioner's, Bombelli's; these men had no place in that life. On my visit to Bombay in mid-February, I noticed, while taking the taxi from the airport, hundreds of small orange flags flying on the roofs of slum settlements on the outskirts, denoting the Shiv Sena's power if not necessarily its popularity. Those flags suddenly had a brightness and a presence: to the Muslim, they signified a certain kind of disquiet about the present and unease about the future; to the non-Marathi, another kind; to the lower-caste Hindu, yet another; and yet another to the representative of the middle class, whose life had generally held no terrors, except nightmares about promotion and his children's school admissions and higher taxes, and to whom, if anyone, India had made sense as a nation and a democracy.

The Shiv Sena—its figurehead, and the derivation of its name—is not to be confused with Shiv, the Hindu god. For, although Shiv is, aptly, the destroyer of the universe, ridding it of civilizations and human beings when they become too corrupt and too many, he is generally a god who spends most of his time alone, meditating and smoking charas (cannabis). The politics of power-sharing, which most of the other Hindu gods are always indulging in, and by which characteristic they so faithfully allegorize Indian politicians, is of no interest to Shiv. No, the Shiv in Shiv Sena refers to Shivaji, a brave Marathi ruler who used brilliant guerrilla tactics to strike terror into the hearts of fierce Muslim kings—or so we learnt from history books, and more vividly from Amar Chitra Katha comics, the Indian version of *Classics Illustrated*. (Amar Chitra Katha means 'Immortal Picture Stories'.) There, Shivaji was shown as a lean man with a pointed beard who smuggled himself into enemy camps in sweet baskets and neatly chopped off villainous heads.

Bombay, in the Sixties and Seventies, had a utopian air about it: it was the only city in India in which everyone was potentially upwardly mobile. We who were born at the beginning of the Sixties, and whose fathers belonged to that corporate class whose activities constituted the commercial life of this sea-front town, grew up with Tintin, Archie and Jughead, Richie Rich, with war films like *Where Eagles Dare* and Westerns like *McKenna's Gold*, with Coke and Gold Spot and later with rock music. The comic-book idyll of Fifties America, of California, with palm-trees, swimming-pools, sunny promenades, sodas and juke-boxes, persisted in that Bombay. Half the life of a human being, they say, is made up of dreams; living in Bombay then, one would have known that half the life of a colonial or post-colonial is made up of dreams of the West.

In the Eighties, Bombay began to change. Increased growth
accompanied continued deprivation. The number of homeless
people, living in makeshift 'bastis' or shanties, multiplied; at the
same time, property prices rivalled those of Tokyo. Young
film-stars, usually the sons of older 'veterans', kept guns in their
houses; there were Mercedes Benzes on the roads and 'bastis'
along the sides, some of them selling 'smack'. The aura of the
colonial city had disappeared from Bombay, replaced by the
feverishness and electric radiance and wealth and destitution of
a Latin American town, the contradictions of a Third World
city. Seventeen-year-olds drove Marutis—a new lightweight car
made with Japanese collaboration, symbolizing the buoyancy
and lift of upward mobility and money—that had been given to
them by their fathers; often they had no licence; often they ran
over and killed or crippled people sleeping on pavements. My
old friends—the comic book generation—either got into drugs
or into business management (a degree in business management
was a symbol of prestige for this generation, just as a degree in
science was for the previous one) or they left for the real
America which they had always dreamt about. It was in this
context, strangely, but perhaps logically, that the Shiv Sena had
its rebirth.

In mid-February, when I was there, Bombay seemed to have
recovered from the riots that had taken place more than a
month before. Half of the upper-middle-class population
seemed to gather each day at the Bombay Gymkhana, to eat
from the hot buffet, and children from the Cathedral school,
which was nearby, and where I had once studied, kept coming in
and sitting in groups, or alone, to study for exams during the
lunch break, while bearers brought them sandwiches. The
members of the club seemed addicted to its atmosphere, to its
cricket grounds, its swimming-pool, its Chinese soups, its
dining-room, and the long veranda, on which everyone sat in
wicker sofas; many of them would not leave till it was night.
Members kept coming in, waving to each other, looking at each

other's clothes; the middle-aged men were like boys, wearing jeans and eating ice-creams, or wearing shorts and swinging tennis racquets. Everyone, in an oppressive but childlike way, enjoyed being on display. Beyond the cricket green to the right, one could see a steady stream of anonymous commuters hurrying to catch trains, either at the Churchgate station which lay on one side, or the Victoria Terminus on the other. When the bombs went off three weeks later, I was back in Calcutta. Once more, it was BBC Asia that first told us about it. I thought, then, about the commuters, for one of the bombs had gone off at the Victoria Terminus, and I also wondered if the members of the Bombay Gymkhana were still able to gather inside it as before, or whether the veranda was more or less empty now. I could not imagine it, though: in my mind, I saw the dream-addicted members still finding their way through the war-torn city to the club in order to re-create their world.

WILLIAM DALRYMPLE

THE CITY OF WIDOWS

VRINDAVAN, UTTAR PRADESH, 1997
The eye of faith can often see much that is hidden from the vision of the non-believer. To most secular visitors, Vrindavan appears to be nothing more than a rundown north Indian bazaar town, its dusty streets clogged with cows, beggars, bicycles and rickshaws. But to the pious pilgrim it is the dwelling place of Krishna, and thus—in that sense at least—an earthly paradise fragrant with the scent of tamarind and arjuna trees.

Devout Hindus believe that Krishna is still present in this temple town with its crumbling palaces and swarming ashrams, its open sewers and its stalls selling brightly coloured lithographs of the God Child. Listen carefully in Vrindavan, I was told by an old sadhu on the riverbank, for if you are attentive you can still catch the distant strains of Krishna's flute. In the morning, said the sadhu, the god can sometimes be glimpsed bathing at the ghats; while in the evening he is often seen walking with Radha along the bank of the Jamuna.

Every year, hundreds of thousands of Hindu devotees come to Vrindavan, making their way barefoot to the Jamuna along the *parikrama* which links all the town's most holy temples and

WILLIAM DALRYMPLE's first book, *In Xanadu*, which he wrote when he was twenty-two, won him the 1990 *Yorkshire Post* Best First Work Award and a Scottish Arts Council Spring Book Award. His other books include *City of Djinns: A Year in Delhi* (winner of the Thomas Cook Travel Book Award), *From the Holy Mountain: A Journey in the Shadow of Byzantium* and *In the Court of the Fish-Eyed Goddess*. 'The City of Widows' is from *The Age of Kali*, a collection of his travel essays, published in 1998.

shrines. Most then head on to another neighbouring pilgrimage site: the mountain of Govardhan, which, according to legend, Krishna used as an umbrella, lifting it with his little finger. It is now not much more than a hillock, but this does not worry the pilgrims; they know the legend that the more sin proliferates in the world, the more the mountain is diminished.

Some who come to Vrindavan, however, never leave the town again. For many Hindus believe that there is nowhere more holy in all India, and therefore that there is nowhere better to spend your final days, nowhere better to prepare for death.

The pilgrims come from many different castes and communities, from amongst the rich and the poor, from the north and south; but one group in particular predominates: the widows. You notice them the minute you arrive in Vrindavan, bent-backed and white-saried, with their shaven heads and outstretched begging-bowls; on their foreheads they wear the tuning-fork-shaped ash-smear that marks them out as disciples of Krishna. Some of them have slipped out of their homes and left their families, feeling themselves becoming an encumbrance; others have fled vindictive sons and daughters-in-law. Most have simply been thrown out of their houses. For in traditional Hindu society, a woman loses all her status the minute her husband dies. She is forbidden to wear colours or jewellery or to eat meat. She is forbidden to remarry (at least if she is of reasonably high caste; low-caste and untouchable women can do what they want) and she is forbidden to own property. She may no longer be expected to commit sati and throw herself on her husband's funeral pyre, but in many traditional communities, particularly in the more remote villages, she *is* still expected to shave her head and live like an ascetic, sleeping on the ground, living only to fast and pray for her departed spouse.

This practice receives a certain legitimacy in the ancient Hindu tradition that old people who have seen the birth of their grandchildren should disappear off into the forest and spend their last days in prayer, pilgrimage and fasting. In modern India the custom has largely died out, but in some parts, notably rural Bengal, a form of it has survived that involves simply kicking bereaved grandmothers out of their houses and sending them off to the City of Widows.

Every day widows from all over India arrive in Vrindavan. They come to seek the protection of Krishna, to chant mantras and to meditate on their own mortality. They live in great poverty. In return for four hours of chanting, the principal ashram will give a widow a cupful of rice and two rupees—about four pence. Otherwise the old women, a surprising number of them from relatively wealthy, high-caste, landowning families, subsist on what they can beg. They have no privacy, no luxuries, no holidays. They simply pray until they keel over and die. There are eight thousand of them at present in the town, and every year their number increases.

'If I were to sit under a tree,' said Kamala Ghosh, a local women's rights activist, 'and tell you the sadness of the widows of Vrindavan, the leaves of that tree would fall like tears.'

'My husband died when I was seventeen years old,' said Kanaklatha. 'He had some sort of stomach disorder. I took him to lots of hospitals in Calcutta but he did not recover. He suffered for a month. Then he died.'

The old lady looked past me, her clouded eyes focused towards the ghats and the course of the holy river Jamuna.

'I still remember his face when they brought him to me,' she said. 'He was very fair, with fine, sharp features. When he was alive his eyes were unusually large, but now they were closed: he looked as if he was sleeping. Then they took him away. He was a landlord in our village, and greatly respected. But we had no children, and when he died his land was usurped by the village strongmen. I was left with nothing.

'For two years I stayed where I was. Then I was forced to go to Calcutta to work as a maid. I wasn't used to working as a servant, and every day I cried. I asked Govinda (Krishna), "What have I done to deserve this?" How can I describe to anyone how great my pain was? After three years Krishna appeared to me in a dream and said that I should come here. That was 1955. I've been here forty years now.'

'Do you never feel like going back?'

'Never! After my husband died and they took away everything I owned, I vowed never to look at my village again. I will never go back.'

We were standing in the main bazaar of Vrindavan. Rickshaws were rattling past us along the rutted roads, past the tethered buffaloes and the clouds of bees swarming outside the sweet shops. Behind us rose the portico of the Shri Bhagwan Bhajan ashram. Through its door came the sound of bells and clashing cymbals and the constant rising, falling eddy of the widows' incessant chant: 'Hare Ram, Hare Krishna, Hare Ram, Hare Krishna . . .' Occasionally, above the chant of two thousand women, you could hear snatches of the soaring Bengali verses of the lead singer:

> Mare Keshto rakhe ke?
> Rakhe Keshto mare ke?
> (Whom Krishna destroys, who can save?
> Whom he saves, who can destroy?)

It was ten in the morning and Kanaklatha had just finished her four-hour shift. In her hand she held her reward: a knotted cloth containing a single cupful of rice and her two rupees. 'We try to remember what we are chanting,' said Kanaklatha, following my gaze, 'but mostly we carry on so that we can eat. When we fall ill and cannot chant, the ashram doesn't help: we just go hungry.'

Kanaklatha said she had got up at four thirty, as she did every day. She had bathed and dressed her Krishna idol, spent an hour in prayer before it, then performed her ablutions at the ghat. Then from six until ten she chanted her mantras at the ashram. After that, a day of begging in the bazaars of Vrindavan stretched ahead.

'I stay with my mother,' said Kanaklatha. 'She is ninety-five. My father died when I was sixteen and she came here then. We have to pay a hundred rupees rent a month. It is my main worry in life. Now I'm two months in arrears. Every day I ask Govinda to help us make ends meet. I know he will look after us.'

'How can you believe that after all you've been through?'

'If Govinda doesn't look after us who will?' said Kanaklatha. 'If I didn't believe in him how could I stay alive?'

The widow looked straight at me: 'All I want is to serve him,' she insisted. 'Whatever we eat and drink is his gift. Without him we would have nothing. The way he wants things to be, that is how they are.'

'Come,' she said, her face lighting up. 'Come and see my image of Govinda. He is so beautiful.'

Without waiting to see if I would follow, the old lady hobbled away along the street at a surprising pace. She led me through a labyrinth of lanes and alleys, past roadside shrines and brightly-lit temples, until eventually we reached a small courtyard house near the ghats. There, on the floor of a cramped, dark, airless room, lay Kanaklatha's mother. She was shaven-headed and smeared with ash like her daughter, but she was toothless and shrunken, lying curled up like an embryo on a thin cotton sheet. Around her were scattered a few pots and pans. Kanaklatha squatted on the floor beside her and gently stroked her head.

'My mother was a strong woman,' she said. 'But she had a haemorrhage two years ago and after that she just withered away. Now she just lies on this bed. If I could afford to give her just one glass of fruit juice she would be better than she is. I want her to die without pain, but I am consumed by the thought that if something bad happens we could not afford medical treatment.'

'It is all fate.' It was the mother speaking, 'When we were young we never imagined this would be our end.'

'We were a landowning family,' explained Kanaklatha. 'Now we have to beg to survive. Even now I'm full of shame when I beg, thinking I am from a good family. It is the same with all the widows. Our usefulness is past. We are all rejects. This is our karma.'

'Only Govinda knows our pain and misery,' said her mother. 'No one else could understand.'

'Yet compared to some of the others . . .'

'What do you mean?' I asked.

'Some of the other widows. At least we are together. But many women I know were thrown out of their houses by their own children. When their sons discover that they are begging on the streets of Vrindavan they are forbidden from writing to their grandchildren.'

'We haven't committed a crime,' said the old lady. 'Why should we go through all this?'

'Sometimes I think even sati would have been preferable to the life of a widow,' said Kanaklatha. 'At the time, burning on my husband's pyre seemed horrible. But after living through so much pain and misery, I wonder whether sati would not have been the better option. Now all I want is to serve Govinda and my mother, and spend the rest of the time in prayer. Here, come inside, see my little Krishna.'

Kanaklatha indicated that I should step over her mother. She pointed to the end of her tiny room. There, raised up on a wooden bench beside a small paraffin stove stood a pair of small brass idols of Krishna, each dressed in saffron dolls' clothes. One figure showed Krishna as a child; the other as a youth, dancing with a flute in his hands.

'Look at his beauty!' said Kanaklatha. 'Every day I bathe him and change his clothes and give him food. Krishna is my protector. He cannot resist the entreaties of any woman.'

She walked over to the shrine and bowed her head before

the images.

'Sometimes when I am asleep he comes to me,' she said. 'I tell him my sorrows and he tells me how to cope. But the moment I awake, he disappears . . .'

That evening, in a nearby temple, I met Kanaklatha's landlord, a Brahmin priest named Pundit Krishna Gopal Shukla.

'If those women die tomorrow,' he said, spitting on the floor, 'I will have to bear the expense of cremation. It should be the ashram's responsibility. They get so much money from pilgrims. I do so much for these widows already. I rent them a room. I even give them free water.'

According to Shukla, the widows' ashrams in Vrindavan were increasingly set up by Delhi businessmen as a means to launder black money. They would give donations to their ashrams and receive receipts stating that they had given much larger amounts, which would be written off against tax. As far as the ashram owners were concerned, the widows were just a means to a financial end, a quick route to a clever tax dodge.

There was no doubting the very considerable funds the ashrams of Vrindavan receive. One medium-sized one attracted donations by undertaking to erect an inscribed marble plaque recording the name of any devotee who gave at least two thousand rupees, and promising that the widows would sing bhajans for the donor 'for the next seven generations'. The resulting plaques covered not only every wall in the hangar-sized building, but also its floor and ceiling. Many of the donors turned out to be British Hindus: next to plaques recording donations from Agra, Varanasi and Calcutta were a number from rather less exotic centres of Hindu culture such as Southall, Northolt and Leicester.

'They treat the old women very badly,' said Shukla. 'They show them no respect. They give them less than the minimum on which they can survive. Some of the ashrams even demand a down-payment from the widows when they first arrive. They say it is to cover the cost of their cremation, but after a death they simply put the woman's body in a sack and throw it in the Jamuna.'

Shukla walked with me along the *parikrama,* through the crowded streets of the town. As we walked, we passed long lines of widows, all shaven-headed and with begging-bowls stretched towards us.

'My family have been priests in Vrindavan for many generations,' said Shukla as we walked. 'The town used to be very beautiful. But now it has expanded and become very dirty and polluted. Before, people came here and they found peace. Now they just find corruption and mental pollution.'

I asked the priest about the stories that appeared occasionally in the Indian press claiming that the ashram managers were in the habit to taking beautiful teenage widows as concubines, or selling them at ten thousand rupees a time.

'It happens,' he said. 'Many of the ashrams are now run by criminal elements. Even some of the sadhus are involved. They lure young girls in, then sell them to local landowners. When the landowners are finished with them, they can sell them to the brothels in Delhi. They pay the police off, so they don't intervene.'

What Shukla said was confirmed by local women's groups: 'Go to the villages around Vrindavan,' said Kamala Ghosh, 'and you'll see that all the landowners have little widows as mistresses. When they tire of them the widows are sold to whorehouses in Delhi and Bombay. And we have had widows here as young as ten.' Among those I talked to in Vrindavan, there was agreement that nothing was being done to save the widows from such exploitation, least of all by the police.

Shukla and I were now standing outside the Shri Bhagwan Bhajan ashram, the biggest of them all, where I had met Kanaklatha that morning. A prayer shift had just finished and the street was full of tired old women in white saris. On the steps of the ashram sat a fat man in white homespun who Shukla pointed out as one of the managers. I asked him about the allegations, but the fat man simply shrugged.

'The widows come here because they love Krishna,' he said. 'After they sing we give them some rice and two rupees. That is our duty. But we are not their keepers. What they do when they go is their business.'

Inside, the ashram consisted of two vast halls. On the floor of each squatted about a thousand widows in their identical white saris. Most of them seemed to be in their fifties or sixties, but there was a thin scattering of much younger women, while around the edge of the hall, leaning against the walls, or occasionally completely prostrate on the ground, were a number of much older women. Some of them were clearly mentally disturbed, letting out high-pitched shrieks like wounded birds, while others compulsively combed their hair or brushed away imaginary flies. The windows of the two halls were shuttered, and the only light came from a pair of naked bulbs suspended from the centre of the ceiling, leaving the edges of the rooms in a deep, Dickensian darkness. The whole establishment stank of urine and dirty linen.

Then a woman stood up in the centre of each room and began clashing cymbals; from another place a bell started to ring. A new shift was beginning. A cantor started up the chant, answered by two thousand widows singing as one, on and on, faster and faster: 'Hare Ram, Hare Krishna, Hare Ram, Hare Krishna . . .'

This form of devotion was the invention of the great sixteenth-century Bengali sage Shri Krishna Chaitanya, an Orpheus-like figure believed by his followers to be an incarnation of Krishna. After Chaitanya's wife died from a snake bite, the sage became a wanderer, travelling to all the sites connected with the life of Krishna, building many new temples and rescuing others from decay, particularly Vrindavan, whose shrines and temples had become overgrown and ruined.

Chaitanya's devotion to Krishna was of a deeply emotional kind, and his contemporary biography, the *Chaitanya Charit Amrita*, is filled with accounts of him falling into mystical raptures, 'breaking into song, dancing, weeping, climbing up trees, running to and fro like a madman and calling out the name of Radha and Krishna'. He encouraged his followers to come together and chant devotional songs called kirtans which, sung with a rising tempo and accompanied by the ringing of cymbals and bells, were supposed to lift the devotee into a mystical rapture. In Chaitanya's own time there are many accounts of thousands of devotees caught up in the mesmeric beat falling in to a state of trance, dancing and jumping as if in a frenzy, carried away in torrents of religious hysteria. So unruly and ecstatic did many of Chaitanya's prayer gatherings become that the Moghul governor of the area tried to ban his cult, and to arrest its leader for disrupting public order. According to the *Chaitanya Charit Amrita*, even the wild beasts were affected by his kirtans:

> *When the herd of elephants saw Chaitanya coming through the woods of Vrindavan they shouted 'Krishna' and danced and ran about in love. Some rolled on the ground, others bellowed. As the master sang a kirtan aloud, the deer flocked thither and marched with him on two sides. Then six or seven tigers came up and joined the deer in accompanying the master, the deer and the tiger dancing together shouting 'Krishna! Krishna!', while embracing and kissing each other. Even the trees and creepers of Vrindavan were ecstatic, putting forth sprouts and tendrills, rejoicing at the sound.*

Yet anything less ecstatic than the singing of today's widows in Vrindavan would be hard to imagine. At the back, the madwomen are shrieking. In the foreground, the exhausted old widows struggle to keep up with the cantor's pitch, many nodding asleep until given a poke by one of the ashram managers walking up and down the aisles with a stick. It is difficult to think of a sorrier or more pathetic sight. Vrindavan, Krishna's earthly paradise, is today a place of such profound sadness and distress that it almost defies description.

At the end of the shift, as darkness was beginning to fall outside, a pair of Brahmin priests walked into the hall and began to perform the arti. Taking a burning charcoal splint, they revolved the flame in front of the idol of Krishna which stood at the centre of the room. As they did so the widows let out an unearthly ululation: an eerie, high-pitched wailing noise. Bringing their hands together in the gesture of supplication, they all bowed before the idol as the priests closed the temple doors for the night. Then slowly the women began to file outside.

'This is not life,' said one old woman who came up to me out of the shadows, begging for a rupee. 'We all died the day our husbands died. How can anyone describe our pain? Our hearts are all on fire with sorrow. Now we just wait for the day when all this will end.'

ALEXANDER FRATER

CHERRA

The driver suddenly paused in his discourse and pointed ahead. 'Cherra!' he said.

He changed gear and took the car slowly up a steep, winding incline. I craned to see and, at the head of the gradient, 1,300 metres above sea level, I finally laid eyes on the wettest place on earth.

It wasn't much to look at. I noted a cluster of low, discoloured hilltop buildings which, as we approached, opened to reveal a tiny bus depot and bazaar. Two battered vehicles boarding passengers and freight bore the 'God's Gift None Can Blot' legend. I jumped out and asked the driver to meet me back here in three hours, noting that many of the market people carried calico-wrapped backpacks suspended from headbands in the fashion of Himalayan porters. Into each headband a furled umbrella had been stuck, giving them a curiously horned appearance, like unicorns. The houses and tea shops were roofed with corrugated iron sheets worn thin as razor blades and crowned by tall tin chimneys; plastic bags had been lashed over the chimney tops to seal them against the rains.

I felt reserve, even hostility. No one smiled. And, though the villagers avoided my eye, I sensed their eyes on my back. The only person to speak to me was a small girl from whom I bought

ALEXANDER FRATER has contributed to many publications, including *Punch* and the *New Yorker*, and was the chief travel correspondent of the *Observer*. 'Cherra' is from *Chasing the Monsoon*, which has also been made into a BBC television travel documentary. His other books include *Beyond the Blue Horizon*.

a handful of peanuts and a ripe·orange; then she reached beneath her table and gravely produced, for my inspection, a tray of carved silver-bowled opium pipes.

Nearby I examined a display of coracle-shaped, raffia-worked 'knups' or sou'westers which, placed over the head and shoulders afforded protection from the rain. I passed on, seeking the Cherrapunji umbrella seller, and found him crouching beside a flight of slippery stone steps. Emaciated, with sore red eyes, he was assembling a whole umbrella from the wreckage of several ruined ones, painstakingly fitting old, rusted ribs into a sprocket clasped between his toes. He was surrounded by bits of oiled silk, coloured and patterned fragments of nylon, and handles both orthodox and fantastic—the heads of ducks, spaniels, horses, rabbits and Red Indian chiefs.

'I'd like to buy an umbrella,' I said.

After all these weeks I still didn't possess one, and this seemed an appropriate place to make good the deficiency.

He didn't want my business. A rack of umbrellas, either new or reconditioned, stood propped behind his stool, but he waved a finger and shook his head. None was available. I knew the market people were watching because the whole place had gone quiet, and I persisted. Eventually, giving me an odd, fathomless look, he reached behind the rack and produced a silver-handled parasol, pink silk and trimmed with lace. It was a fragile European antique, probably made last century to shield some wealthy memsahib from the sun. Against forty feet of rain it would afford as much protection as a knotted handkerchief. I heard a faint susurration of laughter from the spectators behind and handed it back. He took it with a faint, ironic smile. I thanked him for his trouble and headed out of the marketplace to see the rest of the town.

Cherrapunji occupied a spur of flat tableland three miles long and two wide. Waterfalls lined the wooded limestone cliffs at its back, foaming out of the trees into cloud-filled ravines. One fall was reputed to be the world's fourth highest, though so many were parading today that I couldn't isolate it from the others; no fewer than twelve sprang from the glistening, hundred-yard cliff face before me. The reluctance of the cloud to quit the ravines led me to think it might somehow be colluding with the falls, perhaps even taking nourishment from them. Each, after all, discharged billions of cloud particles a second which, when absorbed, added extra body to the swirling precipitation streaks and streamers that kept obscuring the view.

Whenever they parted, more waterfalls appeared. I may even have induced one; dimly, through drifting mist and at the precise point I suddenly willed it to be, I perceived a new cascade emerging from the rock. I had never seen so many, had never imagined that such a profusion of these lovely, diaphanous things could be congregated in a single area. The town, isolated inside this foaming wall, its northern limits demarcated by rainbows, rang with the exuberant sounds of tumbling water.

The southern limits of the spur dropped steeply away to the flooded plains of Bangladesh, now a glamorous Caribbean blue in the afternoon sun. Cherrapunji's lofty elevation gave me a grandstand view of the drowned country below, and I suddenly understood that, with nowhere else to go, the overflow from these hills went surging out across the undefended flatlands. That's what Cherrapunji's rain did. It assisted in the annual flooding of Bangladesh. As I stood pondering again the two sides of the monsoon coin, death and destruction on the reverse of life and continuity, a voice suddenly said, 'What are you doing here?'

I turned. A burly Indian in a rumpled khaki safari suit stood watching me.

'Just having a look around,' I said.

'Where are your papers?'

'Why?'

'Security. You are in a prohibited zone.'

I opened my passport at the Cherrapunji Permission and handed it to him.

He pondered it for some time, then gave it back, frowning 'There has been a mistake,' he said. 'You are not allowed here.'

'Delhi says I am.'

'Unfortunately Delhi is far away. You must leave at once. Many illegals are coming in through Cherrapunji from Bangladesh. The people are angry and things are very tense.'

'Do I look like a Bangladeshi illegal?'

He cocked his head and said, unexpectedly, 'Perhaps a Bangladeshi illegal on a bad day. But they will not make the distinction. They are against all foreigners. They think you are here to steal from them.'

I told him my business and, after I promised to be gone two hours before sunset, he relented. Then, strolling with me, he said the Indian government was proposing to fence off the whole of its border with Bangladesh.

'The fence will be a stout one, best quality steel, and it will run along the slopes here below Cherra. Maybe we will even electrify it, but we are having problems enough generating power for our own needs. And those Banglas are resourceful people, you know; they would probably run wires from the fence to light their damn houses.' He gestured towards the slopes. 'Just a few hundred metres below there is big climate change; the Cherrapunji people grow fantastic tropical fruit—oranges, grapefruit, magnificent bananas, the finest mandarins in the world.'

He left me beside the old British graveyard. A number of tombstones bore the faint, weathered legend, 'Died by His Own Hand'. Cherrapunji had been the first British hill station in the north-east, but its founders had not anticipated the oppressive effect of rain and isolation on the temperaments of young men sent out to administer it . . .

The bungalows hereabouts, like those erected by the British, stood hundreds of yards apart. One had a garden wall fashioned from two halves of a Dakota's wing, another fencing from a Dakota's tailplane. In several gardens I saw Dakota propeller bosses being used as flowerpots; orchids seemed to thrive in them. Then I remembered the kindly Thril transport manager at Faridabad who, as a Dakota mechanic with the Indian Air Force, had served on a base near Cherrapunji and recalled its high accident rate; I guessed, though, that this recycled wreckage had less to do with his handiwork than with the conditions pertaining here during the monsoon. I imagined flying a Dak blind through sheeting rain, with turbulence coming off the hills and windshear roaring up the slopes from the plains of Bangladesh. It must have been a mortally dangerous combination. No wonder so many had crashed around Cherrapunji—more victims, their numbers unknown, to add to its tally of deaths.

The Mawsmai Falls were located on the outskirts of the settlement. On the bluff overlooking them stood a broken stone balustrade, a small, nostalgic echo of a great English estate at which, on fine evenings, the expatriates doubtless gathered to view the pretty cascades across the valley. Here they would have talked, counting the days until the next Home leave, discussing the Khasis (and possibly taking the Hooker line: 'Sulky intractable fellows, averse to rising early and intolerably filthy in their persons'), perhaps shakenly mourning the sudden passing, by gunshot, of a neighbour ('Did he seem dejected to you?') and endlessly comparing notes on how best to keep dry and warm.

Advice on what to wear was available even in London— flannel shirts, woollen undervests, trousers cut from American or Dutch Pepperill unbleached drill, merino socks, stout but comfortable boots, leggings, a waterproof one could ride in, a cashmere coat kept closed to the neck with pearl buttons, shanks and fasteners, and two yards of warm red flannel in case of a sudden chill to the liver. A woven Jaeger, or sanitary belt was held to be a great safeguard against dysentery. They were urged to sleep in flannel and carry umbrellas of strong silk or alpaca.

Beneath the falls Hooker found laurels, brambles, jasmines, oaks and, to his surprise, Khasi miners labouring in hidden coal-pits. Today the Mawsmai was flanked by numerous other falls. Plumes of white water sheeted off the green cliff, vanished into cloud, then reappeared in a foaming burn that went plunging down to nourish the tropical fruit gardens and top up the Bangladeshi flood.

Wapshot might occasionally have joined the expats here, though my impression was of a man not much given to social chit-chat; indeed, if he talked obsessively about the contents of his rain gauge the others may have found him depressing. And what would my father have made of Cherrapunji? Certainly he would have appreciated its similarity to some of the wilder parts of western Scotland, which he loved, and, provided he experienced a few of those famous forty-inch days, might well have regarded it as the trip of a lifetime. Now I had come in his place and, staring out at the falls, I tried to conjure him up. But I couldn't see the shy young doctor who once pitted his wits against the extremes of the tropical weather systems, and who would have pressed me hard for details of Cherrapunji and the Indian monsoon, shaking his head, laughing in that surprised, delighted way that I missed so much.

All I saw was the brave, tired man who knew he had a mortal heart condition and who, stubbornly rejecting the idea of retirement, suffered his massive, inevitable coronary two weeks after joining a new practice in New Zealand; it happened on the steps of an Auckland post office where he had called to mail an affectionate letter to my daughter. I imagined this father looking at me a little doubtfully, privately wondering whether the trip had really been a good idea. Travel writing, eh? Well, perhaps such things serve a purpose. But a need? Hmm. He had wanted me to be a doctor too.

Some youths were leaning on the balustrade, gossiping noisily, and now I became aware that they had fallen silent and were watching me. Two detached themselves and strolled over, umbrellas tucked under their arms, ragged shirt-tails protruding from worn, patched sweaters. One spoke English.

'What are you doing here?' he enquired.

'I've come to see the waterfalls.'

'Come from where?'

'England. London.'

'Are you Methodist?'

'No.'

'I am Methodist. My friend here is animist. He see God in the waterfalls. Where do you see God?'

'Well . . . inside my head, I think. But not very often.'

He nodded, and translated for his friend. The friend, who had a nervous disorder that made him twitch and start, spoke at some length.

'He is telling you he also see the spirits of dead ancestors around here. These are two great-aunts who lived in bottom village far below. One stormy night, after selling their potatoes at Cherra bazaar, they climb down high and precarious cliff ladder beside the Mawsmai—and tumble off.'

The friend spoke again.

'They were drunk!'

'That's a terrible story,' I said.

'Yes.' He gave a merry laugh.

'Your English is very good.'

'Of course. Every day I am listening to BBC World Service. And my teacher was taught by the Methodists. Welshmen. Thomas Jones, father of the Khasi alphabet, gave us our written language and started big fashion for literature in Cherrapunji. Now there are poets working all over the hills.' He nodded at his friend. 'He is a poet. He has written a very good poem about the great-aunts. It is called "Falling".'

I asked for a translation of 'Falling' but thought bemusedly: Welsh? Methodists? I never realized the Methodists had been in Cherrapunji. Would Wapshot have mentioned them in his letters? Undoubtedly, but news of their deeds had not been relayed to me. Perhaps my father thought I was too young to know; tales of Old Testament floods and honey-smeared corpses might be dull but they weren't controversial. I saw Wapshot in a new light. He had been a man under stress, competing day and night with the sonorous, persuasive Taffs and their buttery bardic voices; perhaps they had introduced rugby to the Khasi hills as well. Poor Wapshot. He had certainly had his work cut out.

The boys were discussing their opening stanzas in low, eager voices when, abruptly, the sun went out and a bomb exploded a hundred feet above our heads. The flash and bang almost lifted me off the ground, but they barely glanced up. Casually unfurling their umbrellas they continued talking as, stunned, I watched the approach of the Cherrapunji rain.

A fountain of dense black cloud came spiralling over the hills, then rose steeply into the sky. It formed a kind of tent, apex high overhead, sides unrolling right to the ground. It was very dark inside but I could just discern, trooping towards us, an armada of shadowy, galleon-like vessels with undersides festooned with writhing cables of water. They gave off thundery rumbles and a noise like discharging hydrants, the rain descending in hissing vertical rafts of solid matter that lathered the earth and made the spokes of the poet's umbrella, under which I had taken shelter, bend like saplings.

Standing there, I recalled the words of Y. P. Rao. 'Observations of meteorologists who have visited the area suggest the phenomenal rains at Cherrapunji prevail over a short length of the range, up a small portion of the slope.' He believed they were lured into a unique orographic trap. The wet air, rushing up from the south, struck that small, sloping aspect, then found itself being ducted, willy-nilly, into a

south-facing, funnel-shaped catchment opening in the hills—
a limestone corral from which it could only escape by
shedding its moisture.

I felt little of the excitement I had known when the burst
arrived in the south. Those had been occasions for public
jubilation. This was a routine matinee performance at
Cherrapunji, awesome certainly but exhilarating only to earnest
collectors of meteorological records; such specialists would now
be watching, incredulous, as their gauges foamed like
champagne glasses.

The rain left us enveloped in low, luminous cloud. The poet
and his friend, summoned by their companions, left with the
poem still untranslated. I set off back to the bazaar and,
moments later, saw six men and a woman emerge from the
Scotch mist and troop towards me in single file, all sporting
closed umbrellas tucked into their headbands. After they had
passed, the woman suddenly turned, ran back and placed a
brown, speckled bird's egg in my hand.

1990